Judaism, Education and Social Justice

Also available from Bloomsbury

Pedagogy, Politics and Philosophy of Peace, edited by Carmel Borg and Michael Grech
Critical Education in International Perspective, Peter Mayo and Paolo Vittoria
Transnational Feminist Politics, Education, and Social Justice, edited by Silvia Edling and Sheila Macrine
Capitalism, Pedagogy, and the Politics of Being, Noah De Lissovoy
Critical Human Rights, Citizenship, and Democracy Education, edited by Michalinos Zembylas and André Keet
Education, Equality and Justice in the New Normal, edited by Inny Accioly and Donaldo Macedo
A Pedagogy of Faith, Irwin Leopando
Wonder and Education, Anders Schinkel

Judaism, Education and Social Justice

Towards a Jewish Critical Pedagogy

Matt Plen

BLOOMSBURY ACADEMIC
LONDON • NEW YORK • OXFORD • NEW DELHI • SYDNEY

BLOOMSBURY ACADEMIC
Bloomsbury Publishing Plc
50 Bedford Square, London, WC1B 3DP, UK
1385 Broadway, New York, NY 10018, USA
29 Earlsfort Terrace, Dublin 2, Ireland

BLOOMSBURY, BLOOMSBURY ACADEMIC and the Diana logo are trademarks of Bloomsbury Publishing Plc

First published in Great Britain 2023
Paperback edition published 2024

Copyright © Matt Plen, 2023

Matt Plen has asserted his right under the Copyright, Designs and Patents Act, 1988, to be identified as Author of this work.

For legal purposes the Acknowledgements on p. vi constitute an extension of this copyright page.

Cover image © David Talukdar/Getty Images

All rights reserved. No part of this publication may be reproduced or transmitted in any form or by any means, electronic or mechanical, including photocopying, recording, or any information storage or retrieval system, without prior permission in writing from the publishers.

Bloomsbury Publishing Plc does not have any control over, or responsibility for, any third-party websites referred to or in this book. All internet addresses given in this book were correct at the time of going to press. The author and publisher regret any inconvenience caused if addresses have changed or sites have ceased to exist, but can accept no responsibility for any such changes.

A catalogue record for this book is available from the British Library.

A catalog record for this book is available from the Library of Congress.

ISBN: HB: 978-1-3502-9309-0
PB: 978-1-3502-9313-7
ePDF: 978-1-3502-9310-6
eBook: 978-1-3502-9311-3

Typeset by Newgen KnowledgeWorks Pvt. Ltd., Chennai, India

To find out more about our authors and books visit www.bloomsbury.com and sign up for our newsletters.

Contents

Acknowledgements	vi
Glossary of Hebrew and Jewish Terms	vii
Introduction	1

Part 1 Faith, Justice and Education

1 Paulo Freire's Critical Pedagogy – a Theory of Social Justice Education	9
2 Catholic Social Teaching and Liberation Theology – Theories of Religious Social Justice Education	21
3 Judaism and Social Justice – Religion, Culture and Progressive Politics	33

Part 2 Jewish Social Justice Education – Interviews with Practitioners

4 Critique – the World as It Is	55
5 Vision – the World as It Should Be	77
6 Strategy – Education, Activism and Community Organising	99
7 People – Agents and Beneficiaries of Social Change	133

Part 3 Towards a Jewish Critical Pedagogy

8 Philosophical, Theological and Political Themes	147
9 The Jewishness of Social Justice Pedagogies	179
10 Normative Theories of Jewish Social Justice Education	189
Conclusion	217
Notes	221
Bibliography	235
Index	243

Acknowledgements

I would like to thank the following people and organisations, without whom this book would not have come into existence:

My teachers and colleagues Professor Jonathan Cohen, Professor James Conroy, Professor Judith Suissa and Dr Paddy Walsh, for their guidance, insightful feedback and enthusiastic engagement with my research;

My employers at Masorti Judaism for providing invaluable flexibility, time and funding;

The Philosophy of Education Society of Great Britain for supporting this project through its major grant programme;

My interviewees, for the time and thought they generously contributed to this project, but more importantly for their dedication to the holy work of Jewish education and social justice;

My parents, for teaching me the values that ultimately inspired this book;

And, most importantly, my family: my wife Atira and my children Micha, Asher and Ziv, for their encouragement, support, patience and love.

Glossary of Hebrew and Jewish Terms

All terms are in Hebrew or English unless otherwise stated.

Ashkenazi	Jews and Jewish traditions whose ancestry can be traced to medieval Germany, Central and Eastern Europe.
Bet Midrash	'House of study' – space for Jewish text study, often located in a synagogue, Jewish school or *yeshivah* (see below).
Bible	The Hebrew Bible ('*Tanakh*') comprises the Torah or five books of Moses, the Prophets and the Writings; its content although not the order of its books is identical to the Protestant Old Testament.
Bund	(Yiddish) The General Jewish Labour Bund – socialist, Yiddishist, non-Zionist organisation of Jewish workers in pre–Second World War Eastern Europe.
Chabad	Also known as Lubavitch, a Ḥasidic sect known for its openness to certain aspects of the modern world and intensive outreach operations among non-Orthodox Jews.
Dvar torah	'A word of Torah'. Used to describe a sermon or teaching moment in which the lessons of Jewish texts are applied hermeneutically to the real-life situation of the audience.
Halakhah	The body of Jewish legal literature and the rules contained therein, developed since the first millennium BCE, that governs every aspect of ethical and ritual behaviour for observant Jews.
Ḥasid/ic	'A pious person'. Usually denotes an adherent of the mystical, pietistic Ḥasidic movement that originated in eighteenth-century Poland and forms an important section of contemporary ultra-Orthodox Jewry.
Ḥevruta	(Aramaic) 'Friendship' or 'companionship'. A traditional approach to the study of biblical, rabbinic and other Jewish literature in which small groups – usually pairs – of students independently analyse and discuss the text.

Lishmah	'For its own sake'. Denotes the performance of religious precepts due to their intrinsic value or purpose rather than for instrumental reasons, for example to obtain a reward.
Mahloket	'Debate' or 'controversy'. A characteristic of talmudic and other rabbinic texts, which record legal and theological discussions featuring multiple, contradictory positions, typically without coming to a definitive conclusion.
Maimonides	(Greek) Moses ben Maimon. Thirteenth-century Spanish and Egyptian Jewish jurist and philosopher who wrote the authoritative legal code *Mishneh Torah* and the philosophical work *Guide to the Perplexed*.
Masorti	'Traditional'. A contemporary stream of Judaism, also known as Conservative Judaism, which is committed to traditional, halakhic practice and modern, liberal values, and seeks to grapple with the tensions between them.
Mensch	(Yiddish) 'Man'. A decent human being. *Menschlichkeit* – the quality of being a decent human being.
Midrash	A rabbinic mode of interpreting scripture which involves creative readings and embellishment of the original texts with new narratives. Also refers to the canonical and modern works of Bible interpretation generated by this practice.
Mishnah	A compilation of oral, mainly legal, traditions (see Torah), redacted by Rabbi Judah Ha-Nasi in third-century Palestine. Forms the basis for the entire corpus of *halakhah*/Jewish law.
Mizrahi	'Eastern'. Refers to Jews of Middle Eastern and Asian origin. Often used more loosely to refer to all Mediterranean, North African and Middle Eastern Jewish communities.
Orthodox	A contemporary stream of Judaism characterised by the attempt to defend the integrity of the tradition against the pressures of the modern world. *Ultra-Orthodox* or *Haredi* Judaism generally seeks to minimise all contact with secular, non-Jewish society and culture, whereas *Modern Orthodoxy* allows for a measure of social and cultural integration while resisting modern influences on traditional belief and practice.
Progressive	An umbrella term for non-Orthodox Jewish denominations, particularly Reform and Liberal Judaism. Sometimes loosely applied to other streams such as Masorti Judaism.

Prophets	Characters in the Hebrew Bible who relay the word of God to the people, often concerned with ethical behaviour and social justice. 'Prophetic Judaism' is a modern term for interpretations of Judaism that prioritise interpersonal morality and justice over Jewish law and ritual concerns.
Rabbis	A caste of Jewish leaders whose authority was based on their Torah scholarship and teaching, who emerged in the late first millennium BCE and became dominant after the destruction of the Second Temple in 70 CE. 'The Rabbis' usually denotes the religious authorities of the Mishnaic and Talmudic periods, but the term is also used to describe subsequent and contemporary Jewish religious leaders.
Reform	A stream of Judaism that seeks to recast Judaism so as to conform to modern, liberal values, rejecting the authority of *halakhah*/Jewish law in favour of autonomy and informed decision-making on the part of the individual. In the UK, closely allied with Liberal Judaism.
Sephardi	Jews and Jewish traditions whose ancestry can be traced to medieval Spain and Portugal; often used loosely to refer to all Mediterranean, North African and Middle Eastern Jewish communities.
Shabbat	The Sabbath, the day of rest lasting from sunset on Friday until nightfall on Saturday, on which a wide range of work-related activities are prohibited in traditional Jewish practice.
Talmud	A multivolume series of extended interpretations based loosely on the text of the Mishnah, characterised by multivocal, open-ended discussion and the preservation of minority opinions. Includes halakhic, theological, ethical and legendary/narrative content. The Jerusalem Talmud was compiled in Palestine around the year 400 CE. The more extensive Babylonian Talmud was compiled in present-day Iraq between the third and sixth centuries CE and forms the authoritative basis for all subsequent Jewish law.
Tikkun Olam	'Repairing the world'. A phrase originating in the Mishnah (as '*tikkun ha-olam*'); originally referred to reforms designed to resolve unjust legal anomalies. Influenced also by the term '*tikkun*' as it appears in early-modern mystical texts, referring to human participation in restoring cosmic harmony through

	religious practice. Tikkun Olam now commonly denotes social justice activism inspired by Jewish values.
Torah	'Teaching' or 'instruction'. The Written Torah comprises the first five books of the Hebrew Bible. Oral Torah denotes additional traditions of interpretation, narrative and law that were eventually recorded in the Mishnah, Talmud and Midrash. The term 'Torah' is also often used to describe the entirety of Jewish religious tradition.
Tzaddik	'A righteous person'. Generally denotes someone with the highest standards of ethical behaviour. More specifically refers to the leader of a Hasidic sect.
Tzedakah	'Justice'. The practice of charitable giving, which in Judaism is not seen as a voluntary act of generosity but an ethical and legal obligation.
Yeshivah	A traditional school or academy whose curriculum centres on the study of Jewish texts.

Introduction

Jewish social justice education is an active and growing field of practice, encompassing a diverse range of agendas and practices: teaching Jewish texts and values around issues of refugees, human rights and environmental justice; organising members of the Jewish community to oppose the occupation of the Palestinian territories and support the Israeli Left; advancing gender equality and LGBT+ inclusion within the community through informal education and training; engaging Jewish students in volunteer service learning projects to alleviate poverty in the developing world; building interfaith coalitions to work on local agendas such as housing, crime and healthcare; encouraging a culture of charitable giving and volunteering among Jewish young people; and mobilising Jews in the national and international political arenas around issues such as racism, police brutality, gun violence, climate change, immigration and antisemitism. This work is taking place within synagogues, schools, youth movements, cultural events and adult education programmes in Jewish communities around the world, led by rabbis, teachers, informal educators, political activists, and a plethora of charities and NGOs.

Yet Jewish social justice education remains an under-researched and under-theorised phenomenon. People involved in this area of activity tend to be practitioners rather than scholars, and the limited amount of writing on the subject is relatively lightweight and journalistic rather than academic. To my knowledge, no serious exploration of the relationship between Jewish education and social justice or of the role of Jewish education in promoting social justice has been carried out. This theoretical lacuna has practical implications for the thousands of practitioners across the world who are attempting to achieve social justice ends through the medium of Jewish education but have no well-thought-out rationale as to what this might mean and, consequently, cannot know if it has any chance of success. While this book does not attempt to answer the empirical questions concerning the effects, successful or otherwise, of such educational practices, it takes a first step in remedying this deficiency by asking a deceptively simple question: what might the phrase 'Jewish social justice education' mean? The bulk of the book is devoted to exploring this question by describing and subjecting to philosophical analysis the approaches articulated by thinkers and practitioners who consider themselves to be part of the 'Jewish social justice education' enterprise. This descriptive phase then leads to a normative one in which I propose several possible directions a coherent theory of Jewish social justice education could take.

This book emerges from my own personal, professional and academic background. I grew up in a politically committed, left-wing, largely secular, Jewish family. My route into involvement with Judaism and the Jewish community took two forms. First, as a teenager I joined a Zionist youth movement and spent a significant amount of time in Israel, where I encountered and became convinced by the notion that Jewish identity could be based on national or ethnic rather than religious foundations. I was also exposed to secular, left-wing but Jewishly committed role models for the first time. Second, I became involved with the Masorti (Conservative) movement, a stream of Judaism that seeks to integrate traditional Jewish practice with modern, progressive values. In this context I was able to experiment with, and adopt, religious practices without feeling that I was sacrificing my beliefs or philosophical integrity. My activity as a youth movement leader also helped me develop my lifelong professional involvement in Jewish education: teaching, developing curriculum and training educators within progressive and pluralistic Jewish educational institutions in the UK, Israel and the United States. Today I remain committed to democratic–socialist politics (broadly understood) and left-wing Zionism, active within the Masorti Jewish community, and professionally involved with Jewish education. My motivation to write this book stemmed partly from a desire to integrate and explore the connections between my political, religious and educational commitments.

I have chosen to employ the term 'Jewish social justice education' rather than a variation such as 'Jewish education for social justice' since the addition of prepositions implies unfounded assumptions about the relationship between the concept's constituent parts. Are we talking about Jewish education as a means to the end of social justice, education in the service of a Jewish conception of social justice, engagement with social justice as a vehicle for Jewish education or some other variation? In fact, any interpretation of this nature is grounded in a prior assumption: that Jewish social justice education entails an instrumentalism or a distinction between means and ends (implied by the word 'for'). This is unwarranted, as we shall see. Nonetheless, it is important to clarify the specific ways I will be using the three interlinked terms, 'Jewish', 'social justice' and 'education'.

Judaism is more than a propositional, theistic faith tradition and Jewishness is more than a religious identity. Both concepts are multivalent and can be interpreted to connote overlapping religious, cultural, ethnic or national aspects of identity and practice. Deciding whether particular fields of thought and practice – for example, approaches to social justice or education – are Jewish in any meaningful sense is therefore extremely difficult, particularly in this context, since Jewish social justice practitioners are usually motivated by universal, human issues more than purely parochial concerns. I have therefore chosen to define an approach to education and social justice as Jewish if it explicitly presents itself in the context of ideas drawn from Jewish texts, history or culture, defined as such by its authors or practitioners, and if its stated or implied aim is to pursue its educational and social justice goals within or on behalf of the Jewish community.

I have endeavoured to be guided in my understanding of social justice by the texts and approaches I have surveyed, yet have nonetheless been in need of a working definition so as to limit the field of my research. While social justice is a term often associated with the Left, in particular with egalitarian liberalism and socialism, it can be understood in ways which are so diverse as to be mutually contradictory. For example, the term may be used by thinkers on the libertarian right in ways which are unacceptable from a social–democratic point of view. I have limited the theories of social justice under discussion to those which adhere to, or are in dialogue with, universalist values, see themselves as part of a politically progressive tradition and which are grounded in a basic commitment to the strengthening of social and economic equality. This definition does not stipulate a commitment to Marxism or materialism and is open to ideologies which understand the struggle for equality in individualistic, communitarian or cultural terms, and to approaches which stem from theological conceptions of justice.

In the context of social justice, the term 'education' is to be understood alongside 'politics'. While it is not my intention to offer a comprehensive account of either concept, the ubiquity of these terms in the following discussion makes it necessary to clarify how I comprehend them. I take education and politics to be alternative, complementary or overlapping ways of realising or embodying principles or practices of social justice. The celebrated radical educator Paulo Freire (see Chapter 1) describes social change in terms of *praxis*, which he takes to be a circle or dialectic comprising two poles: reflection on reality and the production of ideas which are implemented in the form of social transformation, leading to the creation of a new reality which then becomes the subject of ongoing reflection and critique. My starting point will be to understand education as the ideational, reflective aspect of Freirean *praxis*, and politics as the material, socially transformative one. As such, education will refer to those aspects of the social justice enterprise that take place in the framework of a relationship between teachers (broadly understood) and learners and that focus on a process of cognitive, emotional or practical development, reflection and change. As education is primarily about relationships and not institutions, this can take place not only within formal settings such as schools and universities but also in the wider context of families, youth movements, literacy circles, cultural and social networks, religious institutions and political parties.

In order to create a level playing field for the analysis of widely varying forms of philosophical, political and educational discourse, I have chosen to relate to the approaches to social justice education surveyed here as forms of *ideology*, embodied in spoken or written texts. Following Terry Eagleton,[1] I have understood ideologies as sets of ideas which advance and legitimate the interests of particular social groups, in conflict with competing groups and interests with ideologies of their own. The focus of discussion here is *utopian* ideologies which, rather than seeking to preserve social conditions, aim to transform reality in line with an explicitly articulated vision. I have employed a hermeneutical methodology in order to facilitate a process of bringing different ideological texts into relationship, interpreting one in light of another, and using this dialogue as a way of fleshing out various theoretical conceptions of Jewish social justice education. I have adopted this approach in order to deal with two interlinked difficulties associated with this area of inquiry. First, since very little has been written about Jewish social justice education, I have chosen to generate texts for analysis by interviewing practitioners. Second, the under-theorised nature of this field means I have had to make decisions about the appropriate theoretical context in which to examine these texts. These two activities create a hermeneutical circle: the generation of texts is conditioned by interview questions inspired by my theoretical background reading, while the choice of this analytical context is prompted by themes that emerge from the interviews. In addition, the process is informed by my own ideological positions, which inevitably seep into the discussion, and which are in turn influenced by what I learn from my research.

I am interested in interrelating four kinds of text (or context). In Chapter 1, I survey the critical pedagogy of Paulo Freire as articulated in Freire's own writing and in that of several important North American successors who have adapted his work for the developed, global North. Chapter 2 covers religious approaches to social justice education, in particular the texts of Catholic social teaching and liberation theology and the educational literature which has developed around them. In Chapter 3 I explore contemporary theological and political writing on the relationship between Judaism and social justice. And in Chapters 4–7, I set out narratives generated by interviewing Jewish social justice education practitioners. The choice of these texts is itself a hermeneutical process. My own interests and initial understanding of Jewish social justice discourse and practice informed my choice of relevant theoretical contexts: critical pedagogy, Catholic writing on social justice education, and literature on Judaism and social justice. These framed my interview questions and analysis of the resulting texts, went on to influence the ways in which I understood the theoretical context itself, and helped me shape a dialogue that resulted in a fertile mixture of philosophical, theological, political and pedagogical themes. These will be covered in Chapters 8 and 9.

Finally, in Chapter 10, I propose three normative theories of Jewish social justice education: 'Jewish politics in a renewed public sphere', 'Jewish education for relational community building' and 'Jewish critical pedagogy for cultural emancipation'. By fleshing out these theories and applying them to thorny contemporary political and educational issues – Israel/Palestine, LGBT+ inclusion and the culture wars – I hope to provide a rich array of answers to the question: what is Jewish social justice education?

Part 1

Faith, Justice and Education

In the coming chapters, I will introduce the three bodies of work which form the context for my analysis of Jewish social justice education: the educational–political ideology of critical pedagogy; religious approaches to social justice education based on the traditions of Catholic social teaching and liberation theology; and the theological, philosophical and cultural backdrop as represented in contemporary Jewish approaches to social justice.

1

Paulo Freire's Critical Pedagogy – a Theory of Social Justice Education

Freirean critical pedagogy – embodied in the work of Brazilian educator Paulo Freire and several of his successors who extended and reinterpreted his work in the context of democratic, industrialised countries – is a relevant, illuminating context for Jewish social justice education for several reasons. It is a comprehensive, convincing account of the relationship between education and radical politics, motivated by universal, humanist values, firmly grounded in theory and fully fleshed out in terms of practical pedagogy. It acknowledges the deep, complex nature of the relationship between politics and pedagogy and avoids simplistic, instrumentalised formulations of education's function within the social justice enterprise. Finally, critical pedagogy articulates several themes that dovetail with the approaches of Jewish social justice writers and practitioners and which form a fruitful foundation for developing a theory of Jewish social justice education. These themes are the concepts of humanisation and dehumanisation; cultural questions of colonialism and race; the challenges of populism and the antidote offered by democratic socialism; the importance of *praxis* and dialogue as modes of engaging in education and politics; and the development of a problem-posing, critical pedagogy in contrast to dominant modes of oppressive educational practice.

Humanisation, Dehumanisation and *Praxis*

Paulo Freire's approach is grounded in an explicit anthropology – a set of ideas about what it means to be a human being. He asserts that, in contrast to other animals, human beings have the unique potential to be subjects: they not only adapt to reality but are also able to make decisions and transform the world.[1] Human beings' subjective consciousness and this potentially transformative relationship to reality stem from *praxis*, a dialectic of reflection and action on the world. Reflection facilitates understanding, analysis and diagnosis; it points to possible directions for action, and creates the insight that it is possible to transform reality. Human action, inspired by this reflection, creates a new reality, which then becomes the object of reflection. This process takes place through dialogue, in which the world mediates between the participants in the conversation.

Just as human beings are neither disconnected from nor merged with the world, they are influenced and conditioned by reality but not determined by it.[2] Freire rejects mechanistic objectivism and believes that while free will operates under the limitations of objective reality, it always preserves its independence. Just as existence is marked by unfinishedness, so too human existence is characterised as a process of becoming, or of the realisation of a person's human-dialogical presence in the world. Human beings' vocation to act in and transform the world emerges from the awareness of this unfinishedness. Freire believes that the essence of humanity is decision-making and action in light of the tension between good and evil, where good is defined as liberation or humanisation, and evil is understood as oppression or dehumanisation.[3]

The humanisation–dehumanisation axis is the backbone of Freire's world view.[4] In the conceptual framework outlined above, humanisation is the process whereby a person realises her human potential – subjectivity, dialogue, *praxis* and ethics. Dehumanisation is the negation of this potential and the relegation of a person to the status of an object. However, these concepts cannot be understood in relation to a single human being but only in a wider socio-cultural context.

Colonialism and Race

Freire sees culture as a field or mechanism for social oppression, which he depicts in binary terms as a conflict between the oppressors and the oppressed.[5] He claims that dominant social groups preserve class privilege by strengthening cultural differences, consolidating internal class homogeneity by nurturing distinct class-based cultures. The social elite identifies its own culture as superior and presents it as the exclusive national culture, while condemning what it considers to be the inferior cultures of subordinate social classes. This hierarchical cultural field provides the foundation for the perpetuation of social inequality. For example, in countries under colonial or neocolonial domination, a 'culture of silence' emerges in which the director society silences the object society, while the local elite reproduces this process by silencing the indigenous masses. The thought–language in these societies (Freire sees thought and language as one integrated phenomenon) reflects the world of the director society rather than local reality. The imposition of the oppressive class's thought–language prevents any possibility of the oppressed relating authentically to the world and engaging in revolutionary *praxis*. A similar dynamic motivates the phenomenon of illiteracy, which Freire sees as a dehumanising form of class oppression.

While Freire, writing from the late 1960s to the 1990s, primarily addresses the situation of postcolonial societies in the developing world, Donald Macedo attacks the same phenomena in the United States of the 1990s and 2000s. He critiques conservative positions such as those advanced by Allan Bloom and E. D. Hirsh, which in his view deny the ideological nature of schooling and claim that multiculturalism is tearing apart a formerly existing universal, European American culture. Against this, he argues that in reality this kind of homogeneity never existed and that the idea of the melting pot is a form of cultural genocide. In fact, Americans are heirs to a tradition of cultural conflict which the Right is trying to shut down in the service of the dominant ideology.[6]

Populism, Socialism and Democracy

Freire's diagnosis relates to various stages in the evolution of society. If absolute dehumanisation and oppression characterise agrarian and illiterate societies under colonial or local autocratic rule (in Freire's terms, 'closed' societies), the initial emancipatory struggle gives rise to a new form of oppression: populism and the mass society.[7] Freire's prescient diagnosis of populism presents it as the reaction of political leaders to the awakening of the masses in which the rulers manipulate the people in order to bolster their authority. While this movement has the potential either to evolve into authentic revolutionary democracy or to pave the way for a right-wing coup, populism itself perpetuates dehumanisation by moulding the public into a malleable, unthinking mass which tries to act on reality without engaging in reflection. This 'massification' is connected to the advertising industry – today we would emphasise the role of social media – and to manipulative myths with which it turns human beings into domesticated, conformist observers; instils fear; and destroys their ability to love, think critically, form communities and intervene in historical processes of change.

Whereas Freire's critique is grounded in the South American context, for Henry Giroux, a leading theorist of critical pedagogy in the United States, it is no less relevant to the 'democratic' North. Giroux associates this kind of analysis with the critique developed by Theodor Adorno and the Frankfurt School in the 1930s. Adorno uses the term 'culture industry' to expose the fact that rather than emerging from the masses, culture is produced for them by economic interests who standardise and rationalise it, reduce it to 'amusement' and use it for purposes of domination; rather than being an escape from the mechanised work process, culture becomes an extension of it.[8] Writing in the 1980s, Ira Shor draws attention to one practical consequence of this situation: the phenomenon of 'accelerated perception' among students, caused by overexposure to mass culture, from video games to escalators and microwaves (again, this analysis anticipates the rise of social media). As a result, students find it hard to carefully read and examine texts, events and ideas; teaching such students necessitates 'deceleration mechanisms,' including journal keeping, cooperative group work, reading out loud with discussion, process methods for writing and narrative rather than numerical evaluation.[9]

Against this kind of populism, Freire promotes a vision of democratic socialism. His loyalty to radical, democratic positions stems from what he refers to as his religious faith, which he identifies with values such as freedom, humility, consistency and tolerance.[10] For Freire, socialism is impossible without democracy, and vice versa. Just as true social equality is bound up with a deep-rooted democracy, it is impossible to bring about a process of democratisation in the absence of a solution to social and economic problems.[11] Freire believes that the job of progressive governments is to assist those in need by means of inclusive, not fatalistic, economic development, where the term 'fatalism' serves to express Freire's opposition to the neoliberal axiom that growth is incompatible with egalitarian policies and economic democratisation. Progressive governments must avoid 'assistencialism' – attributing the needs of the oppressed to natural causes or their own personal failure, rather than seeing their situation as the result of the political and economic impotence which arises from public policy and power relations in society.[12]

This kind of social and historical transformation does not mean taking power but reinventing the idea of power. This process requires the democratisation not only of the regime but also of the economy and the field of cultural production in order to give expression to a range of voices – including illiterate ones – which constitute society. Freire assigns an important role to civil society: not to replace the state but to hold it to account, while generating a broad dialogue between all sectors of society, including both progressive and conservative elements.[13] Yet Freire also distinguishes sharply between democracy – the opposite of authoritarianism – and permissiveness, in both political and educational realms. Democracy involves not only freedoms but also authority – albeit democratic authority rather than the authoritarian, silencing variety. Democratic discipline is halfway between the authoritarian negation of freedom and an anarchic absence of authority. It is connected with modes of democratic behaviour – organisation, mobilisation, critique – which are all essential for correcting the evils of capitalism. The dialectic of authority and freedom gives rise to autonomy – disciplined self-rule.[14]

Leadership, Dialogue and Identity Politics

For Freire, truly revolutionary action always involves humanisation, generated through *praxis* and dialogue. The leadership of an authentic revolution (as opposed to a putsch) must initiate dialogue with the people; the depth of this dialogue determines the revolutionary character of the movement. This approach stems from the intersubjective nature of revolutionary *praxis* in Freire's system: it is impossible to think *for* the people, only *with* the people. Liberation can have no objects, only dialogically constituted subjects. The people's engagement with *praxis* and dialogue together with their leaders avoids the danger of bureaucratisation and the transformation of the revolutionary leadership into a new class of oppressors.[15] Revolutionary action therefore implies a pedagogical position. Revolutionary leaders need to engage with the people not in order to teach or instil a particular world view but to learn together about the world and to resolve differences of opinion through dialogue.[16] The resulting unity of leaders and oppressed is based on class, but class consciousness emerges only from people's awareness of their oppression as individuals; this awareness is generated through *praxis*.

If unity is the key to revolutionary victory, the value of tolerance takes on central importance. Freire distinguishes between a radical politics of unity and tolerance which is able to withstand the attacks of the Right, and a fractious sectarianism.[17] In the same context, he discusses multiculturalism and identity politics, welcoming the emergence of feminist, ecological and peace movements, and calling on the parties of the Left to form alliances with and learn from them.[18] Freire accepts elements of an identity politics or intersectional perspective, recognising that there are 'hierarchies of oppression' with some people simultaneously occupying oppressor and oppressed positions. However, he makes clear that rather than working for emancipation only from each other, oppressed groups should work out how to engage in collective struggle for the emancipation of all.[19]

Giroux extends this discussion of tolerance and sectarianism, supplying it with theoretical foundations.[20] He seeks to question the politics of binary oppositions and construct what he calls a 'border pedagogy', a politics and pedagogy which can acknowledge multiple, complex subject positions. An obsession with binary polarities, he continues, is not only evident in neoconservatism but can also be discerned behind much radical thinking which seeks to prioritise one kind of oppression over another, setting oppressed groups against each other. Drawing on Bakhtin's idea that language – the constitutive feature of identity – is fundamentally heteroglot, irreducible to a unity and always the site of struggle, Giroux wants to help students become 'border crossers', understanding otherness in its own terms and creating borderlands where cultural identities can be reshaped. Yet this kind of borderland is not an end in itself but a place where multiple subjectivities and identities exist within a wider, solidary democratic project and where difference is a means to the end of a struggle for equality and justice. Giroux believes that postmodernism (alongside feminism and specifically African American feminism) is an important resource for emancipatory pedagogy in that it is epistemologically open, non-axiomatic and anti-elitist; it, therefore, facilitates challenges to Eurocentric master narratives and enables more critical explorations of identity and otherness. Unlike Freire, Giroux does not limit dialogue to the oppressed; 'border crossing' seems to be a liberatory process in which the 'coming to voice' of oppressors and oppressed (inasmuch as the suspicion of binary oppositions allows us to draw a line between them) is dialectically related.

Oppressive and Emancipatory Pedagogies

For Freire, political oppression is associated with an oppressive pedagogy: a dehumanising 'banking education' which stands in opposition to dialogue and *praxis*.[21] Freire claims that true learning combines the production and the apprehension of knowledge. He rejects the possibility of 'pre-packaged' knowledge which can simply be 'acquired' and insists that authentic knowledge is always produced by learners in the framework of dialogue and reflection on reality. Banking education disrupts this gnoseological circle and presents education as the acquisition of objective knowledge by distant intellectual authorities and the depositing of this knowledge (hence 'banking') into students who are seen as passive, empty vessels.

Banking pedagogy serves the ideology of oppression.[22] Since it prevents critical thinking and encourages the automatic acceptance of received wisdom, it facilitates the propagation of capitalist ideology while presenting this world view as objective and neutral. Even the educational process itself is presented to students through a capitalist ideological lens: the aim of education is not learning per se but preparing students for integration in the labour market. As such, banking education serves capitalism by means of instilling capitalist concepts, in this case the idea that the value of any action is the attainment of some material, financial reward which is external to the action itself. The transmission of ostensibly fixed, objective knowledge encourages learners to adopt a fatalistic attitude: the idea that the world, with all its shortcomings, is not dynamic or open to intervention and transformation but static and unchanging. Instead of getting involved and changing the world, the students' job is to adapt to it. Banking education creates hierarchical relations between authoritative, knowledgeable teachers and submissive, ignorant students, thereby instilling in learners feelings of inferiority and powerlessness in the face of what is perceived as legitimate and omnipotent authority. Moreover, this kind of pedagogy also operates in relation to the oppressors so as to perpetuate domination. While the lower classes are kept submissive and marginalised by means of competency-based banking-style literacy education, elite students are prevented from becoming critical through specialised technical education which discourages holistic, interconnected thinking; prevents the development of critique; and turns them into technicians for the dominant order.[23]

In contrast to banking education whose goal is the transfer of pre-packaged knowledge from teacher to students, Freirean, dialogical education enables learners to interpret the world through dialogue with a teacher, where the subject matter mediates between the participants. In Giroux's critical–theoretical language, this entails the replacement of positivism with dialectical, self-critical or reflective thought which seeks, in Walter Benjamin's phrase, to 'brush history against the grain', finding its cracks and fissures, that is, locating possibilities and images of emancipation and otherness within the oppressive reality of dominant society and culture.[24]

This kind of education involves a certain tension between the learners' freedom and the teacher's authority.[25] On the one hand, the learning process is grounded in the lives and culture of the students themselves, where the aim is to encourage them to think critically about topics which affect their lives (Freire assumes these topics will touch on the social and the political). This dialogue does not involve the domination of one person by another but the collective domination and transformation of the world by all the partners to the conversation.[26] On the other hand, the process is emphatically not child-centred nor free of boundaries. Freire insists on serious, critical and rigorous study and on a scientific attitude to reality.[27] Teachers are expected to expose students to their own, clearly presented, political–ethical positions, even if this has the potential to influence the students' own views (this is on condition that the teacher grants legitimacy to student narratives which may be different from those of her own). The educational process should give the students direction, while encouraging critical thinking and avoiding manipulation.[28] Freire thus sees education as a synthesis of structured, systematic teacher knowledge and the as-yet unstructured knowledge of the students, formed through dialogue. Freire expresses this position using a quotation from Mao: 'We must teach the masses with precision what we receive from them with confusion.'[29]

As this quotation perhaps implies, while problem-posing, dialogical pedagogy necessitates a significant role for learners, Freire does not focus on the role of students as agents. In contrast, Henry Giroux elaborates on the question of agency as opposed to structure and, as such, puts more emphasis on the active role of students as producers of culture and as mediators of their own oppression.[30] In an essay written with Roger Simon, Giroux argues for a conception of pedagogy as a form of cultural production and exchange, which deals with the question of how students actively construct the categories – both affective and cognitive – which prefigure their production of, and response to, classroom knowledge. Ignoring the knowledge students bring with them to the classroom – essentially popular culture – implies silencing and disempowering them.[31] Giroux's focus on students as agents gels with a wider political concern about the place of young people under neoliberalism. Whereas concern for youth and investment in young people were central concerns of the modernist, democratic project, neoliberalism's destruction of the social contract goes hand in hand with a reconceptualisation of youth as a threat; rather than attempting to solve social problems, the neoliberal state now punishes those who suffer from them – not least young people.[32]

Conscientisation

The relationship of education to the process of social and political change can best be understood by examining Freire's concept of conscientisation: the evolution from a naïve to a critical consciousness. Naïve consciousness is marked by an 'ideological' perspective (where ideology distorts reality in line with the interests of the ruling class), the failure to understand connections between different social phenomena, fatalism, the belief that culture (the product of human activity) is an unchangeable part of nature and seeing human beings as objects embedded in a reality from which they are all but indistinguishable. For the naïve consciousness, power relations and social oppression are incomprehensible and unchangeable facts to which one must simply adapt. In contrast, critical consciousness sees reality as dynamic and historical, as a system of problems which the human subject, distinct from material reality, can understand and overcome. A conscientised person is aware of himself and of the fact that his situation is due to oppression – power struggles in society – and not the state of nature.[33]

The path to critical consciousness is literacy, a variety of humanisation, the transformation of human beings from objects to subjects. Freire's literacy process is political; 'reading the word' is always accompanied by 'reading the world', and in fact a person has to learn how to read the world before becoming able to read the word. In Freire's original literacy programmes in Brazil, illiterate people learned to read the word and the world by analysing codifications – simple visual and verbal texts which describe aspects of the learners' lives. By analysing codifications, students acquire a critical distance from their reality and learn to see it as a set of problems which require solutions. This enables them to understand themselves as subjects who are capable of intervening in reality. They begin to understand their limitations (described by Freire as 'limit situations') not as immovable obstacles but rather as constraints which can be broken by means of 'limit acts', which produce a new reality complete with a new set of limit situations. This is *praxis*, through which understanding the world leads to transforming it.[34]

Freirean conscientisation involves not only the unveiling of the world and human subjectivity but a reflective process of reconceptualising previously held ideas. Human beings need to engage in meta-cognition and recognise their own cognitive acts. For example, oppressed people tend to reject the codifications that are presented to them in favour of their previously held convictions.

Gradually, the learners come to understand that this rejection stems from the internalisation of the oppressors' world view; in order to get critical distance on this perspective and neutralise it, culture must be transformed from an internalised factor which unconsciously influences behaviour to an object of knowledge whose impact can be recognised.[35]

Education and Politics

The connection between education and politics, between conscientisation and political–social revolution, is not self-evident. Despite being a pedagogue, Freire limits the role of education and gives precedence to politics, which he understands as action intended to take state power. He writes that awakening critical consciousness is a condition of social change but is not emancipatory in and of itself.[36] Freire argues that education is unable to generate social change precisely because of its potential power to do so. Schools do not determine the shape of society, the reverse is the case: the authorities in an unemancipated society will not permit education to threaten their status.[37] Yet despite his assumption that political change must precede any deep educational shift, Freire believes in the possibility of ideological change before the structural transformation of society. This change cannot be sharply distinguished from the material transformation but constitutes its initial stage; altered consciousness is the first step in problematising existing reality.[38]

In this context, before the revolution, education plays two roles in the process of liberation. First, conscientisation unveils for the oppressed the nature of their oppression, prepares them to participate in *praxis* and develops in them a commitment to social change. This role becomes even more important in the 'transitional phase', characterised by populism, bureaucratisation and the absence of dialogue. This kind of society features rebellious rather than critical consciousness; this does not lead to *praxis* (the dialectic of thought and action) but to activism – activity which is not grounded in an analysis of reality. In this context, the role of conscientisation is to enable a transition from naïve to critical consciousness, to guarantee a dialogical relationship between the revolutionary leaders and the people, to preserve the democratic character of the revolution and to prevent a takeover by a new, oppressive, leadership group.[39]

Second, since schools are sites for the reproduction of capitalist ideology, dialogical education has the power to subvert this process, in particular at the margins of the education system.[40] Giroux sharpens this view by adding that in addition to exposing capitalist and other oppressive ideologies, the radical potential of schools is to begin constructing more emancipatory social relations and practices as the basis for a democratic public sphere. This kind of potential for radical intervention is amplified by Giroux's take on Freire's implicit position that there is a distinction between schooling and education. While the radical potential of schools is limited by the fact that they are state institutions which essentially serve the interests of the dominant order, education in the sense of creating alternative public spheres, and the struggle for social and economic democracy can be carried out with adults outside of the school framework.[41] In fact, capitalism's insistence on education and lifelong learning actually provides opportunities for subversion as the authorities can never totally control what is being learned.[42]

* * *

Critical pedagogy's coherent, fleshed-out conception of education for radical social change forms an important context for my inquiry into potential theoretical foundations for Jewish social justice education. In particular, Freire and his successors raise several important issues that, as we will see below, resonate with themes articulated by Jewish writers and practitioners. Humanisation and dehumanisation connect with the idea that humanity reflects the image of God and with the moral imperatives that flow from this. The intersection of economic, cultural and political dimensions of oppression is reflected in the intertwined concerns of Jewish thinkers around economic inequality, racism, antisemitism and the complex interactions between privilege and disadvantage that stem from the various identities experienced and adopted by Jews. Critical pedagogy's dynamic, dialectical view of liberation as an ongoing process echoes a reluctance on the part of Jewish writers to articulate clear, utopian social visions, and the concomitant tendency to understand social change or progress as an ongoing challenge rather than a journey to a well-defined destination. The centrality of particular forms of *praxis* and dialogue, in particular Freire's brand of problem-posing education, dovetails with Jewish pedagogical approaches such as *dvar torah* (bringing traditional texts and ideas to bear on contemporary reality), *hevruta* (relational, pair-based study) and *mahloket* (a culture of controversy and disagreement). Finally, Jewish practitioners are preoccupied, like Freire, with the relationship between education and politics, and the various strategies of social change that emerge from this encounter.

In the next chapter, I explore a second important context for the study of Jewish social justice education: faith-based approaches inspired by Catholic social teaching and liberation theology.

2

Catholic Social Teaching and Liberation Theology – Theories of Religious Social Justice Education

Religious social justice education is, self-evidently, a relevant context for Jewish theory and practice. Writing on this topic is predominantly Catholic in orientation[1] and draws specifically on two traditions: Catholic social teaching (CST) and liberation theology. CST comprises a body of authoritative texts – mainly papal encyclicals and episcopal pastoral letters – dating from Pope Leo XIII's *Rerum Novarum* in 1891 and drawing on the biblical and theological traditions of the Church.[2] While aside from a few isolated references these texts do not address explicitly pedagogical issues, CST has inspired an educational literature, emanating largely from the Catholic universities in the United States. This literature consists mainly of theoretical attempts to elucidate the curricular and pedagogical implications of CST, alongside accounts of practical bids to implement CST principles in educational settings. In contrast, liberation theology emerged in Latin America in the late 1960s and early 1970s as a radical, religious response to the contemporary extremes of poverty, economic inequality and political oppression,[3] and has also inspired a smaller corpus of explicitly educational writing.

In this chapter, I will set out some of the key elements of a religious approach to social justice education as understood through the lens of these traditions, emphasising those themes that have the potential to enter into fruitful dialogue with Jewish approaches. These topics include the roles of the poor and the non-poor in the social justice enterprise; a spiritual, communitarian view of social justice; the centrality of *praxis*; the tension between individualist and structural conceptions of injustice; and the relationship between character education and more explicitly political forms of progressive pedagogy.

Poverty as a Religious Category

Catholic thinkers see poverty as a barometer for the spiritual health of wider society: injustice towards the poor means we have forgotten who God is, while returning to God requires us to experience poverty and relearn how to care for the poor.[4] In the same way, poverty is also an inducement to, or a trigger for, faith. Seminal liberation theologian Gustavo Gutierrez writes that liberation seeks to remedy three problems: first, material poverty and injustice; second, those things which limit human beings' 'ability to develop themselves freely and in dignity' – Freire might term this dehumanisation; third, selfishness and sin.[5] But is social and political liberation nothing more than a means to the end of spiritual salvation? In other texts (see below) it becomes clear that liberation theologians in particular define faith itself in terms of solidarity with the poor and the pursuit of justice. However, poverty is not only an economic indicator of a moral malaise; it is an inherently spiritual phenomenon. For Gutierrez, poverty means premature or unjust death, a negation of life as the prime human right and as a gift of God which is to be defended. Other writers have noted that Catholic responses to poverty are spiritual and communitarian rather than liberal in tone. Human beings created in the image of a triune God are understood to be fundamentally relational. Poverty is therefore unjust not because of the material deprivation it involves but because it means exclusion from the economic life of the community. Being treated as a non-member of the community – perhaps as a non-person – is the meaning of injustice.[6]

In the framework of Catholic thought, however, poverty is not only a social problem to be combatted; it is also a religious ideal. Roger Bergman, for example, cites the teaching of Jesuit leader Pedro Arrupe that the obligation to imitate and follow the poverty of Christ requires human beings to undergo an internal change under the influence of the Holy Spirit, developing solidarity with those who suffer and enabling them to be 'for others', living not for themselves but for Christ who died for the world.[7] Solidarity with the poor, then, seems to require in some sense the imitation or the assumption of poverty. This can be interpreted in two different ways: either taken literally as the renunciation of material goods for the sake of the spiritual benefits this brings, or understood as identification and solidarity with the poor in their pursuit of justice. The first of these two options implies a spiritual critique which focuses on the moral damage wealth causes to its owners (and possibly also on the spiritual damage which poverty wreaks in terms of human indignity and exclusion). The second option involves a direct attack on the material suffering of the poor in which the ideal of poverty does not require the renunciation of riches but rather the development of solidarity and the commitment to justice, which perhaps involve an emotional if not a physical detachment from one's possessions.

Critique of Enlightenment Individualism, Capitalism and Marxism

CST not only privileges the spiritual over the economic and the political, it is also built on a set of anti-individualist, communitarian assumptions. While the Church's attitude to private property evolved over the course of the twentieth century, papal encyclicals reflect an unchanging commitment to the primary values of human dignity and collaborative work for the common good and to the subordination of private property to these goals. These principles, rather than a materialist commitment to economic justice, explain CST's progressive views on the dignity of labour, unemployment, unionisation, the role of the state in social and economic management, global poverty and international development. In its more radical moments, CST's spiritual and communitarian principles bring it into direct conflict with capitalism. At the same time, CST has always defended the principle of private property so long as it is employed for the common good, and explicitly set itself up in opposition to Marxism and as a means of combatting the influence of communism among the poor.

Liberation theology's attack on capitalism is far more radical and thoroughgoing: it claims that capitalism has failed to meet the basic needs of most human beings and that socialism is more compatible with Christianity.[8] Whereas mainstream, canonical CST emphasises the responsibility of the rich and poor to work in harmony, liberation theology considers capital and labour – what it terms the 'civilisations of wealth and poverty' – to be inherently in conflict, and believes that this conflict will lead to the replacement of the sinful market economy with the Kingdom of God. Liberation theologians such as Gutierrez and Petrella argue that capitalism's commitment to profit as the highest value instrumentalises human life and as such is a form of idolatry which is incompatible with Christianity.[9]

Catholic approaches to social justice, then, reflect a variety of approaches to capitalism and Marxism: at one end of the spectrum, an acceptance of capitalism tempered by a critique of its inhuman and un-Christian excesses, combined with a resolute opposition to Marxism; at the other, a rejection of capitalism as intrinsically sinful or idolatrous, an affinity with socialism and a cautious acceptance of some Marxist ideas. What these approaches have in common is an anti-materialist, communitarian orientation, and a rejection of individualist, instrumental approaches associated with the Enlightenment.

Social, Economic and Spiritual Vision: God and the World

While Catholic approaches assume the priority of the spiritual over the material, this has clear moral and social implications. Fred Kammer, for example, writes that CST is grounded in the biblical model of the Jubilee year, in which slaves are set free and all land is returned to its ancestral occupants.[10] Manifested through this vision of redistributive justice is a spiritual notion that property is subordinate to humanity: since the land belongs to God, human beings' claim to it is temporary and relative. More broadly, Catholic social justice writers connect the spiritual to the moral and social through the concept of *imitatio Dei* – the ideal of imitating God or God's attributes. This means human beings share in God's work of creation through their responsibility for stewardship over the world and participate in God's fundamentally relational nature through their relationships within the covenantal community. These ideas drawn from the Hebrew Bible are amplified in Jesus's universalisation of the covenantal community, its extension particularly to the *anavim* (the poor or oppressed) and the notion that we find God by caring for each other.

Moreover, CST and liberation theology also contend explicitly with social and economic issues. Papal encyclicals and other CST documents draw on underlying spiritual and moral values to set out clear political and economic visions. *Quadragesimo Anno*, for example, calls for the just distribution of resources in line with the common good. This includes profit sharing, fair wages, a share in company ownership for workers and a collaborative economic model to alleviate the problem of class conflict. *Pacem in Terris* advocates a regime of economic rights such as the opportunity to work, just wages, the right of workers to own property, the right to life, food, clothing, shelter, medical care and social security; these demands are based on concepts of human dignity and universal natural law. *Populorum Progressio* sets out a vision of international development based on planning, cooperation and interdependence rather than free trade, reflecting an economic order built on solidarity between the rich and the poor.[11] In contrast, perhaps because of its origins as a response to the traumatic abuses of the Latin American dictatorships, liberation theology has tended to articulate an uncompromising cry of denunciation rather than a constructive political programme.¹² This avoidance of any specific, concrete social vision seems also to reflect an aversion to straightforward utopianism. Gutierrez, for example, implies that the fulfilment of his social vision is a meta-historical event which is prefigured by historical acts of liberation that lead towards but never quite realise it. He writes that the envisaged new fraternal society *manifests itself* in historical deeds that lead towards liberation, but that the roots of oppression will not be destroyed unless the advent of the Kingdom is a grace, that is, a gift. If so, the social vision inspired by Gutierrez's conception of the relationship with God is unattainable other than in the acts of people working in the here and now towards its realisation.¹³

Several Catholic writers have addressed the role of community, culture and religion in a just society. Bergman,¹⁴ for example, cites Alasdair MacIntyre's critique of Enlightenment individualism and his claim that a coherent moral identity can only be sustained within a tradition and a culturally or communally informed, teleological conception of human life. This implies a politics which enables local communities to survive by sustaining a life of the common good against the destructive, modern forces of the nation state and the market. It also involves a communitarian conception of human rights in which rights are defined as minimum conditions for life in community, as reflected in the US Bishops' pastoral letter *Economic Justice for All*.¹⁵ In this context, Christian conceptions of justice as the reign of God provide communal, relational alternatives to universal, liberal and individualist perspectives.

Social Justice Education as Personal and Moral Development

Any discussion of the educational and other strategies proposed by Catholic social justice thinkers must be contextualised against the tension between personal and structural conceptions of social justice; in other words, the relationship between individual actions and social structures as causes of injustice and as arenas for change. Beginning in the 1960s, liberation theology and then CST began to diagnose poverty and injustice in terms of social or structural sin. The market economy, for example, can be seen as a structure which necessitates and rationalises sinful behaviour. While individuals are responsible for these structures, they cannot be rectified solely through individual effort.¹⁶ However, in the 1980s, more conservative forces in the Church sought to contain what they considered to be an overly radical notion. In the Congregation for the

Doctrine of the Faith's *Libertatis Nuntius* – Instruction on Certain Aspects of the 'Theology of Liberation', Cardinal Joseph Ratzinger (later Pope Benedict XVI) admits the existence of structural sin but asserts that structures are consequences, not causes, of individual actions. Individual morality is therefore the primary concern and cannot be neglected until after a process of structural change.[17]

In this context, it is possible to identify two overlapping, interlinked approaches in the liberation theology and CST literature: social justice pedagogy as a process of personal and moral development, or as a form of radical, political education.

Social change as a process of personal and moral development is exemplified by Roger Bergman's book *Catholic Social Learning*.[18] Alongside the CST canon, Bergman draws on Ignatian pedagogy (named after St Ignatius of Loyola, sixteenth-century founder of the Society of Jesus) as articulated by Jesuit Superior General Pedro Arrupe in the 1970s. Ignatian pedagogy operates according to the 'see, judge, act' pastoral cycle. This process involves the teacher guiding students to distil their understanding on the basis of their existing experience, and directing them towards new experiences and information in order to expand their knowledge. Next, students engage in reflection in order to grasp the essentials of what is being learned, to understand the connections between different areas of knowledge and to learn how to learn. This period of reflection should be a formative process which impels students to the third stage, action. Here the teacher's role is to provide action opportunities which lead to further experiences, reflection and action. The process is valuable even if it does not lead to concrete social change, as its purpose is to transform how the students live in the world, impelled by faith to seek the greater good.

Bergman illustrates this pedagogical strategy through a case study following students from a Catholic university on a service learning semester programme in the Dominican Republic and Haiti. Bergman reports that the students' experience of real poverty during this programme got theology down 'into the pit of the stomach'. This is an attempt at 'Freirean empowerment' of privileged students, by creating a context in which 'heartbreaking personal relationships with the poor seem to necessitate personal transformation'.[19] The programme was deeply unsettling for students as it put them in unfamiliar social, cultural, linguistic, economic and communal settings, opening them to new ways of being and energising the intellectual exchange of the classroom. The learning process focused, for example, on students' feelings of guilt upon realising that the average annual income in the Dominican Republic was equal to the sum they had brought with them as spending money. This forced them to acknowledge that they were complicit in the world's inequalities, despite their best intentions.

The feeling was intensified by the insight that despite their desire to serve, there was nothing they could do to help their Dominican friends; in fact, they were the true beneficiaries of the process in terms of their inner transformation. The emotional scars left on the students formed their most important learning points. They came to understand their distress theologically, as a parallel to ancient Israel's crying out to God. Learning to cry, feeling and articulating the pain of others, is in itself an educational goal and practice. Yet while there is a sense in Bergman's writing that the feelings of guilt and distress are a primal reaction to the suffering of other human beings, his account makes clear that this emotional response is contingent upon social analysis: guilt results when students understand that there is a causal relationship between their privilege and their friends' suffering.

Bergman claims that this process has deep foundations in Catholicism, being connected in his view not only to Freirean *praxis* and hence to the roots of liberation theology but to Aristotelian *phronesis* (a type of knowledge acquired through reflective practice – see Chapter 8) which, he notes, has been dominant in Catholic social ethics since Aquinas. He argues that this kind of service learning most closely parallels Aristotle's process of habituation followed by a phronetic critical assessment and refinement which takes into account an analysis of the structural roots of injustice. Drawing on Alasdair Macintyre's neo-Aristotelian ethics, Bergman goes on to argue that since personal-moral identity cannot exist apart from a tradition of practices and a teleological or vocational narrative which embodies that tradition, learning about the virtues involves observing them in the narrative context of other people's lives. As such, learning to emulate moral exemplars or role models is a core component of justice education. Learning from exemplars operates partly on the affective plane in that it evokes shame in the young person that she does not measure up, alongside an imaginative aspiration to emulate them.

Bergman's approach contains an unacknowledged contradiction between the goal of educating students for a life of service by means of an experiential, affective process which informs social analysis on the one hand, and the lesson which the experience teaches on the other: that personal service in the form of volunteering is impotent in the face of structural injustice. While Bergman tacitly endorses an evolutionary model of social change based on individual moral action to improve the world, this tension implies a more revolutionary conclusion. If individual service is powerless to address structural inequality (and therefore to assuage the sense of guilt to which structural injustice gives rise), then a habituative/phronetic character education for social justice makes little sense. The alternative implied by his argument is an experiential-affective process whose goal is the development of critical social analysis as a means for conceptualising and working towards the realisation of radically alternative ways of structuring a just society.[20]

Social Justice Pedagogy as Political Education

The second variety of Catholic social justice pedagogy can be characterised broadly as political education. If the approaches surveyed above emphasise the character education of the non-poor for a life of service in pursuit of the common good, the pedagogies under discussion here seek to work directly with the poor or oppressed and enable them to participate in the politics of radical social change. The fundamentals of this approach are illustrated by Daniel Schipani's book, *Religious Education Encounters Liberation Theology*.[21] Since many aspects of Schipani's work superficially resemble Bergman's approach as outlined above, a comparison of the two will make clear the fundamental differences between these models of social justice pedagogy.

Schipani sets out what he calls a liberationist perspective for doing religious education, based on a similar model to Bergman's Jesuit pastoral cycle. However, while Bergman implicitly conceives of the poor as a means to the end of this process of character education for social justice agents in training, Schipani emphasises the importance of solidarity and true dialogue if educators are to play a genuine part in achieving social change. For him, social justice education means enabling the poor themselves to transform the world. He describes conscientisation, the core of this process, in religious terms, as a movement from storytelling to history-making, whereby people come to inhabit emancipatory stories such as the Exodus and the Resurrection and assume authorship of them. Drawing on Freire, he emphasises that educators must face the challenge of immersing themselves in the life situation of the people they serve, focusing on their real issues and themes, and engaging in authentic dialogue based on listening, open conversation, mutual caring and community building. Biblical or theological input can play a role in informing and transforming the discussion, but only in non-authoritarian, non-indoctrinating ways, such that Christian principles renew themselves no less than imposing themselves on their environment. This dialogue enables people to see alternatives to the limit situations they face, paraphrased by Schipani as learning to see God's presence in the world.

Although liberation theology involves the poor reclaiming the Bible, the liberationist hermeneutic means that Scripture takes second place to the people's concrete experience. Schipani describes a hermeneutical circle between the biblical text in historical context (A) and the contemporary context of the ecclesial community (B). B shapes the reading of A, which in turn enables us to transform B, in light of which we reread A anew. Where Bergman focused on the transformation of students in light of their experience of somewhat objectivised poor people, Schipani grants epistemological privilege to the oppressed as subjects, in that their situation is closer to that of the Bible's original audience. This perspective reflects the epistemological centrality of *praxis*. Schipani articulates the well-known theological idea that religious faith or knowledge of God is to be understood as obedience to the will of God and *imitatio Dei* – imitating the divine attributes. He argues that this represents a rejection of the cognitive model of knowledge (equated with Freire's banking education) which for Schipani is reflected in the Old Testament and which Jesus encountered at the hands of his authoritarian Jewish teachers. Schipani's conception of theological knowledge as essentially practical and relational derives from two principles: the idea that 'walking the path leads to understanding the path', in other words, that cognitive knowledge can only derive from experience or *praxis*, and from a commitment to transformation rather than rationality as the goal of knowledge.[22]

Community is central to religious political pedagogy. In Latin America, the kind of popular education described by Schipani was intimately connected with the Ecclesial Base Community (EBC) movement.[23] Particularly in periods of dictatorship and often in tension with the Church hierarchy, the EBCs forged a connection between spiritual renewal and social commitment, combining the seeing–judging–acting (and celebrating) method with participation, democracy and leadership training. Pastoral agents were engaged in training local leaders, thereby reducing dependence on clerics and increasing participation and responsibility. They also worked to involve their communities in local, neighbourhood issues, using the pastoral cycle to share issues, reflect on them in light of Scripture in order to understand that God is on the side of the oppressed and take action in the wider, secular community.

The Role of the 'Non-poor'

In contrast with liberation theology, CST-based educational approaches tend to emphasise the role of the non-poor in the social justice enterprise. It is important to understand this position in the broader context of research on the role of social justice education with non-poor or oppressor groups. The importance of working with non-poor or privileged groups has been noted both in terms of their relative access to power and their capacity to support social change initiatives, and in light of the history of non-poor individuals taking up the leadership of radical movements.[24] However, there is no consensus over the role of the non-poor in working for social justice and the educational processes they need to undergo in order to take this function on.

Some scholars have used multicultural or intersectional models in which intersecting class, gender, racial, religious and other identities form a matrix in which each individual takes on both oppressor and oppressed positions, which are situationally specific. In this context, unlearning privilege and addressing social justice are good for the privileged because they too are seen to suffer from oppression.[25] Taking issue with this approach, Ricky Lee Allen notes that privileged students reading Freire's *Pedagogy of the Oppressed* often assume that they are in the role of the oppressed – a 'delusional space' which ignores structured hierarchies and adopts a postmodern position in which we cannot value one form of oppression more than any other.[26] Against this, he argues that Freire clearly distinguishes between dehumanisation and oppression, setting up an 'oppression-humanisation' dialectic in which the terms are related but not conflated. Oppression is specifically about access to power and privilege and, accordingly, while the privileged may be dehumanised, they are not oppressed.

For Allen, the solution is to move oppressors towards critical consciousness. Indeed, he points out that multiculturalism is undergoing a 'turn' in the direction of the oppressor, trying to create a sense of radical agency among oppressor groups by focusing on the construction of white identity or masculinity, for example, as oppressive structures and convincing oppressors that they are accountable for their racially or gender-conditioned privilege. Using members of the oppressor class to challenge oppression in this way is potentially empowering. However, the process is inevitably difficult because the oppressors' myths insulate them against humanisation, and they hang on to these and their oppressor identity at all costs. Recognising cognitively that one is an oppressor does not automatically lead to action or to solidarity with the oppressed. This requires concrete action in which the privileged work against oppression, become 'class traitors' risking retaliation, accept the knowledge claims of the oppressed, follow their leadership and demonstrate genuine love for them. In Freirean terms, this process is one of ongoing humanisation, conversion and 'rebirth'.

CST-influenced writers tend to reject both these perspectives – the multicultural and the Freirean-conversionary. Instead, they distinguish between the poor and their implicitly non-poor advocates – the justice activists – and often tacitly grant this latter group the dominant role in achieving social change. While poverty is held up as an ideal, this is often interpreted as a psychological detachment from material goods and a commitment to working for justice, rather than a demand to cast off one's possessions and actually join the ranks of the poor.

A range of more nuanced Christian approaches is evident in *Pedagogies for the Non-Poor*,[27] a series of reflections on mainly Church-based social justice education initiatives aimed at middle-class participants in North America. Some of the projects surveyed in the book are designed to effect attitudinal or behavioural change among the participants, along the lines of the character education approaches surveyed above. These include an initiative to nurture small groups of 'peacemakers' and to educate the community in a local parish towards peace activism, and study programmes which seek to sensitise participants to social justice issues through travel in the Global South or by facilitating contact with academics from developing countries, thereby leading to educational and political action. Other projects aim directly at mobilising non-poor participants for political action, for example, lobbying politicians about global hunger. A third category emphasises relationship-building, leading to social and political action, for example, an initiative to enlist the support of middle-class churches to respond to factory closures, and a family justice network which sought to connect with activists in Central America. While these projects all grant agency in the process of social change to the non-poor, one example hints at a more 'conversionary' or solidary perspective: a classroom-based educational programme led by nuns which aims to encourage wealthier participants to let go of the resources needed by the poor and to support their struggle for housing, healthcare, education and security.

* * *

In his book *Educating for Life*, Catholic educationalist Thomas Groome writes that as well as proposing a philosophy of education for Catholic communities, he hopes to draw from the 'depth structures' of Catholic Christianity in order to contribute to a broader conception of a universal, spiritual, humanising education.[28] These depth structures include a positive anthropology, the sacramentality of life, the importance of relationship and community, spirituality and working for justice. In this chapter I have surveyed some of the central educational themes of CST and liberation theology that have the potential to serve a similar role in my exploration of Jewish social justice education.

Certain ideas will become particularly important in the ensuing discussion. The relationship between *praxis* and cognitive learning taps into the Jewish principle of *Torah lishmah* – learning for its own sake – and the complexities this creates for the ways education relates to social action. A religious appraisal of poverty and exclusion is important in different ways to Catholic and Jewish thinkers. Writers and practitioners from both traditions are preoccupied with a critique of modernity, in particular individualism, capitalism and Marxism, and conversely with the articulation of a social vision based on spiritual and moral values. Catholic and Jewish approaches are both caught up in the relationships between individualist and structural understandings of injustice and the concomitant tension between character education and political education approaches. Finally, Catholic writers are interested in the role of the poor as opposed to the non-poor in social activism; this theme is taken up by Jewish thinkers, whose approach is complicated by the ambiguous range of historical and current positions taken by Jews along the privilege–oppression axis.

In the next chapter, I explore a final important context for the study of Jewish social justice education: contemporary theological, philosophical and political approaches to the relationship between Judaism and social justice.

3

Judaism and Social Justice – Religion, Culture and Progressive Politics

The final context for an exploration of Jewish social justice education consists of Jewish theological, cultural and political approaches to social justice. The notion that social justice values spring organically from Jewish tradition or even that Judaism is primarily a call to social activism is, perhaps unsurprisingly, commonplace among politically progressive Jewish thinkers. However, in reality the relationship between Judaism and social justice is more complex. Traditional Jewish literature is replete with xenophobic and patriarchal content and this is reflected in the prevalence of right-wing, chauvinistic and even racist trends in contemporary Jewish discourse. Readings of Judaism as a universalist social justice tradition, like any contemporary political construal of the tradition, must therefore be seen as the result of an interpretive process, best understood through a hermeneutical lens. Accordingly, in this chapter I will locate contemporary Jewish ideas of social justice within the dialogue between Judaism and modernity that began in eighteenth-century Europe, specifically the encounter between Jews and political ideologies such as liberalism, socialism and nationalism.

The Jewish Encounter with Modern Politics

Modern Jewish history in Europe (and extending by the late nineteenth century to Russia, North America and the land of Israel) is marked by the encounter with political movements and ideologies. From the mid-1800s, Jews developed a strong affinity for liberal, republican and constitutional politics – the forces behind Jewish emancipation and the acquisition of equal rights.[1] While many Jews retained these liberal loyalties, the late nineteenth century saw the emergence of an even stronger political relationship: between Jews and socialism.[2] For members of an often impoverished, persecuted and marginalised community, the attraction of radical politics was clear. Many Jews sought to immerse themselves in the general socialist movement, taking on universalist left-wing positions, joining social–democratic and, later, Communist parties. While some Jewish radicals were undoubtedly influenced by vestigial prophetic and rabbinic ideals of social justice, this initial encounter with socialism was more often associated with the weakening of religious and cultural commitments. Integration into the internationalist, cosmopolitan and anti-clerical Left frequently meant abandoning particularistic Jewish loyalties and identity.

As a result of this cosmopolitanism and perhaps, conversely, because of tacit nationalistic and antisemitic attitudes, radical movements tended to neglect the cultural needs of the Jewish population and the specificity of the problems faced by Jews. Marxists, for example, typically asserted that antisemitism required no special attention, being little more than a symptom of capitalism that would wither away after the revolution. These tendencies, alongside the Jewish community's historically ingrained inclination towards autonomous forms of organisation, prompted the emergence of explicitly Jewish forms of socialism. The best known of these was the Bund, the General Jewish Worker's Union, founded in Lithuania in 1897, which soon became the most powerful Jewish political movement in the Russian Empire. The Bund's commitment to mobilising Jewish workers led it to organise in Yiddish, the language of the Jewish masses. This began as a pragmatic, tactical decision, but over time the Bund became increasingly concerned with specific issues of Jewish rights, antisemitism and the importance of secular, proletarian Jewish culture. By 1901 it had adopted a form of Diaspora nationalism, calling for extra-territorial, cultural autonomy for the Jewish community in the framework of a multinational, federal state.[3] While the Bund remained vehemently anti-religious and anti-Zionist, it therefore came to represent an attempt to do radical politics in a distinctively Jewish way.

Jewish Socialism, Socialist Judaism

The synthesis of Jewish and socialist ideologies, however, reached its apogee in the convergence of socialism with another form of nationalism: Zionism. Contemporary Zionism has come to be associated to a significant extent with the political and religious Right. However, perhaps unsurprisingly for an essentially utopian movement, Zionism was strongly influenced from its inception by left-wing politics. Three of its founding ideologues – Moses Hess, Nahman Syrkin and

Ber Borochov – were committed socialists. For these thinkers, Zionism was not only a solution to the particularly Jewish problems of antisemitism and alienation but was a means for advancing a universal vision of social justice – by definition a distant prospect – by creating a socialist Jewish state in the here and now. These formulations of socialist Zionism cemented the idea of an intrinsic connection between Jewish national or cultural identity and the values of social justice. It is worth exploring briefly some of the more interesting ways this notion was developed by Labour Zionist ideologues: Berl Katznelson, Aaron David Gordon and the leaders of the Religious Kibbutz Movement (Martin Buber was another vitally important progressive Zionist thinker; his work will be covered in more depth in Part 3). In different ways, each of these ideologues sought to articulate not only a genuinely Jewish socialism but an explicitly socialist Judaism.

Berl Katzelson was one of the most important leaders of the pre-State Jewish community in Palestine. He integrated socialism with the ideology of cultural Zionism, pioneered by thinkers like Ahad Ha'am, which sought to bring about a renaissance of Judaism as the secular-national culture of the Jewish people.[4] He applied the concept of 'revolutionary constructivism' to the act of building a socialist society from the ground up and to the reconstruction of Judaism based on what he saw as its positive, progressive cultural heritage. Katznelson took issue with those members of the labour movement who sought to abandon Jewish tradition or to transform it in excessively radical ways. Instead, he argued that rituals such as Jewish festivals were uniquely suited to become carriers for socialist Jewish values, and were amenable to reinterpretation and evolution into new, secular forms of practice while retaining this authentic content. He saw the festival of Passover, for example, as the embodiment of the Jewish people's yearning for freedom, understood not only in terms of national emancipation but as the 'liberation from the oppression of class by class'.[5]

A. D. Gordon, a Polish-Jewish immigrant to the land of Israel in the early 1900s, created a different but equally intriguing synthesis of nationalism, religiosity and progressive politics.[6] Gordon's core values of labour, solidarity and social equality stemmed not from Marxism, to which he was adamantly opposed, but rather from a nationalist commitment to creating a new, healthier form of Jewish collective life. Gordon believed that Diaspora existence had crippled the Jews, cutting them off from their land, an essential source of sustenance, and forcing them to survive through the dried-up resources of history and religion. The revival of the Jewish people necessitated the re-establishment of the bond with the land by reintroducing Jews to manual, agricultural labour. However, this particularistic reformulation of Jewish identity also had a deeply universalist complexion. Gordon believed in the organic unity of the cosmos, of nature and of all people, and that human beings have degraded and profaned the universe through corrupted, capitalist social relations and the commodification and exploitation of nature. The regeneration of universal nature required the regeneration of individual human nature, which was itself to be attained through the immersion of human beings *in* nature. The reclamation of agricultural labour was therefore a vehicle not only for Jewish national rebirth but for social justice, the reshaping of human nature and the redemption of the world.

The Religious Kibbutz movement, founded in 1935 as a framework for the creation of Orthodox agricultural communes in the land of Israel, sought explicitly to create a dialogue between socialism and Judaism, while preserving the authenticity and integrity of the Torah as a distinctive tradition.[7] Like Gordon, its leaders were keenly aware of a rift between Judaism and modern, human existence, and addressed themselves to the challenge of closing this gap by revitalising religious life under conditions of Jewish independence. However, they were aware of the distance between the Torah's pre-modern context and largely ritual–ethical character on the one hand, and the nature of capitalist society and modern political ideologies on the other. They therefore resisted the impulse to read modern values such as socialism into Judaism in an artificial way. Instead, they recognised that Jewish jurisprudence contains interpretive tools (e.g. the concepts of 'beyond the letter of the law' and 'the spirit of the law') which allow for the expansion of the Torah's remit into progressive social approaches without threatening its integrity. For example, the laws of *tzedakah* (charity) tacitly accept the existence of poverty and inequality, whereas the spirit of the law aspires to a classless society. The method adopted by these thinkers was to understand the Torah's social principles (such as the sovereignty of God and the consequent contingency of private property) in their original context, conduct an analysis of contemporary capitalist society and then implement the Torah's principles in a way that was appropriate to modern conditions; in their view, this meant a socialist response. Preserving the distinctiveness of the Torah's moral–religious discourse in the face of political ideology was important in an additional sense. The Religious Kibbutz movement's leaders believed in a dialectic of personal-moral and social renewal; individual transformation was necessary for political change and vice versa. This represented a synthesis of distinct Jewish and political–materialist approaches and reflected their conviction that socialism without a moral, religious base would inevitably become oppressive.

* * *

The foregoing survey of attempts to synthesise Judaism and modern progressive politics is an important backdrop for an exploration of contemporary Jewish social justice discourse. However, the next phase of the discussion has to take into account a radically changed context. Jewish socialism emerged as a political force in the large Yiddish-speaking Jewish population centres of Eastern Europe under conditions of rising nationalism and antisemitism, growing poverty and mass migration. Since then, the Jewish world has been transformed by the physical destruction of Eastern European Jewry by the Nazis and its cultural degradation under Communism, the establishment of the State of Israel, the collapse of the Soviet Union and the concomitant disruption of socialist politics, and by the growth of multiculturalism and the progressive social and economic integration of Jews in the democratic West, particularly in the United States.[8] Finally, Judaism has been profoundly influenced by the emergence of feminism and movements for racial justice: civil rights, anti-apartheid and Black Lives Matter. In the remainder of this chapter I will explore the relationship between Judaism and social justice in the work of thinkers operating in this contemporary, Western, post-Communist, Diaspora setting. I have largely excluded Israeli writing that specifically tackles social justice issues in that country; while there are significant, politically progressive Jewish thinkers and practitioners operating in Israel, the conditions of Jewish majority status and cultural dominance frame the relationship between Judaism and politics in ways that lie outside the scope of this study. And despite biblical and rabbinic literature's rich treatment of justice-related issues such as social ethics, obligations to the poor, *tzedakah* (charity) and civic responsibility, I have steered away from these pre-modern texts in their own right – although contemporary Jewish thought clearly exists in intensive dialogue with this traditional material.

The following survey addresses three core themes which characterise contemporary Jewish social justice discourse: the tension between utopianism and incremental, reformist or pragmatic approaches to social change; structural and collective versus individual and interpersonal conceptions of justice; and finally the nature of the relationship between Jewish tradition and social justice concerns.

Revolution or Reform?

Contemporary Jewish social justice thinkers can be located on a spectrum between those who advocate radical, utopian visions, often accompanied by a revolutionary approach to social change, and those who adopt pragmatic, incremental and reformist views. This tension encompasses two interconnected questions: how radically different is the ideal, envisaged future from current reality, and is the transition between current reality and the envisaged future to be achieved gradually or abruptly?

Israeli philosopher Avi Sagi explores these questions by analysing the concept *tikkun olam* ('repairing the world'), which originates in rabbinic and mystical texts and which has become a popular label for Jewish social justice work.[9] Sagi distinguishes between two understandings of the term: as a utopian ideal and as a social–historical process. Utopian thought involves transcending or rejecting reality in favour of a clearly imagined alternative and then returning to reality in order to rebuild it. He argues that this risks presenting culturally specific ideas as universally valid, ignoring the complexity of reality and the diverse needs of different people and groups and, in the absence of agreement and compromise, resorting to violence and coercion to impose a particular vision. In contrast, Sagi prefers to conceptualise *tikkun olam* as a process of socio-cultural criticism concerned with achieving reform in a particular society rather than the entire world. This is reminiscent of Freire's understanding of utopia as an ongoing, dialectical process of social change driven by *praxis* – critique of existing reality as the basis for action which, in turn, leads to the creation of a new reality and a new target for critique. In this formulation, *tikkun olam* tends towards pluralism, since it is grounded in the complexity of empirical, human reality. As such, it avoids the dangers of the utopian model and, as a response to concrete suffering, tends to be more effective at prompting action than an abstract set of ideas.

Mapping this philosophical discussion onto the Bible, Michael Walzer describes how the Exodus story has been used to buttress both bold, utopian and more cautious, pragmatic positions.[10] Moses putting the people to the sword after the sin of the golden calf (Exodus 32) has been used as a justification for purges and revolutionary violence by groups as diverse as Calvinists and Leninists. A social–democratic reading of the story, in contrast, portrays Moses as a dialogical leader who educates and debates with the people, gradually leading them to redemption during their forty years of wandering in the desert. While Walzer does not specify if social–democratic Moses is any less utopian than Leninist Moses (theoretically, moderate methods could be used to achieve revolutionary results), in Sagi's formulation, utopian vision is associated with revolutionary tactics and violence.

Perhaps for this reason, contemporary Jewish social justice writing tends towards pluralism, pragmatism and reformism. This distinguishes it from the radical, utopian visions articulated by nineteenth- and early-twentieth-century

Jewish socialists. While some Jewish authors clearly believe in a radical reshaping of society along non-capitalist, egalitarian, communitarian lines, most focus on social critique and the articulation of religious and moral principles rather than expressing a clear-cut, utopian vision. They also display a preference for personal transformation, community building and reformist politics over revolutionary change. This reflects, no doubt, the context in which this literature has been produced: largely middle-class, liberal, religious communities within relatively stable democratic societies. However, this moderate bias also indicates a theologically grounded tendency to prioritise relationships over ideology. Michael Lerner, the founder of *Tikkun*[11] magazine, reflects that the world's flaws need to be healed by flawed human beings and that the mission to transform the world must therefore always be accompanied by compassion for others and for ourselves.[12] Reform theologian Eugene Borowitz invokes the kabbalistic idea that in order to create the world, God's power first had to be directed towards itself, creating the *tzimtzum* (withdrawal or contraction) necessary to make space for existence. Drawing on this teaching, he argues – in terms reminiscent of Freire – that leadership should not be thought of in terms of the accomplishment of plans but in line with the humanising effect it has on those being led. People should not be seen as the means to the end of the leader's goal but as co-creators, nurtured by the leader, working on common aims.[13]

Structural and Personal Approaches

In light of the generally pragmatic, gradualist tone adopted by Jewish social justice thinkers, we might perhaps expect them to adopt individualistic, ethical and interpersonal approaches to social change. While much of the literature can be characterised in this way, a number of writers in fact emphasise collective, political and macro-economic perspectives.

This structural strand in Jewish social justice thinking is based on the assertion that the social and economic system itself is a matter of religious or ethical concern. Abraham Joshua Heschel,[14] for example, invokes the biblical prophets to insist that God is primarily concerned with commonplace, everyday issues of economic justice in education, housing and jobs. This kind of spiritual commitment leads several writers to critique capitalism and propose various forms of values-driven economics. Capitalism is criticised in that it evaluates human activity in solely economic terms and neglects the religious importance of work as a means of achieving human dignity and responsibility.[15] Its economic crimes against the poor constitute a form of humiliation and a direct affront to their human dignity.[16] Free market economics and the belief that narrow self-interest leads to public benefit undermine the halakhic (Jewish legal) principle that individuals are to be held responsible for damage, including damage to the environment.[17] Similarly, if globalisation is not the result of human agency but rather the product of the invisible hand or chaos theory, how can it be judged morally? As such, capitalism is held to be incompatible with Torah, not because it contradicts the details of a putative halakhic economic system but because the idea of doing 'the right and the good' would place such restrictions on private property as to make it unprofitable and therefore untenable.[18] Jewish feminism also exhibits this kind of structural tendency. Thinkers such as Judith Plaskow[19] and Tamar Ross[20] have engaged in a thorough critique of patriarchal structures in Jewish theology and *halakhah* (law and practice), suggesting systemic reform as a necessary antidote. While much Jewish feminist writing is dedicated to the project of reshaping Judaism itself, some writers have applied Jewish feminist principles to wider, structural issues such as healthcare and social justice[21] and intersectional analyses of race, class and sexuality.[22]

As well as emphasising the significance of economic and social systems, structurally minded thinkers tend to argue that the collective, specifically the State, has an important role to play in advancing social equality. *Tzedakah* (charity or poverty relief), for example, is seen not as a voluntary act but as an obligation for the collective as well as for the individual. Just as this duty was discharged in the pre-modern period through the coercive power of the self-governing Jewish community, in modern times this obligation is to be taken on by government.[23] Similarly, Judaism's primary aim of regulating human behaviour through law, combined with its communal and national collectivism, predisposes it against individualism and in favour of state action to achieve welfare. However, this approach is set against a marked suspicion of state authority (embodied in biblical laws designed to control abuses of royal power) which means government intervention needs to be limited.[24] One solution to this tension is a vision of social and economic policy shaped by the Maimonidean principles of moderation and pragmatism, in which government's role is to regulate markets away from extremes and to balance competition and profit with cooperation and social responsibility.[25]

However, even these somewhat ambivalent statist, collectivist positions are contested by authors who advocate for a more personal, intimate conception of social justice. Elliot Dorff claims that Judaism rejects the secular separation of private and public and seeks to pursue *tikkun olam* – repairing the world – in the context of the family, based on the idea that God cares about all aspects of our lives and that people cause harm to each other in their personal relationships no less than in their social ones.[26] Jonathan Sacks takes up this personal orientation and uses it to make an explicitly anti-structural, anti-political argument:

> There is nothing wrong with our economics or our politics. The failure lies with our unwillingness to make sacrifices in the short-term to ensure the health of our families and communities in the long-term. … No government can make us solicitous, law-abiding, honest, public-spirited or reliable. No law or economic incentive can make families stay together, or neighbours help one another, or parents spend more time with their children. … The politics of hope is born the moment we locate responsibility within ourselves, knowing that we can change and that we are not alone.[27]

Sacks argues that we need to move away from a redistributive politics focused on money and towards a civic liberalism that strives for social integration and civic virtue and which requires relationship- and institution-building, not statist redistribution. He claims that resuscitating the common good requires us to reject Aristotle's conception of human beings as political animals and the State as a contractual arrangement designed to address the clash of competing, self-interested agendas, and instead to adopt Maimonides's view of human beings as social creatures whose identities are shaped by relationships based on kinship and *hesed* (covenantal love).

As Sacks's ultimately relational, covenantal approach illustrates, it is possible to find intermediate positions between the structural and personal perspectives set out above. Several writers articulate such a view by focusing on the importance of community or civil society as ways of mediating the dichotomy of the individual and the State. In his book *Justice in the City: An Argument from the Sources of Rabbinic Judaism*, Aryeh Cohen points out approvingly that in the Greek tradition cities are important because they enable the perfection of the virtues, both by providing an interpersonal framework within which people have the opportunity to perfect their individual virtues, and by enabling the aggregation of individual imperfect virtues so as to create perfection on a collective level. A just city is a community of obligation in which the privilege of citizenship means the assumption of the city's collective responsibility towards workers, the homeless and the poor who, despite often being invisible or marginalised, are constitutive parts of the community.[28]

Cohen cites a talmudic discussion of the moral problems associated with the obligation incumbent upon residents of a city to build a gatehouse,[29] emphasising the rabbis' concern that gatehouses threaten to prevent decent people hearing and responding to the cries of the poor, who are thereby effectively excluded from the community. He notes the historical shift in antiquity from a classical conception of civic responsibility in which residents of a city were expected to take responsibility for their neighbours as fellow citizens, to a Christian ideal of caring about the poor as a distinct group. The Jewish challenge of recognising and reaching out to marginalised people as fellow citizens, not as recipients of charity, is a subset of the broader malaise of social atomisation in contemporary society. Arthur Waskow addresses this issue by drawing on the biblical motif of fringes (the obligation to wear *tzitzit* or fringes on the corners of clothing and the duty of *pe'ah* – supporting poor people by allowing them to harvest the corners – or fringes – of fields) and argues that this idea symbolises the lack of a hard boundary between people: we are all connected to each other and, on the basis of this kinship, have an obligation to support each other. Waskow asks how it might be possible to build a new form of interpersonal fringes in our modern, urban world, where rich and poor constantly rub up against each other but usually share no meaningful relationship.[30]

These broadly communitarian perspectives represent one way of mediating the tension between structural and personal approaches to social justice. Another way is to conceptualise personal growth and social or political change as interconnected and mutually reinforcing processes. In an article on the relationship between morality and spirituality, Jonathan Wittenberg comments that while *tikkun ha-nefesh* (repair of the soul) leads to *tikkun ha-olam* (repair of the world), sometimes the process is reversed: actions in the world lead back to motivations, feelings and meaning.[31] This approach is fleshed out by David Jaffe who gives a detailed account of the personal change processes individuals need to undergo in order to become effective social activists. His prescriptions are based on the teachings of Hasidism and the nineteenth-century Mussar movement, a theology that sought to enlist the emotions as well as the intellect in the process of personal, ethical transformation.[32] Michael Lerner writes that spiritual enlightenment and the struggle against oppression are one and the same. This implies that the personal should not be seen as merely a means to the end of the political or vice versa, but that both are vital, interlinked arenas for transforming people and the world. As such, liberation requires not only political action but personal psychological work. Becoming emotionally healthy, Lerner argues, enables us easily to distinguish between the true, just, voice of God and the distorted voice of cruelty that traps us in oppressive behaviours. So too, eliminating concrete instances of oppression and cruelty is vital if people are to develop in emotionally healthy ways.[33]

The Relationship between Judaism and Social Justice

We have now explored some of the ways in which social justice themes have been expressed by Jewishly engaged writers in explicitly Jewish terms. However, the precise shape of Judaism's relationship with social justice concerns – first raised in the context of the encounter between Jewish culture and modern political ideologies – remains unclear. This relationship is conceptualised by contemporary writers in three main ways. Some see the values of social justice as an innate, core theme that emanates from Jewish history and the textual tradition. Others understand Judaism to be fundamentally oppressive, for sociological or theological reasons, and advocate reform of the tradition in light of social justice values that originate outside Jewish culture. The third perspective – in a way a synthesis of the first two – understands that Judaism contains both egalitarian and reactionary ingredients and sees social justice as a theme that needs to be drawn out hermeneutically by interpreting the text with politically progressive intent.

Several thinkers, then, understand justice to be a core, authentic message of Judaism. Elliot Dorff comprehensively catalogues a variety of ways in which faith in God provides Jews with reasons to care for others.[34] For example, God is the creator and owner of the world; all property is therefore on loan and refusing to use it to help others means denying God's sovereignty – essentially a form of idolatry. God commands us to care for others, both in our actions and in our intentions, and sanctions this with rewards and punishments. Human beings' creation in the divine image means we should treat each other as being of worth and recognise God's love for us. It also requires specific moral behaviours, in particular the recognition of the sanctity of life and human dignity. Jews have additional responsibilities to care for each other that stem from the covenant, both as the result of the original promise made at Sinai, and because of their ongoing relationship with God and other Jews. Finally, Jews' obligation to ethical behaviour is based on more than obedience, contract, covenant or community; it derives from the Torah's aspiration to holiness and *imitatio Dei* – emulating the moral attributes of God.

This framing of moral obligation in theological terms is given a vivid, political complexion in Abraham Joshua Heschel's analysis of racism.[35] Heschel writes that in contrast to religion, a unifying, universal force that sees humanity as the child of God, racism means dismembering the flesh of living humanity and attempting to honour the father by torturing his child. Racism is a spiritual disease, the profanation of God's name, a form of blasphemy, satanism and unmitigated evil. In contrast, Jews are called to act like the prophets – interfering, speaking out, not minding their own business, showing zero tolerance of wrongs done to others, feeling them as if done to ourselves. They must proclaim that God is a God of pathos and is affected by the injuries people inflict on each other. For Heschel the problem of racism 'is God's gift to America, the test of our integrity, a magnificent spiritual opportunity'.[36] There is clearly no distinction for him between religious and social or political issues.

Michael Lerner writes that *tikkun olam* (repairing the world), humanity's central task, is to be achieved by breaking the cycle of cruelty and by treating the stranger and all marginalised people justly.[37] Lerner reads the story of the binding of Isaac (Genesis 22) as Abraham's struggle to distinguish the true voice of God – the call to compassion and humanity – with the voice of cruelty that emanates from his own internalised trauma. At the crucial moment in the narrative when Abraham is about to murder his son, he finally manages to break out of the cycle of cruelty and to hear the authentic divine injunction not to hurt the child. Jewish law serves to embed the principles of love and justice in concrete behaviours, adherence to which is bound up with a sense of commandedness and partnership with God. These truths, for Lerner, can only be articulated in religious language and cannot be expressed adequately in secular terms. Yet Abraham's struggle is reflected in historical Jewish experience which is marked by the battle between the pristine message of justice and the potential for organised religion to be corrupted and co-opted by social elites, who misinterpret it and use it to enforce economic, racial and gender-based oppression.

Michael Walzer draws a commitment to progressive politics from the Bible in a different way, arguing that the structure of the Exodus narrative, undeniably central to Jewish theology and self-understanding, naturally lends itself to radical, political interpretations.[38] As opposed to most pre-modern, circular mythologies, the end point of the emphatically linear Exodus story is radically different from its beginning, thereby conveying the message that oppression is not inevitable but springs from human choices. This linearity and the secular or political nature of the people's redemption (the promised land is not the messianic kingdom) explains the story's appeal for radicals and progressives throughout history.

For Eugene Borowitz, Judaism's inherent concern for justice stems not only from the textual tradition but from the experience of modern history. He writes that the Emancipation – the granting of civil rights to European Jews during the eighteenth and nineteenth centuries – is to be understood as revelatory and theologically significant in that it changed Jews' understanding of what God wanted from them in relation to all humankind by setting them in new social circumstances. It enabled Jews to realise fully their duties to God in relation to human society as a whole, rather than being restricted to acting only within the confines of the Jewish community. The horrors of the Holocaust, paradoxically, reaffirmed this new understanding in that for Borowitz it could not be understood in purely particularistic terms but rather elicited a humanistic, universalist, moral response.[39]

Other writers base their understanding of Judaism as a religion of social justice on specific details of rabbinic tradition. Sid Schwarz argues that 'justice is to religion what love is to family': it is the quality that makes the institution worthwhile.[40] He adds that the fundamental commandments are the ones that 'jump out as essential expressions of the Jewish commitment to the cardinal values of righteousness and justice'[41] and enumerates seven core rabbinic values which underpin this Jewish commitment to justice. These include *hesed* (lovingkindness motivated by empathy and *imitatio Dei*), *kvod habriyot* (the dignity of God's creatures, the principle underlying all the interpersonal commandments), *bakesh shalom* (seeking peace), *lo ta'amod* (the prohibition on standing idly by while others suffer), *darkei shalom* (the creation of harmonious social relations with non-Jews), *ahavat ha-ger* (loving the stranger, in particular the vulnerable and oppressed) and *emet* (truth, moral honesty and integrity).[42] Jill Jacobs claims that rabbinic authorities in Judaism's seminal, talmudic period (the first six centuries CE) implicitly rejected the kind of injustices that characterise contemporary American society; they were simply unable to imagine phenomena such as working poverty, homelessness or mass incarceration of criminals. Rectifying these problems is therefore a basic requirement of Judaism.[43]

In contrast to the position that social justice is an innate Jewish value, other thinkers argue that Judaism has become, or is inherently, oppressive. Shmuly Yanklowitz, for example, claims that in the twenty-first century it has become dangerous for a rabbi to criticise capitalism, argues that many American Jews are imprisoned in a 'pandemic of money worship' and notes that despite the Torah's clear commitment to the imperative of healthcare, most Orthodox Jews have opposed healthcare reform.[44] Some writers attempt to explain this phenomenon on sociological or historical grounds, for example, through the claim that the process of modernisation that transformed the Jewish people in the nineteenth and twentieth centuries caused the various elements of Jewish identity – ethical universalism, group identity, spirituality – to break apart, each coming under the 'ownership' of a different constituency or denomination.[45] By implication, some Jewish groups emphasise universal ethical issues at the expense of community cohesion or ritual observance, while others prioritise the particularistic and ignore social justice concerns altogether. The distance between Judaism and social justice commitments has also been explained in terms of socio-economic and ideological shifts within the US Jewry. Since the Second World War, American Jews have experienced growing ideological dissonance as a result of the tension between their increasing prosperity and commitment to welfare capitalism on the one hand, and the heritage of Jewish socialism and Jews' self-image as runaway slaves on the other.[46] The complex, ambivalent ways in which Jews are positioned – and position themselves – within a discourse of privilege and discrimination will emerge as a vital issue for Jewish social justice educators (see Part 2).

These perspectives potentially accord with Lerner's analysis of real-world Jewish religion as the product of a conflict between a genuine, progressive core and inauthentic, oppressive elements which have accumulated as a result of external, social and political dynamics. However, other authors argue that Judaism as a religious tradition is inherently reactionary. Discussing the issue of homophobia, for example, Jay Michaelson suggests that homosexuality poses a fundamental religious question and threatens a core principle of 'mythic' or fundamentalist religion: the idea that sexual order mirrors the divine order.[47] This idea forces religious people to deny sexual equality, deny religious truth or redefine religion in a post-mythic way. The discussion of gay rights is really, therefore, a discussion about the nature of religion. The lack of commitment to justice issues on the part of many Orthodox Jews is, in this reading, not coincidental, since progressive religious positions (such as those which underlie the application of traditional texts to contemporary questions of equality and inclusion) cannot appeal to conservatives because their interpretive and moral content flatly contradicts the Bible. This clash reflects the irreconcilable difference between two different systems of thought: the mythic/fundamentalist/literalist on the one hand and the post-mythic/non-fundamentalist/metaphorical on the other.

Feminist scholar Tamar Ross blurs the line between oppressiveness which is sociologically induced and that which is inherent to the system.[48] She argues that traditional Judaism's patriarchal character can be explained historically by the fact that women have been systematically excluded from influencing Jewish legal norms. However, this dynamic has shaped the content of Jewish law and practice, erasing or subordinating women's experiences and roles to those of men, and effectively casting women as means to the end of male religiosity. While Lerner might argue that this represents an inauthentic distortion of an imagined, pristine, egalitarian tradition, the Judaism that actually emerges from this process is, at its core, fundamentally sexist.

As against these claims that Judaism is either inherently progressive or reactionary, many thinkers recognise that modern concepts of social justice emerge from Judaism only as the result of a hermeneutical process. For some modern Jewish thinkers, for example, Hermann Cohen[49] and Erich Fromm,[50] the potential for justice represents the pristine core or apex of the tradition which needs to be distilled and isolated from conservative and reactionary accretions and substrata. Other variants of this position are less hierarchical and recognise that Judaism is a complex, multifaceted tradition which contains both emancipatory and oppressive potential. This connects to a debate over the very nature or purpose of Jewishness. J. B. Soloveitchik, for example, makes a distinction between two biblical paradigms of covenant.[51] The covenant of fate (*brit goral*) originated with the Exodus from Egypt and assumes that Jews are bound together by outside forces and the need to survive. Against this, the covenant of destiny (*brit ye'ud*) began with the revelation at Sinai and implies a voluntarily accepted, values-driven commitment to a transformational relationship with God. While Soloveitchik does not address specific questions of social justice, he rejects the notion of a purely survivalist mode of Jewish identity. Sid Schwarz similarly differentiates between a 'tribal' Judaism which is based on feelings of familial solidarity among Jews, and a 'covenantal' perspective which calls for the realisation in the wider world of the universal values taught by Jewish tradition.[52] These thinkers recognise that Jewish tradition contains multiple positions; drawing out one perspective rather than another is inevitably an interpretive act.

In fact, even writers who claim that Judaism has an inherently progressive or oppressive essence recognise the complexity of the tradition and the impossibility of reading it other than hermeneutically. This raises the question as to which modes of interpretation are legitimate. Attacking naïve attempts to enlist Judaism for the cause of modern, political liberalism, for example,

Borowitz argues that what American Jews considered to be 'Jewish ethics' until the 1960s was actually no more than a restatement of secular, liberal values in Jewish language.[53] Other writers[54] criticise what they see as a failure to distinguish between the values of Judaism and those of progressive politics, for example, the tendency to uproot concepts such as *tikkun olam* ('repairing the world') from their textual sources and to blur their precise legal or theological meanings in an effort to use them to 'Judaise' what are essentially secular political commitments. These comments are essentially criticisms of an unsophisticated hermeneutics.

Similar forms of critique often originate with scholars such as Yeshayahu Leibowitz[55] and Tamar Ross[56] from within the Orthodox world, who are concerned that the loose, interpretative application of the tradition to contemporary problems steps outside the normative limits of the formal halakhic (Jewish legal) system. Authors featured in the Orthodox Forum's volume on *Tikkun Olam*[57] carefully consider whether social justice commitments are actually required within Jewish law by exploring the question of whether Jews have any obligation towards non-Jewish society and, if so, what the halakhic rationale for this position might be. Based on an analysis of various classical Jewish works, Gerald Blidstein, for example, suggests three possibilities: that Jews are responsible for social change only within the Jewish community; that through faithfulness to God Jews are expected to set an example for non-Jewish society; or that Jews are obliged to encourage or even compel non-Jews to comply with the Noahide laws (the legal code established by the rabbis for non-Jews living within or alongside Jewish communities).[58]

Other thinkers, often but not always non-Orthodox, welcome a looser kind of interpretive discourse. Jill Jacobs[59] argues that Judaism must be lived in the world, not just studied in the *bet midrash* (study hall), and favours a dialogue between rabbinic texts and contemporary justice issues within which a specifically Jewish approach to economic and social issues can be developed.[60] This method involves deriving social, political and economic principles from classical Jewish texts, then applying these to contemporary situations, often analogically, even where the text itself would not have considered it appropriate to do so (e.g. because the rules involved originally applied only to relationships between Jews). Borowitz implicitly endorses the importance of finding ways to apply traditional content to contemporary issues with his claim that it is important to pay careful attention to, and preserve, the differences between Judaism and Western liberalism. He argues, for example, that acts of individual freedom are not always ethical and not all ethical acts (e.g. Jewish/non-Jewish intermarriage) are Jewishly acceptable. Since universalist humanism is not self-evident but is, in his view, grounded in Jewish monotheism, we must ensure that our universalism does not become so radical that it undercuts its own Jewish foundations. In other words, the specificity of historical Judaism – including those elements which would be considered regressive from a liberal standpoint – must be preserved if it is to play a meaningful role in any contemporary moral and political conversation. This dialogical approach implicitly characterises the work of many writers who draw on classical texts to address contemporary social and political issues.

* * *

This survey of contemporary Jewish social justice writing has highlighted several important themes. In contrast with nineteenth- and early-twentieth-century Jewish socialists, contemporary thinkers tend away from visionary utopianism and towards pragmatic, critique-focused, gradualist approaches to social justice. This does not necessarily imply a lack of radicalism: even Freire, even as a self-defined revolutionary, advocated a dynamic, dialectical view of liberation as an ongoing process, rather than a unidirectional movement towards a predefined end. Radical tendencies can indeed be discerned in the recognition by many Jewish writers of the importance of structural social and economic issues and in particular a robust, principled analysis of capitalism's incompatibility with Jewish moral values. However, this radicalism tends to be accompanied by ambivalence about the role of the state; recognition of its indispensable role in shaping social equity is matched by suspicion of its capacity to overreach and encroach on the realm of interpersonal relationships and individual responsibility. In general, these authors emphasise the role of covenantal relationships, communities and civil society institutions as ways of curbing state power and as the proper arena in which to work for social justice. Similarly, Jewish thinkers find themselves caught between the relative importance for social justice of personal, ethical and spiritual transformation versus collective, political change. While some opt to prioritise the personal over the political, a more characteristic move is to conceptualise these options as poles of a dialectic, recognising that personal growth and social change are both indispensable components of one holistic process. Finally, this literature is marked by debates over the very nature of the relationship between Judaism and the values of social justice. While some thinkers attempt to cast Judaism as inherently politically progressive, the majority recognise that the tradition's pre-modern context is far removed from our own, that it contains both potentially emancipatory and oppressive elements, and that the values of social justice can only emerge as the result of a hermeneutical process.

Having surveyed the relationship between faith, social justice and education as they appear in the discourses of critical pedagogy, Catholic social teaching and liberation theology, and politically progressive Jewish thought, I now turn to an exploration of these issues as articulated in interviews with Jewish social justice practitioners.

Part 2

Jewish Social Justice Education – Interviews with Practitioners

While the connection between Judaism and social justice has been amply discussed, very little has been written about the role of (Jewish) education in relation to these issues.[1] Any exploration of theoretical approaches to Jewish social justice education therefore had to be preceded by a process of generating material to analyse. I achieved this by interviewing a number of UK-based educators, activists, religious leaders and community organisers and asking them to reflect on their work. The next four chapters are taken up with an analysis of texts generated in interviews with the following practitioners (all names are pseudonyms):

Andrew	Director of a charity funding human rights work in Israel
Annie	Volunteers and runs training for a Jewish LGBT+ organisation
Calley	Community organiser working with Jewish communities within a broad-based, multi-faith alliance
Craig	Former director of a foundation providing philanthropic funding for Jewish social justice projects
Danny	Director of a Jewish student organisation; formerly managed campaigns at a Jewish social action charity
Emma	Director of a Jewish anti-racism charity
Francesca	Writes curriculum and runs sessions on gender within Jewish schools on behalf of an orthodox-feminist group
Jacob	Masorti rabbi who teaches, writes and campaigns on environmental and refugee issues
Jodie	Director of a charity engaging Jews in international development through volunteer programmes in Africa
Joe	Activist with a non-Zionist, radical left-wing campaigning and cultural group

Manny	Parliamentarian and veteran community organiser
Rachel	Reform student rabbi and leader of a rabbinic social justice network
Sally	Head of informal education at a Jewish secondary school; runs volunteering and charity projects
Seth	Education director of a Jewish human rights charity
Shalom	Orthodox rabbi who manages local interfaith and social action projects and runs sessions on social justice in Jewish schools
Stuart	Founder of various anti-racist and international development organisations in the Jewish community
Tamar	Runs an organisation advocating for a two-state solution to the Israel–Palestine conflict

I employed an in-depth interview approach, based on a flexible topic guide that allowed for a combination of open and guiding questions together with free-flowing conversation, challenge and debate. The topic guide consisted of the following questions:

- Tell me about your work, what you do, what challenges you face and what you're trying to achieve.
- How did you come to be involved in this work?
- Which authors, books or texts have influenced your approach and how do you understand them?
- What issues and problems are you trying to address? What 'injustices' are you focused on?
- What is your vision? What do you understand by the term 'social justice'?
- How do you understand the relationship between Judaism and social justice? What difference does being Jewish or working in a Jewish setting make to you as someone involved in social justice?
- What strategies and actions do you think should be employed to advance social justice?
- What is the role of education in social justice? What about Jewish education specifically?
- What is the educational process for you? What happens when you 'do education'?
- Who do you work with? Who are the subjects of your work, the beneficiaries, your partners and allies?

I have presented the interview narratives within a framework inspired by the Israeli philosopher of education Zvi Lamm,[2] who suggested that any ideological discourse can be broken down into four dimensions: diagnosis or critique, eschatology or vision, strategy and people – who enacts and who is affected by the ideology. Rather than interpreting or analysing each interview as a self-contained text, I have gathered all the passages across the interviews that relate to each of the headings in Lamm's typology before embarking on a process of coding based on motifs that emerged inductively from the interview texts themselves. Sorting and thematising the issues addressed by the interviewees enabled me to find common themes, create connections and construct virtual dialogues between them. These dialogues were further enriched by theoretical insights gleaned from the background literature.

It is important to note that this concept of educational ideology implies a rejection of models which clearly distinguish between non-educational (philosophical, moral, political) principles and the pedagogical practices which flow from them.[3] Instead, I assume that values-driven educational approaches incorporate a mishmash of religious, political, ethical, pedagogical and other ingredients, and need to be understood holistically. For this reason the following analysis addresses not only explicitly educational topics but a wide range of social justice–related concerns. Accordingly, in the coming chapters I explore my interviewees' responses under the following headings: critique – the world as it is; vision – the world as it should be; strategy – education, activism and community organising; and people – agents and beneficiaries of social change.

4

Critique – the World as It Is

The critique – or description of the world as it is – articulated by the Jewish social justice educators I interviewed touches on several core themes: inclusion and exclusion, capitalism and inequality, the breakdown of relationships and institutions, the gap between Judaism and social justice, and questions relating to Israel and Zionism.

Inclusion and Exclusion

Inclusion and exclusion are core issues that preoccupy Jewish social justice educators. While the terms are used primarily in relation to issues of gender and sexual orientation, some interviewees also refer to discrimination on the basis of class or economic status, ethnic identity, or political and religious beliefs. Various implications of exclusion are discussed: harm to the identity and well-being of individuals and to the ideal of an inclusive, welcoming Jewish community; the connection between exclusion, privilege and social inequality; the impact of exclusionary language and role modelling; institutional resistance to change; tension between egalitarian social norms and discriminatory religious ones; and a critique of rigid social roles and the culture of identity politics. It is notable that despite the availability of relevant theological frameworks – as made clear in the previous chapter – most interviewees do not frame their critique in explicitly Jewish terms.

The discussion of inclusion and exclusion is rooted in the concept of privilege. Annie, a trainer with a Jewish LGBT+ organisation, uses Peggy McIntosh's metaphor of a backpack to describe the collection of assets and advantages that people who occupy privileged positions in terms of race and gender carry around with them unknowingly.[1] The absence of this privilege results in exclusion or discrimination. Annie recalls,

> I remember when I first did an exercise with privilege, one of the [statements] that was read out was … 'I have never bought flesh coloured plasters and found that they didn't match my skin colour'. And it was just … I'd just never thought about it. Ever. I've bought plasters more times than I can remember, and never once has it occurred to me that … plasters are described as flesh coloured, and actually they are my skin colour, but they are not everybody's.

For several interviewees, exclusion is an issue that relates specifically to the Jewish community. Annie, for example, rails against what she sees as the Jewish community's failure in the area of LGBT+ inclusion:

> I love being Jewish, I love being a part of a community. It pains me that we're pretty shit at this. And this is … for me … of one of the things that's holding us back from being the community that we could be: diverse, positive, open, welcoming, inclusive. I just think we're failing. And I don't like seeing something I care about so much fail at something I think is important.

Joe, an activist with a non-Zionist, radical left-wing campaigning and cultural group, echoes Annie's perspective in relation to exclusion from the Jewish community and applies it to the issue of political beliefs. When asked to explain his statement that he wants to make British Jewish 'more left wing', he says,

> You can call it a selfish motive if you like in the sense of most of us have grown up being in synagogues where we've felt a left-wing tiny minority, certainly in regard to Israel, but in regard to other things. It would be much more fun for us if that wasn't the case. If we go to a synagogue full of people who are more like us then we can talk much more openly about how we feel about politics and not have to separate our Judaism from our politics – that would be great!

As well as being an obstacle to equal opportunities, Joe suggests exclusion also has an impact on the inner life of the individual, in this case, a requirement to artificially segregate two important aspects of one's identity, and perhaps even deny one of them.

Francesca, an educator working with a Jewish feminist group, is preoccupied with issues of exclusionary representation and role modelling in the context of gender roles within the Orthodox school system. She concurs with Annie's insight about the impact of discriminatory role modelling for both equality of opportunity and the emotional well-being of the students. She describes, for example, a visit she made to her son's nursery class during *Kabbalat Shabbat* (the ceremony for inaugurating the Sabbath):

The teacher said 'Okay who wants to do *hamotzi*' [the blessing over bread] and all the kids, especially the girls put their arms in the air kind of waving back and forth. And the teacher said 'Oh no the boys do it,' and the same thing happened with *kiddush* [the blessing over wine]. So I went up to her afterwards, the teacher, she is lovely, and I said to her 'That was a lovely *Kabbalat Shabbat*. I just want you to know that in our household I *do* do *kiddush* and *hamotzi* and I said it's ... I am not suggesting that you have to do that here, but the way you said it was negative. First of all that is not correct halakhically [in terms of Jewish law], but also you are sending a message that this is not appropriate, and this is what we do at home.'

Francesca describes the potential impact of experiences like these, particularly within educational institutions which offer no avenue for dealing honestly with the issues they raise, in terms of

kids not having conflict between what they are learning in school and at home. And if they see things at home ... and they are told at school that those things are inappropriate and that's emotional dissonance, cognitive dissonance, and that's complicated. Kids, people learn to deal with that, but it is healthier for them to have mechanisms to address these kinds of questions, about what does it mean to be a modern Jewish person and if you have gender differences what do you do about it?

Alongside the impact on emotional well-being, these forms of dissonance also have implications for equality of opportunity. For example, Francesca relates what happened when she asked members of a student council at an Orthodox school to brainstorm names on the subject of 'Jewish leaders':

For about five minutes they went through twenty, thirty Jewish leaders, Abraham, Ben Gurion, Bibi Netanyahu, who ... and they never, they didn't mention a girl. No woman. And then one of the girls said; at some point she said 'Can I say girls' names?' She had to ask that question. And I said 'Well I just said Jewish leaders' so she hesitated for a moment and then she said 'Okay well what about Esther and ...' So I thought that was a perfect example of the kids not ... it not being obvious to them that there are female leaders in different formats and things have shifted over time.

For Francesca, the school has failed to promote models of female leadership, thereby narrowing these students' horizons and negatively affecting their sense of agency, self-esteem and awareness that they have the potential to take on leadership roles in the Jewish community.

Finally, several interviewees articulated a critique of labelling, stereotypical thinking and crude assumptions about personal identity. Annie notes that we often fail to take account of the nuanced ways in which people want to express their gender and sexual identities. Joe reports that his organisation rejects many of the categories and definitions within which the Jewish establishment operates, for example, the clear distinction between Jew and non-Jew. Francesca applies a similar critique to preconceived notions of gender roles in Jewish religious life. This stems from a holistic, 'multiple' conception of identity[2] as vital for personal well-being and communal vitality:

> A Jewish person who is an integrated self, and has a part of them which is not able to participate and be actively kind of central to that part of themselves, means that a part of them is not being utilised, which is not healthy for the Jewish world, and it is not healthy for them. So it is like having a limb which you can't exercise.

This position is grounded in Francesca's theology:

> Is there a Jewish aspect to my feminism? Yes. There is definitely. That all people were created in the image of God. ... I mean I think that there's something definitely comforting in knowing that God is not male or female. God is God. So God cannot be one or the other, and God has classically male and female attributes. ... And if all people are created equal then that means that we have to recognise the divinity in all people ... not only on a religious level, but on an individual level that all people are unique.

The rejection of labelling and compartmentalisation segues for some interviewees into a critique of identity politics. Danny, the director of a Jewish student organisation, asserts that excessive emphasis on sectional identities itself has discriminatory potential. He argues that identity politics has created an alternative hierarchy in which privilege and the right to speak out derive from being perceived as oppressed on account of a racial, gender or sexuality marker. In contrast, while he is aware of the need to recognise distinct challenges facing specific groups, Danny feels that combatting discrimination requires us to refrain from further embedding these sectional forms of identity. Danny's thinking disrupts the narrative of identity politics which, to him, entails a clear hierarchy of privilege between oppressors and oppressed, and within which Jewish experience does not neatly fit. Specifically, his experience as a Jew points to the shortcomings and the exclusionary potential of this kind of politics and enables him to consider a broader critique of what he considers to be crude, dichotomous thinking.

Capitalism and Inequality

A common strand running through many of the interviews is a critique of social inequality in general, and capitalism in particular. For some interviewees this stems from a broader analysis of modernity as a social and cultural condition.

Jodie, the director of a charity engaging young Jewish people in international development through volunteer programmes in Africa, draws on an article by Zygmunt Bauman[3] to reflect on the difficulty of achieving concrete social change. Bauman argues that in pre-modernity, the city was a place of fixed abodes and well-defined roles and obligations. In contrast, modernity has dislocated and alienated everyone from this pre-modern sense of place, so that even while physically in the city, we remain fundamentally in the desert, with the concomitant requirement that, as pilgrims, we create our own identity. In postmodernity, the difficulties involved in creating identity in the context of an ephemeral culture transform into a refusal of long-term commitments and responsibilities. Progress, and any commitment or work in the service of progress, therefore becomes obsolete. For Jodie, this feature of the contemporary world is related to the breakdown of community:

> Right, I want to make change, I want to make a footprint but how would I do that in that context? So then you start thinking how do you anchor people in sand dunes, how do you give them the capability to? You need to create a little sand castle to protect it. You need community, then you can envision things.

A similar point is developed by Danny, who locates his argument within an understanding of modern history. He conceptualises modernity in terms of three major developments: industrialisation, urbanisation and the emergence of nationalism. While industrialisation and urbanisation are associated with economic and social progress, they also throw up novel problems such as inequality, environmental damage, famine and mass migration, together with more abstract issues such as alienation, social atomisation, the separation of the means of production from the people who benefit from them, and the meaning of life being reduced to the search for profit. In contrast, nationalism is the key to a potential solution, inasmuch as the source of many of the problems Danny identifies can be traced to the absence of factors which are able to mediate between individuals and a faceless, global society. Nation states and communities are, for Danny, contenders for this vital role.

Several interviewees are concerned about problems of structural, social inequality and the question of privilege, understood in economic terms. Andrew, for example, runs a charity funding human rights work in Israel. He discusses the connection between an array of social problems in Israel and the inequitable distribution of government funding to marginalised groups. He argues that any analysis of social problems which does not take account of economic inequality is bound to be inadequate. Tamar similarly recognises the injustice of privilege which derives from the luck of being born rich in an economically unequal society, and recognises that this economic inequality makes equality of opportunity unobtainable.

The problem of self-interest and commitment to the status quo among privileged groups – including much of the Jewish community – is raised explicitly throughout the interviews. Calley, a community organiser working with Jewish communities within a broad-based, multi-faith alliance, argues that a largely middle-class community no longer has much interest in the disadvantaged people it interacts – or fails to interact – with: 'What has it become that it took so long to get even one synagogue to go Living Wage? We never think of buying ham in our synagogues to save money and yet we've come to a place where we weren't paying our cleaning workers, our security guards a living wage.' However Calley also discerns a great deal of nuance and ambivalence around the perceived self-interest of the largely white, middle-class Jewish community. She is clear that 'people are broader than their own class interest' and in some instances are able to develop solidarity with disadvantaged groups as a result of their 'ability to make human to human relationships'. Moreover, for Calley, Jewish narratives have a unique role to play:

> Sometimes I meet lovely, middle-class people whose opening biographies begin with – and mine's similar – 'my family came as refugees'. And this is part of what being Jewish means to them, but they're trapped in this weird space where part of them really identifies with this 'I'm part of the poor and dispossessed' narrative, and part of them is living in this six bedroom house in Hampstead [an affluent area of London] and is struggling to reconcile that. But I think that is also part of what it means to be the Jewish experience.

The discussion of privilege and self-interest is mirrored by a concern about the disempowerment and denigration of the poor and destitute. Emma, the director of a Jewish anti-racism charity, bemoans the fact that the poor are not treated with respect and that the issue of poverty is widely understood within the narrative of 'scroungers and strivers, good and bad, the takers and those who contribute'. She feels that as a result society is becoming a 'mean place', where the 'bonds of social solidarity and [the sense] that we have a responsibility one for the other ... are broken'. Jacob, a Masorti rabbi, makes a similar point in relation to the refugee crisis and the commonplace distinction between asylum seekers and economic migrants, which evokes the Victorian concepts of the deserving and undeserving poor:

> Why should a person live in some place which is extremely poor, which lacks opportunity, which is become poorer and lost a lot of its indigenous culture because of the way the northern and western nations treated it during the colonial era, or the way multinationals exploit it ...? Why should that person not want to do their best for their children in the way I want to do the best for my children? What argument can I really make morally that they shouldn't come here?

This moral delegitimisation of the poor and the implicit denial of their rights is related to another motif: the tendency of people in power and even of social change activists to ignore the voices and perspectives of the poor. Jodie believes this makes effective interventions impossible. For example, in the context of overseas development work:

> So it's kind of like if you really want to make change you have to invest in people ... Look they don't have a school, 'I'm going to build a school'. Turns out they don't have teachers either. Turns out the parents don't value education. So why on earth would you rock up and build a school if you haven't even talked to the local people about what it is that they want and they think they can see a way out?

As noted above, much of the Jewish writing on social justice emphasises the dynamic by which poor people become invisible, unrecognised and humiliated. This prevents the possibility of relationships between rich and poor and erases poor people as subjects of communal concern and responsibility. While the failure to listen to the poor and powerless therefore has practical implications for effective philanthropy, politics and social change work, it also has a moral or philosophical component. Jodie conceptualises the importance of relationships for social justice by drawing on the thought of Martin Buber and Emmanuel Levinas.[4] For Jodie, Buber's philosophy requires us to create holy, purposeful communities based on ever-deepening relationships with others. She understands Levinas's thought as a brake on this aspiration, as a warning to avoid assimilating them in the course of pursuing a relationship with them. In her words,

> You can overstate that relationship of 'I know you' and I think [Levinas] comes to say 'No, you don't know the other person, you don't know the full aspect of

them' and to make too many assumptions is too abuse them in some sense. ... Buber says 'Get into relationships' and Levinas seems to say 'Don't take it too far, you really can't, at some point you have to leave space for them to be them.'

Jodie seems to be pointing to the ethical imperative of forming relationships as well as to the danger that our very efforts to know the poor can result in becoming deaf to their authentic voices.

The Breakdown of Relationships and Institutions

This preoccupation with the nature of relationships between rich and poor points to a broader theme: the breakdown of relationships and social institutions seen not only as a cause or symptom of economic inequality but as a problem in its own right.

Manny, a parliamentarian and veteran community organiser, describes a campaign he was involved in to prevent the privatisation and sale of the port of Dover, in which he became aware of the weakness of relationships among local institutions and within the community:

> The government wanted to sell the port of Dover, unbelievably to the French. That's why I got involved early on when I became a peer and that was a very demoralised community down there, which had a sense of powerlessness, so they just thought that their inheritance, 'The White Cliffs of Dover', the port of Dover was going to be privatised, and they would have no control over their town. And that was a case of engaging local churches, businesses, trade unions, political people in trying to work out what would be for the common good? How they could have the civic inheritance?

Social injustice is linked in this view to the deterioration of community relationships and the concomitant absence of a unifying narrative which articulates a common self-interest and a conception of the common good. Manny also sees this among groups that are emphatically not oppressed. He reflects on his experience of entering politics and becoming a peer:

> And I realised that there wasn't an establishment anymore, so a lot of my work is trying to reconstitute some sense of common purpose. ... I was brought up to believe that ... the head of the Bank of England, and universities, and heads of political parties ... basically knew each other, and had some sense of holding the centre together, but they don't. They are completely lost in their own institutions.

Joe diagnoses this kind of social unravelling and conflict in psychotherapeutic terms, arguing that there is relationship between trauma and social injustice:

> I guess I am quite optimistic with human nature that I tend to think people are quite decent underneath but they're damaged, and it's about repairing those damages, repairing that trauma which encouraged them to be selfish. And it's only through bringing people together and building trust that you'll start to do that.

One element of the breakdown of community and institutions is a perceived process of bureaucratisation and failure of leadership. Leadership is understood here as a relational practice according to which a leader is defined as someone with followers. In the absence of leaders there is no way of rebuilding social relationships or pursuing justice. Manny notes that this diagnosis applies even to the inner life of membership-based communities. He critiques a transactional model where people tend to see themselves as passive consumers rather than active members or leaders who are in relationship with each other. The goal of much of his work has been to

> resist in some way the increasing administrative tendency of Jewish community life [which] was that you just paid your fees and you didn't have to do more. And I think that's had a very interesting life in terms of developing new … communities, on giving people responsibilities. Jews have forgotten how to do it. We are part of the general structures of western liberal capitalism where ultimately, either the State does it, or you pay.

This kind of bureaucratisation is seen as both a symptom of an inherently unhealthy society (where social health is defined in terms of strong, relational communities) and a strategic obstacle to the effective pursuit of political change.

Another phenomenon which both reflects social injustice and prevents effective social change is a perceived tendency within some parts of the Jewish community to avoid interfaith work and relationships with non-Jews. Calley reflects that Jews often shut themselves off from wider society out of a feeling of vulnerability. She gives examples of new Jewish schools which, perhaps from concerns about security, are built in a way which physically cuts them off from the surrounding community. This breakdown of relationships has, for Calley, a direct impact on the way the Jewish community engages (or fails to engage) with social action projects. Commenting on what she sees as the difference between the effective activism of some South African churches compared with the ineffectuality of many synagogues, she says that the difference was that the churches

> knew their people. That was the thing that was most amazing to me. In my synagogue we used to have a *tzedek* [justice] committee and we'd say, what issue should we pick? And we'd sit around a table and randomly pick something after someone's thought, you know, someone's aunt had this charity. And these churches were out meeting people in their neighbourhood every day. I sometimes go to synagogues and I say, what are your relationships like with the people who live on your street? And quite often they'll say to me, we don't know anyone who lives on our street.

Antisemitism

Alongside the issue of relationships between Jews and non-Jews, some interviewees are preoccupied with a related social problem: antisemitism. Emma, for example, sees progressive politics as a way of countering anti-Jewish prejudice. She expresses embarrassment at the spectacle of visibly Orthodox Jews protesting inappropriately against what they see as left-wing antisemitism (e.g. heckling participants on TV panel discussions or picketing anti-Israel theatre productions) and argues that this kind of overly assertive behaviour – particularly coming from people who in her view are unlikely to be involved in social justice and interfaith work – is likely to provoke hostility towards Jews.

Calley relates a story which relates to antisemitism as a reaction to Jews' behaviour in a different way:

> So there's a really wonderful school. ... Comprehensive, poor school, graded outstanding. ... And they're doing this project called City Safe where they go and make safe havens. And they bring a woman ... whose son ... was stabbed to death in north London a couple of years ago. And they go in and they say we'd really like this shop to be a City Safe haven, will you agree? And on [the nearby high street] there are a lot of kosher and Jewish shops. And this one guy goes to [the woman], look, if your son was killed, that was God's plan. I can't do anything. If someone runs in here and someone wants to kill them, that's God's plan, it's out of my hands. And the students go back and they are struggling with this. They have signed up every shop that isn't a Jewish or kosher shop on that street, and they haven't signed up one that is a kosher or a Jewish shop. And their question is what can we do to ... they're frustrated, they feel uncared about, they don't understand why the people who work on the street that is literally next to

their school don't care about these kids. And it's probably worth saying about this school that it's in the middle of [an Orthodox Jewish neighbourhood] and has one Jewish child in it at the moment. And you know that is hard. The deputy head calls me in and we have a conversation about like what are we going to do about this, because the kids come back like Jews don't care about us. None of the Jews … care about us. And I'm obviously mortified and angry all at the same time. I'm completely humiliated that these kids have seen … I think of my community as so caring and so great, and these people have just refused to stand up for these kids.

Both Emma and Calley are concerned that what they see as reactionary attitudes and behaviours on the part of Jews have the potential to stir up antisemitic hostility. However, while Emma implies that justice and interfaith work are means to the end of rehabilitating the Jewish community's progressive credentials, Calley is preoccupied with the students' hurt feelings and the failure of the shopkeepers to live up to the highest ideals of Judaism as an end in itself.

The Gap between Judaism and Social Justice

A theme related to the critique of Jewish/non-Jewish relations is the idea that the Jewish community and perhaps Judaism itself have become disconnected from the values of social justice. Emma, for example, is appalled by what she sees as the mainstream Jewish community's indifference to social issues and its reflexive adoption of insular, conservative positions. She reflects on conversations she has had which have taken the following turn:

'Oh, that government minister … has just demolished a lot of community groups', and someone saying, 'Well he's been good to the Jews'. Well no, it's not good for the Jews. You know? It's not good for the Jews if there's poverty. It's not good for the Jews if people are sleeping in doorways. It's not good for the Jews that people are homeless. It's not good for the Jews if there's racism. So I think I want a different definition of what is good for the Jews.

Tamar applies this critique to the official leadership of Anglo-Jewry and its failure to respond, in her view, to the Syrian refugee crisis: 'The thing I found so sickening about the migrants drowning is that the Board of Deputies[5] didn't say anything and for fuck sake, all of us got to this country on boats, how it can be that we have nothing as an institution to say about this?'

While they express differing attitudes to Jewish particularism, various interviewees argue for the inadequacy or unacceptability of a Judaism which is purely tribal or survivalist. Craig, the former director of a foundation providing philanthropic funding for Jewish social justice projects, advocates a universalist conception of Jewishness while making clear that there is no contradiction between this and a particularistic commitment to Jewish well-being; in fact, he claims that these two components of Jewish identity have the potential to be mutually reinforcing. He illustrates this perspective with a story about a rabbi who responded to his foundation's support for a memorial to the Rwandan genocide:

> He said 'You care more about black children in Africa than you do about your fellow Jews. I'm doing this work on Holocaust memorials in Auschwitz. ...' About nine months later he wrote us a note and the same rabbi said 'I've just been to the genocide memorial in Kigali on a trip that was organised by an organisation outside the Jewish community and I saw the name of your foundation on the door of the Kigali memorial. And now I understand what you are doing. Now I understand why ... your concerns about remembering the genocide of Rwanda are not at the expense of remembering genocide in Nazi Germany, but are very much part of the same effort'.

However, a thoroughgoing universalism is not the only alternative to narrow tribalism. Jodie, for example, references the idea that relations between Jews and non-Jews are often regulated within rabbinic literature under the rubric of *mipnei darkei shalom* – for the sake of peace.[6] Ethical behaviour towards non-Jews is understood not as a categorical imperative but as a way of protecting the reputation and physical integrity of the Jewish community. While Jodie is uncomfortable with this position, it has been argued that the ostensibly particularistic paradigm of *mipnei darkei shalom* has the potential to serve as a framework for more fruitful relations between Jews and non-Jews.[7] It might in fact be possible to construct a multicultural or pluralistic conception of Jewish/non-Jewish relations based specifically on Judaism's particularism and its consequent indifference towards, or de facto acceptance of, the religious identity and behaviour of non-Jews.

The diagnosis of a break between Jewishness and social justice values is related to a critique of the way some organisations are perceived to be pursuing social change work not as an intrinsic good but as a tactic for engaging young people in Jewish life. Several interviewees are suspicious of this position. Craig, for example, recalls that his foundation colleagues

> felt it was insincere to be looking at it in instrumental terms. I think some of the American foundations we came across ... saw instrumental benefits in terms of

Jewish engagement and continuity. That was not the approach we adopted. And we didn't adopt that approach not only for moral reasons, but for pragmatic reasons, that younger Jews can see when you are being authentic and when you are not being authentic. And for us this was an authentic attempt to really engage with these [social justice] issues, because that's how you are meant to express one's identity and to be Jewish.

Jodie points out that the instrumental use of social justice work impacts not only on the Jewish participants but on the poor beneficiaries or partners, for whom it entails a process of objectification. Noting that some young people react to their experience of volunteering in developing countries with feelings of euphoria and the sense that they are heroes, she comments, 'Ooh. Who is the real hero of the story of the developing world changing? Because it really oughtn't to be the white guy rocking up. It really ought to be that people are their own heroes of their own story.' She reflects that while some agencies seek to exploit the fact that young people want to get involved in international development work in order to 'give them a Jewish education', this is where her organisation draws the line. For her, 'building Jewish identity on the back of poor, black Africans ... is obscene'.

While Craig and Jodie attack the inappropriate elision of Jewish education and social justice work, other interviewees claim that Jewish literacy and commitment to justice very rarely coexist. Some Jews are literate, knowledgeable and religiously observant, while an almost entirely separate group is involved in social action and wider, public issues. Shalom, an Orthodox rabbi who manages interfaith and social action projects, reflects,

> When I walk into a class [at a pluralistic cross-communal secondary school] I say, how many recycle, they all raise their hands pretty much, because their parents have taught them already. So it's very different walking into a Stamford Hill [an ultra-Orthodox neighbourhood] ... *MP: There they don't recycle?* Shalom: Not very much. Or how many of you think that climate change is an issue that we should be spending time and energy working on? You know, really high turn-out from [the non-Orthodox school], really low turn-out from girls at [an Orthodox school]. So what's going on there?

Shalom points to a fundamental disjunction between traditional religious teaching and the kind of moral education which he feels is necessary for developing social awareness:

> You don't need a Torah background to feel the way we treat the poor, poor children, you know the way food banks are ... all those issues, which are real issues, you don't need to be, you know, those are embedded, you raise your

children right, they're going to pick up on those issues. That's who I'm assuming is a good person above all. The Torah model is where they go into school, they *daven* [pray], and they have a sense of how to read the Talmud, their Hebrew's good, but they may not have used those skills to look or care or think about global issues. In fact sometimes the opposite.

Francesca confirms this sense, claiming that *halakhah* (Jewish law) is often experienced in Orthodox educational institutions as a barrier to progress on inclusion and equality. She often encounters educators who conceptualise the legal tradition as an unbending set of rules and who use it to resist progress and to draw a line under their refusal to entertain unfamiliar views on gender. 'One teacher said … "But …" – this is the classic line and it is almost a way of stopping conversation – "at the end of the day there is *halakhah* and *halakhah* means that women can't read Torah. That's the bottom line."'

If Orthodox schools stand accused of focusing exclusively on religious education at the expense of social awareness, the progressive Jewish world can be accused of the opposite problem: engaging with justice issues while failing to engender basic Jewish knowledge. Stuart, the founder of various anti-racist and international development organisations in the Jewish community, recalls that he once created information sheets on social issues for distribution in Reform synagogues. He recalls his assumption that, while his readers had a prior interest in issues of homelessness or human rights, they were unlikely to be Jewishly literate. Stuart's aim was to promote the idea that these two areas can and should come together, based on his insight that 'we've got lots of members who are engaged now in the wider world, and we've got some members who are engaged Jewishly, you know, they're mostly two completely separate worlds'.

However, the dichotomy of religious commitment and social involvement is not clear-cut. Shalom notes that many people who care about global issues and *tikkun olam* (repairing the world) are not actively involved in social change: Referring to non-Orthodox educational frameworks he says, 'they're good on concepts but not good on getting the kids to go out and make … radical differences on the ground'. In contrast, the ultra-Orthodox community is in his experience characterised by a network of '*gamahs* [collection points for goods and money for the needy] on every street corner' and a comprehensive network of support for community members. Masorti rabbi Jacob agrees that the distinction between non-Orthodox Jews who care about justice and Orthodox Jews who ostensibly do not falls away in light of the ultra-Orthodox community's 'powerful capacity to care for its own weakest members … which isn't equalled outside the Orthodox world'. Perhaps the precise locus for this critique, then, is not the mutual exclusivity of religious commitment and social involvement but of religious observance and literacy on the one hand and commitment to universal, 'non-Jewish', global justice issues on the other.

The disconnection between the Jewish community and social justice values evokes a broader issue: the idea – criticised by several interviewees – that faith should be divorced from politics. Stuart recalls that the first attempts to engage the organised UK Jewish community with social justice issues in the 1980s took place against a conservative, ostensibly apolitical, backdrop:

> But the main agenda, for me the main agenda was shifting the Jewish community. ... But it was about could we shift synagogues; could we shift the Jewish mind-set? And I think we really did, because at that point the argument was, we should not be getting involved in politics at all. Anti-Apartheid, now we think it's axiomatic, anybody with a social conscience must have been a part of the anti-Apartheid campaign. ... But it wasn't true at the time. You know, we're talking about the Thatcher years, in which the government of the day ... was vehemently opposed to the anti-Apartheid movement. ... And the Jewish community, very conservative, small 'c' ... thought, you know, we don't want to rock the boat. And that was the mind-set.

The notion that the Jewish community should refrain from political involvement on justice issues rests on an assumption that faith or religion can be separated from politics. Jacob forcefully attacks this position, drawing on empirical, historical arguments and articulating a principled, theological position:

> To fail to make the moral and ethical case that Judaism has a say on a particular issue is negligent. I think you have to. Ethics have been in debate with political realities always in Judaism, and to say that religion should have nothing to do with politics is absurd. Because politics are where decisions are made on issues of compassion. Just look at the budgets. Issues of social justice, issues of how you treat minorities. To have no voice, to say we shouldn't have a voice, you shouldn't speak out about such things, that's got to be wrong. I mean it's convenient but that doesn't mean that one shouldn't be talking about Shabbat and prayer and the inner life, but I think it's negligent not to have things to say about the major issues of the common good. And I think Judaism always has and the prophetic tradition has also been fearless, and actually the question of moral courage is a very humbling issue.

Joe expresses his Jewishness in a more secular, cultural way but shares the goal of intertwining Judaism with progressive politics. He argues that 'being left wing doesn't lead to being less Jewish or abandoning Jewishness, that actually there can be a really rich Jewishness within a left-wing politics, and I think some people are really afraid of that actually. That "left" and "assimilation" are kind of tied up and we're trying to really pull those two apart.' One of Joe's goals is to combat the idea – which he sees as assimilatory and, in the context of a multicultural ideology, implicitly discriminatory – that Jews have to abandon their particularistic identity in order to participate in left-wing politics.

Israeli Policy, Zionism and Israel–Diaspora Relations

Israel is a recurring motif in the interview texts. Echoing the perceived disjuncture between religious commitment and involvement with justice issues described above, several interviewees suggest that within the Jewish community Israel–Palestine activists (of all political stripes) and social justice campaigners are often mutually exclusive groups. This observation chimes with the argument made by Peter Beinart in his influential book, *Crisis of Zionism*,[8] that progressive American Jews are being pushed away from a relationship with Israel due to the influence of the Occupation; the deterioration of Israeli democracy; the dominance in US Jewry of a right-wing elite which effectively marginalises critical, liberal Zionist positions; and the fact that young Jews insist on thinking about Jewishness in terms of ethics, not only survival. Sid Schwarz fleshes out this position, claiming that conflicts over Israel between American Jewish liberals and conservatives result from the tension between survivalist ('Exodus') and covenantal ('Sinai') conceptions of Judaism, where the imperative of Jewish survival is taken to be at odds with ethical demands.[9]

Seth, the education director of a UK Jewish human rights charity, claims that because the mainstream Jewish community is preoccupied with Israel, it ignores other political issues:

> In many ways for the UK Jewish community, human rights of other people is not in its priorities. Its priority is being a conversation around Israel, whatever that looks like, and protecting the Jewish community from antisemitism, and I guess the legacy of the Holocaust. … And then add into that the idea that in some sense human rights is a bit of a dirty term for some parts of the community because of its relationship with Israel, or because people think human rights, and their immediate connection is Amnesty, and they think Amnesty, anti-Israel, antisemitic, we don't want anything to do with human rights.

At the same time, some interviewees criticise the tendency of Jews who are involved in social activism to ignore justice issues in Israel and Palestine. Tamar, for example, notes the centrality of Israel/Palestine to most human rights and international development organisations and, in contrast, its marked absence from Jewish social justice discourse:

> What was weird about the Jewish community, which was unlike any of those other organisations, is that Israel is over in one corner and everything else like social justice is in another corner and God forbid they should mix. If you are working for Christian Aid, Oxfam etc., the Israel/Palestine thing is part of the rubric of your organisation. … It was really a sense of, okay, as Jews who are engaged in talking about social justice, can we any longer ignore this major issue of social justice? What was going on inside the only Jewish state in the world?

In contrast, most of the activists interviewed here do connect their social justice agendas and relationships with Israel and are deeply concerned about attacks on democracy, human rights and civil society in the Jewish state. Tamar emphasises the need for UK Jews to respond to these issues:

> How do you give a voice to people who want to be able to speak out in support of their values? And even if that sometimes means being critical, actually giving people a space where they feel comfortable doing that. Whether that is for example, being able to say actually as Jews we really have a problem with the Nation State bill[10] and we think it's going to destroy the democratic fibre of the State of Israel, or whether that is saying to the Board of Deputies, buses have just been segregated going in and out of the West Bank and surely as Jews who believe in equality and human rights we have got something to say about the fact that buses are being segregated and that keeping *shtum* [silent] is basically complicity in supporting it.

While emphasising the need to support Israel in the face of attacks, Jacob also sympathises with this position:

> So the other side of it is that Israel's perpetrating things which are deeply unjust and inculcating a level of racism which is … well, the arson attack and murder of that baby[11] is a symptom; it's not just a one-off event. It has to be regarded as a symptom and an outcome of an unacceptable rhetoric, and though the acts which don't include murder but they do include destroying people's homes for example, or refusing to allow them to build. So there's some of the most unjust things going on and I find that very painful, and it's extremely difficult to know how to address these things and how to take your community with you because the other side is that it's also true that Israel has enemies around it. It's constantly threatened.

Alongside a more general concern about anti-democratic practices and social injustice, several interviewees focus their criticism on the specific issue of the Occupation. For Tamar, the Occupation is not simply an instance of general social injustice. She diagnoses the Israeli-Palestinian conflict in terms of psychological trauma and a cycle of fear:

> For me one of the things that is going on in the conflict, there is massive amount of psychological trauma, on both sides. That creates a whole other narrative that is beyond the injustice/justice piece and power thing. And it plays into it, which is you have, you know, the Jewish people suffer I think from some sort of post-traumatic stress disorder which is from the Holocaust and being kicked out in the pogroms and from being kicked out of the Middle East, which is from fighting wars inside Israel, and that that has a massive impact on collective thinking and collective action. There is no shadow of a doubt that the Palestinians suffer from a collective trauma too. … Sometimes I think, if only you could give post-traumatic stress therapy to the entire Jewish people wouldn't we deal with this differently? … And so I think that what the trauma and fear probably does is obscure the clarity of thinking. I think if you want to approach it as a non-scarred, not-carrying-the-trauma-of-Jewish-history person you'd see it in a much more – our ability to not have that trauma is quite low – you would see it quite differently.

All the interviewees who express views on Israel are critical of the social, diplomatic and/or military policy of the right-wing Israeli government. However, this criticism falls into two categories: Zionist and non- (or post-)Zionist. Andrew, for example, defines himself as a secular, socialist Zionist, a commitment he traces back to his time in the youth movement Habonim-Dror and to formative experiences in Israel as a child and as a young adult. 'If we are a Jewish people,' he argues,

> there is a clear connection, we see Israel as the homeland of the Jewish people, therefore even if I don't live there it is a very strong part of my identity. There is a values piece, which is the founding values of Israel are values that I think are incredibly important and are values that. … Going back to the values of human rights, you know [Israel's] Declaration of Independence is basically a Jewish version of the UN Declaration of Human Rights. . Incredibly profound language and that always sat incredibly comfortably for me.

Tamar illustrates the idea that progressive politics can coexist with a commitment to the State of Israel with a story about a participant on one of her organisation's trips to the West Bank

> who is a hard core Jews for Justice for Palestinians activist and is not really Jewish. She is halachically [in terms of Jewish law] Jewish but is a churchgoer,

but she has a Jewish grandmother in that way that annoys a lot of people (myself included) who claims her Jewishness despite the fact she is a practising Christian to slag off the State of Israel and even I can't stomach that. She came on the trip and her world view was really challenged by the other nine women who were middle of the road, second homes in Israel some of them, grandchildren living in Israel because their kids have made *aliyah* [emigrated to Israel], women deeply concerned by the Occupation and with a level of empathy to the state of Israel and the Jewish people. It was a really big deal to her to suddenly be surrounded by people that were as concerned as her about the reports on the West Bank but weren't prepared to say that Hamas was a vegetarian liberation organisation that meant no harm.

Other interviewees are suspicious of the possibility of synthesising Zionist and progressive principles. Craig, for example, argues as follows:

What I think is harder to sustain is this notion that the Declaration of Independence outlines a vision that is consistent with actually historical and conceptual tensions embedded with Zionism itself as a settler-colonial ideology that would privilege one group at the expense of others. ... [L]ooking at the logic and nature of Zionism both from historical and conceptual lens it's very hard, and increasingly hard, to sustain the idea that liberalism and Zionism can be fused. Therefore I think you either have to embrace your Zionism and abandon liberalism, or you have to embrace your liberalism and abandon Zionism.

Joe's attitude to Zionism and Jewish nationalism is also critical but in some ways more nuanced. He is critical of the way Zionism functions as a hegemonic ideology of Jewish life in the Diaspora but certainly does not reject all expressions of Jewish nationalism:

If you see Zionism as the big super-structure that sustains the mainstream of Jewish life, we'd soon find ourselves in opposition to that super-structure. Even if ... personally I would say there are some elements of historical Zionism which are quite interesting that we might not reject, but that's not all we're talking about. We're talking about the super-structure, Zionism as it has become.[12]

While rejecting the idea of a territorial Jewish nation state (alongside a more general suspicion of state power and militarism), he is not opposed to Jewish nationalism per se:

I've now come to a much more anti-essentialist view [of Jewish culture] which I've come to think of is a little bit nationalist in the way of perceiving Jews as more like a nation. By which I mean the people are sovereign, the people can do what they like by our own fate without relation to religious rules of rabbinic leaders. I wouldn't have thought I would say that ten years ago but I think I've come to realise that you don't have to be a Zionist to be a Jewish nationalist actually, and there was a whole strain of Diaspora nationalism that was not territorial, and particularly the Bund… it's kind of autonomy. It's kind of Autonomist thinking or like the Workmen's Circle folk. If you like [a] folk Judaism … [a] bit like Mordecai Kaplan, Jewish cultural rituals, folk culture, Jewish cultural pride without necessarily requiring territory, without requiring religious obligation.[13]

As Joe implies, Zionism was more than the movement to create a Jewish State; it aimed more broadly at a reshaping of Jewish identity not only in Israel but also, for many Zionist thinkers, in the Diaspora. As such, it is unsurprising that several interviewees assert that British Jews' engagement with Israel and Zionism is often a proxy for working through issues of local Jewish identity and status. For Andrew, this connection is explicit. 'For me as a secular Jew,' he explains, 'Israel is an integral part of my Jewish identity and I think it needs to be a really integral part of this community's Jewish sensibility and Jewish practice.' This position leads him to critique the behaviour of the UK Jewish community:

Coming out of last summer [2014] with the war on Gaza and the rockets. What happened? People were immediately focused on what was going on in Israel. And then as soon as the conflict either died down or it became normalised because it was for such a long period of time … people suddenly shifted the focus to think what does it mean here? Whether that was the Tricycle,[14] whether that was the media, whether that meant the debate within the community, and actually no one was focusing on what it was doing to Israel, what it was doing to Gaza for that matter, what it was doing to the people.

Andrew argues that the response of many UK Jews to events in Israel is, in fact, an attempt to manage their feelings about their own identity and status in British society. This analysis implies a judgement about the relative importance of Israeli and Diaspora issues and a claim that local Jewish self-interest is at least to some extent out of place in a conversation which purports to focus on a more important centre of Jewish life, the State of Israel.

For Tamar, the preoccupation with antisemitism and Jewish/non-Jewish relations emerges from the same set of historical conditions which gave birth to Zionism itself but which have, for her, now lapsed:

I think there is increasingly a younger generation that doesn't feel the trauma of Jewish history. I think I feel it less than my parents, my dad particularly. I think our students feel it less than me. I suppose what it is – it's the power thing again – is that my dad was born into a world of Jew equals powerless and I was born into a world of Jew equals powerful. And therefore your approach to the whole thing is totally different.

By implication, the fact that many Diaspora Jews remain overly concerned with antisemitism and are unable to relate objectively to events in the Middle East indicates that they have failed to internalise this shift from Jewish powerlessness to powerfulness.[15]

* * *

The various forms of critique articulated by the interviewees can be woven together to form a diverse but reasonably coherent narrative. This narrative starts out from the problem of exclusion: the absence of recognition, the tendency to stereotype and box people into preconceived categories rather than recognising the diversity and fluidity of human identity, and the discrimination that this brings about. Economic inequality is understood not only as a material problem but as a delegitimisation and dehumanisation of the poor and a failure to build relationships with them and hear their voices. More broadly, the breakdown of relationships, communities and tradition is seen as an obstacle to meaningful social progress and building a good society. This is reflected in the perceived disjuncture between Judaism and social justice; refusing to take on justice commitments is interpreted as a misinterpretation or dismissal of the values of the tradition. The tension between Jewish identity and justice commitments is exacerbated by the challenge of Zionism and Israeli politics, which sharpen the challenge of negotiating a path between inward looking, survivalist and universal, ethical conceptions of Judaism.

The pedagogical implications of these themes will be discussed in due course. In the next chapter, I move on to an exploration of the interviewees' vision – their conception of the world as it should be.

5

Vision – the World as It Should Be

The treatment of vision – the world as it should be – by Jewish social justice educators touches on the following themes: pluralism, redistributive and economic justice, individual moral behaviour and personal development, civil society and covenantal relationships, and a conception of Judaism as a social justice tradition.

Pluralism

Vision is a problematic category for many Jewish social justice practitioners. They tend to be torn between utopianism and pragmatism, occupied with the need to balance competing ideological approaches, and somewhat resistant to articulating prescriptive visions of a just society. These tensions all raise questions related to the concept of pluralism.

Several interviews reflect a tension between a pragmatic attitude to social change and the need for a clear understanding of ultimate objectives. Stuart, the founder of several Jewish social justice initiatives, relates that when he first got involved in social change work in the 1970s,

> you had all the purists … you know, *The Life of Brian*? You know, the Marxist, Leninist, Trotskyist splinter groups, dozens of them, and that was not my scene at all. I wasn't quite sure what my scene was. And when I went to work on inner city playgrounds I think I decided what my scene was, was I am a practical, pragmatic person, wanting to make a difference at grass roots. I am not a political purist. And I think that was a kind of a learning experience, and a conscious decision, which has stayed with me. I've never been very good with orthodoxies; I've never been very good with authority; and I'm much more comfortable in a more pragmatic space, practical and pragmatic, what can we do?

At the same time, Stuart takes issue with social change activists who do not have a clearly defined goal:

> I think for me you've got to have an eye on the end game. You know, what is it we're ultimately trying to achieve? If we're ultimately trying to achieve a complete eradication of extreme poverty in the world, then that can only mean structural and systemic change. And that has got to be political. … What are we trying to do in the world? You know, are we trying to help a few people? Well I think we're trying to do more than help a few people, I think we're trying to radically change the way the world works.

Rather than simply managing the tension between political idealism and pragmatism, other interviewees see the inherent value of competing ideological approaches and diverse voices, and seek to balance or respond to them as a matter of principle. Shalom, an Orthodox rabbi who is involved with interfaith and social justice education, articulates this as follows:

> If you look at a page of Talmud, you have all the different voices all adding to this conversation. … I loved the idea that you had to listen to the other side before you make your mind up, and there's more than one voice happening, and one side never has the answers. … And sometimes I think … a lot of social action isn't about I think, boys and girls in the classroom, recycle! Or take care of the poor! It's *listening* to the poor. What do they need? This whole notion of microfinancing. You don't have to tell them what to do. Just give them the means to do it. They'll tell you what to do.

For Shalom, pluralism is related to justice because both involve listening to the Other. Similarly, Rachel, a Reform rabbinical student and founder of a rabbinic social justice network, sees Jewish intellectual tradition as a resource for critiquing linear, dichotomous Western thought and the culture of individualism. Her study of Judaism has led her to appreciate the limitations of her previous training as a lawyer:

> The world is full of nuance, and it always should be, and … actually the grey is what life is. … [As a lawyer] you're supposed to try and prove a point, and have a coherent argument. Whereas actually I think in Judaism it's almost the opposite really. Like the Talmud is full of just loads of arguments for the sake of it … without really a conclusion. And it's certainly not coherent. … We've all been trained in this very Western way of thinking about the world, which is very Greek, and actually … it's kind of opposed to a lot of Jewish teachings.

The polarity of talmudic versus Greek thinking is connected, for Rachel, with a tension between the dominant transactional or consumerist framework of modern society and the radical, spiritual alternative offered by Judaism, which puts a premium on people, their relationships and the stories they tell.[1]

Danny, the director of a Jewish student organisation, in an alternative formulation, is committed to two values which often come into tension: marriage equality for LGBT+ people and freedom of religion. As a result, he appreciates the decision of Masorti Judaism, for example, to enable gay people to sanctify their relationships in the synagogue while refusing to do this in the traditional framework of a Jewish wedding (*kiddushin*). He comments,

> I'd like to see a world where people could be a bit more embraced with that complexity, because I think some of how I hear people talk about those issues, I just feel ... 'So you think every religion should just abandon all of its understanding so that gay people can get married?' ... That's not the only thing I care about. I also care about diversity, and freedom of religion. ... So it's about each finding it in their own way.

Some interviewees' commitment to the liberal values of personal autonomy and diversity means they are reluctant to define a prescriptive vision or end-goal for their social change work. Sally manages informal education programmes in a Jewish secondary school, where one of the objectives is to instil in her students the values of charitable giving and volunteering. She was asked whether she would make a value judgement about two different hypothetical graduates of her programme:

> MP: A person who spends all their life working as hard as they can, to earn as much money as possible in order to give their children everything they need and treating their partner well, and treating their children well, and that's their emphasis. And they don't do anything but that, and they don't give to charity, and they don't volunteer because it is all about the good of their family and their work ethic. As opposed to another person who ... spends a lot, he is charitable and philanthropic and does volunteer work, and has a different attitude about what he needs to be a good person in society. Sally: I don't know about for the school. I mean that is a really interesting question. Honestly, personally I think just my innate liberal doesn't, you know doesn't really ... like I don't ... mind.

How would she respond to a graduate of the school who adopted a racist position associated with the Israeli far-right?

> You know I think if you are being religiously pluralist, if you are being a pluralist in an 'orthodox' way, you have to find a way to hear that voice. I mean, I think I would want that voice to be coming from a place of experience and knowledge

and understanding and dialogue, but ultimately if you are truly committed as a pluralist, you have to be able to hear that voice.

Sally, like several other interviewees, is unwilling or unable to articulate any concrete vision which underlies her work. She reflects that her school's educational process reflects 'plurality within boundaries that we are consciously or unconsciously managing' but when asked 'can you define what those boundaries are?' replies 'no'.

Redistributive and Economic Justice

The majority of interviewees feel that a formal, rights-based conception of social justice must be supplemented with a redistributive approach to social and economic equality. Emma, the director of an anti-racism charity, argues that we need 'a fairer society that is working towards equality'. She continues, 'Things are not going to be perfect, but we need to be a part of a society that has the will to say, "Child poverty is unacceptable. Homelessness is unacceptable. And this is what we're going to do."' Masorti rabbi Jacob articulates a similar, egalitarian vision based on the conviction that all people have fundamental economic rights:

> We live in a world where most people in most parts of the world can have access electronically in minutes to seeing how anybody lives in any other part of the world. This didn't even exist twenty years ago. So you can see there's that over there, there's this here, I want to go there. Why morally not? So actually a real moral vision has got a price to it for people like me, like us. Am I keen to pay that price? If I'm really honest, probably not. So I'm not sure that I'm just not being hypocritical. I'm not sure about it, and that's why certain compassion and environment issues may be easier, or dealing with my neighbourhood may be easier than the universal picture, but the universal picture has to look like freedom from hunger, freedom from squalor and if there are basic medical services, they're available for everybody. ... [B]ut who's worked out what the price is and whether we're prepared to pay it?

Jodie, active in the field of international development, reflects on the extent of her egalitarian ambitions: does it make sense to envision a radical transformation of the world and the elimination of poverty? Alluding to the book of Isaiah, she says,

> So that prophetic thing of the lamb and the wolf. I do like it. I have always liked it. I am quite an idealistic person. You know, it does motivate you. The world could be different. But it basically says the social order will be completely

changed. Radically changed. Like it is completely unnatural, that a wolf will lie down with a lamb. That is one of those things that I struggle with. There is a bit of me that is a socialist or even a communist that says the social order needs to radically change but I think it actually goes against nature. I don't think people can give altruistically, always. So there is a bit of me that says no, that is too idealistic, we need to live in a more pragmatic world. So an example is when I came to the organisation three years ago, the tag line, the vision was 'The eradication of extreme poverty'. The eradication of extreme poverty. A just world, with the eradication of extreme poverty. I can't remember the exact wording. We changed it. … The vision is 'the active involvement of the Jewish community in the reduction of poverty'. … It's kind of you take that ideal 'there can be a different order' and you say 'no we're not ready to hear that message but we can reduce'. You can play your part in reducing poverty. I can play my part in reducing poverty.

In addition to the moral imperative of equality, some interviewees consider the economic and political structures which are needed to bring it about. Despite his involvement in philanthropy as a mechanism for social change, Craig articulates a statist conception of a just society:

And I think my view of social justice, I mean for me justice, as I understand it, is about fair and equal distribution of resources … And in order to have justice, you need an important role for a state, because a state is collective, it is universal, it is comprehensive and it can ensure through the involuntary use of taxation, that public goods can be distributed fairly.

Craig argues that as opposed to people on the Left who tend to connect justice with equality and therefore with state intervention, liberal and libertarian thinkers have typically been warmer towards philanthropy, which they associate with freedom.

Community organiser and parliamentarian, Manny, articulates a social vision which rests on the foundation of a strong civil society and is at once non-statist and collectivist:

So the definition for me of being rich is that you pass on an inheritance to your children that you pass on, not just money and land but some form of education and belonging and social networks and these things. And so how do we create an inheritance for the poor? How does the poor have some kind of future? So that's got to involve housing, but above all it has got to involve work and this is the socialist aspect. That the rich cannot avoid the poor because they need their labour. So I do a lot of work on vocation, on the representation of workers on corporate governance and running of larger companies, on regional banks, on endowing assets to local and poor places, so people can have access to money and start businesses.

Radical activist, Joe, in contrast, sets out a non-statist vision that emphasises individual freedom:

> I envisage a society where everybody has enough to fulfil their basic needs and thrive. So personally I really support constitutional economic rights where you have the right to have ... probably a basic income is my big thing, where everyone gets given let's call it twelve-fifteen grand a year, whatever, enough to live. So in that sense I'm not a statist, I quite like solutions which are not dependent on the state running everything but like a sort of libertarian socialism. But you know, I think it's fairly standard left wing stuff, re-distribution of wealth basically and public ownership where it's the best way of doing things. ... I just want to create the most egalitarian society I can with freedom as an important part.

Individual Moral Behaviour and Personal Development

The relationship between individual moral behaviour and social justice is a source of contention in Jewish social justice writing, both in relation to which is intrinsically more important and in terms of the causal connection between them. Several interviewees stress the importance of individual behaviour as a means to the end of justice. Jodie, for example, offers this reflection on the approach of rabbinic Jewish tradition to issues of justice:

> Yes, I think there is probably a clear vision of wolves and lambs lying down together. But isn't it interesting that the rabbis – do they talk much about the prophetic ideas and vision of what the world will look like? I am not sure they do. They talk about, look after the orphan. ... So does it ... I wonder ... it doesn't go into what happens when the wolf lies down with the lamb but it will definitely talk about the biblical bit that if there is an orphan somebody needs to look after that orphan. But who needs to look after that orphan? Who has that responsibility? For sure the Talmud does that.

Judaism, she feels,

> takes something like justice which is really quite difficult to get your hands around and then just takes really practical examples, so how then do you do this, that and the other? How would you bring. ... What does it mean to be involved and care about another person? ... I think Judaism has the answers. I really like

that about Judaism. It's prepared to say, yes, if somebody puts out their hand and says they need some money, give it to them.

Similarly, Manny claims that a just society based on cooperative ideals depends on individual, moral virtues. Discussing the Jewish roots of 'Blue Labour', a conservative, communitarian movement within the British Labour party, he draws both on the heritage of the Bund, the Eastern European Jewish socialist movement which for him emphasised the values of democratic, grassroots organising, and the tradition of civic-minded, Western European Neo-Orthodoxy:

> So I'm arguing that the Cooperative Movement was completely compatible with *'Torah im Derekh Eretz'* [the motto of Neo-Orthodoxy: literally 'Torah with the way of the land' but used colloquially to mean 'Torah with good manners' or 'decent behaviour'] – that there is self-organised, very respectable ... that's the conservative side of Blue Labour: that you have to be honourable. You have to be honest. You have to have ethics in the work that you do. You have to ... *Menschlichkeit* [a Yiddish term meaning 'humanity'] is the key concept ... I mean there you go. *Menschlichkeit* was the key concept that unites Samson Raphael Hirsch [the leader of 19th century German Neo-Orthodoxy] and the Bund. *Menschlichkeit* [means] just being a proper person in the world, to take responsibility for others and to pass it on.

While Jodie and Manny locate moral virtues in a broader context of social change, Sally, the director of volunteering and charity programmes in a Jewish secondary school, implies that righteous individual behaviour is an end in itself:

> So the first thing [students] are told when they come to the school, in the kind of ethos of the school, is be a *mensch* [human being or decent person]. And then one of the first things we do with them in informal Jewish education is we try and unpick what that means, what does that mean to be a *mensch*.

For Sally, social activism and pluralism are both connected to being a *mensch*. She argues that a person's conception of what it means to be a mensch should develop and become more sophisticated over time. For an eleven-year-old, it means 'don't bully people and you don't hit people, or you don't talk when other people are talking. You don't humiliate people'. For someone in their late teens, the concept is less clear but, Sally implies, it should evolve to include a willingness to listen to diverse voices and an openness to other people's experiences.

This process of personal development is for Sally an end in itself. She notes that the aim of involving students in volunteer work with the elderly and people with special needs is to provide them with a bank of experiences. She says, 'I think for us the aim is they'll replicate it in their adult lives. I think it's about imprinting certain experiences so that when they have more power over what they do in their lives, those experiences will be positive experiences that they've had.' Sally illustrates this principle with the example of a student who she asked to compere a high-profile awards ceremony for young volunteers:

> Now he's … dyslexic, he's dyspraxic, he's … you know, he's a bit of a nebbish in the school. … And his name sprung to mind straight away, because … we set up volunteering opportunities, and they sign up, his name was top of the list all the time, like throughout the year his name was top of the list. And so I put him forward to compere at the award ceremony. … Like his head of year was like, 'Really? That kid? He's a bit shlubby. Is he going to look like a mess in his school uniform?' And I was like, 'No no no, it'll be fine'. And then his mother spoke to me at the ceremony, and she was like, 'He is never the child that is picked for this. You know? Like he is never the one who's … Like you have changed his life. Like the honour … the honour of him being able to be this compere, and being recognised for what he's done', she was like, 'He's walking differently. He's talking differently'. You know? Like properly transformative. … And you know, that whole experience of being … like standing up and being the compere at this thing, and recognising the fact that he's a kid who gives his time to others, has been really … a really powerful experience. His mum was in tears. … It was amazing.

Several interviewees locate the ideal of personal development in a religious or spiritual context. Jacob articulates the following approach to personal development and social involvement:

> I think an aim of spiritual leadership has to be to help people find the depths of their own hearts and the passion of their own conscience, and to validate people on that path. … Alongside that is a question which is challenging of *mitzvah* [commandedness]: I feel myself commanded to do certain things and ultimately I believe life is about service. Now, I'm 57 and it's taken me a long time to formulate that very, very simple statement: life is about service. I think life is about satisfaction, life is about what I want to do, life is about happiness, life is about my spiritual journey. In the end it's become clear to me that people I know who are happy are people who find meaning in what they do for others. Now that might be compassion, that might be social justice, that might be both. How does one work against a culture of individual autonomy and 'I do what I want' towards a culture of compassion and moral imagination and obligation? And how does one do that in a way which enables people to find their fulfilment

in that way? Where you're not saying to people, 'This is what you want to do but you shouldn't be doing that. You should be doing something else.' We need to say … and of what you really care about – the most meaningful way you can do it is [this]. That comes back to why I think it's important that the issues with which people engage are issues they care about intrinsically and deeply.

Civil Society

A recurring motif throughout the interviews is the vision of a reinvigorated civil society which is able to act as an antidote to the dominance of the market and the state.

Sally emphasises the importance of empowering individuals for a life of active citizenship. When describing the outcomes of a project in which students were asked to research charities and then pitch for their chosen charity to receive a donation from the school, she comments, 'I definitely think that they felt empowered. Like in a very real way. … And … I think that was back to the cash.' She continues,

> I think what we're trying to do is give them the experience of knowing what it's like to volunteer your time, and what it's like to raise money. … And you know, actually having that experience. You know? And I really relate it to my experience, that every time I take a group of kids to a care home I don't want to do it, I don't want to do it, I can't be bothered, I feel a little bit resentful, until I get there, and I see it, and I'm reminded. I'm reminded of … you know, reminded of its value. Of its value for the care home residents, but its value for the students as well.

For Calley, a broad-based community organiser, nurturing empowered citizens is not enough. She wants participants in her campaigns to understand that the issues they face are collective, not individual. For example, in the context of a campaign to improve access to mental health services she comments,

> I want them to get a sense that this isn't just private to them. This is a public, broader issue, which various kinds of public spaces therefore have something to say about. So in a house meeting we might have a rabbi – in this one we had a priest who opened it with a statement about why should communal institutions care about this stuff. Why is this an issue which is not just about between you and your doctor but is something about our broader health. And I think for me that's also part of where I see Jewish community stuff, very de Tocqueville style. I re-read Jonathan Sacks' piece from last week[2] … and he basically makes

de Tocqueville's argument. ... But he makes an argument that what Jewish communities do that is radical, or any community ends up doing which is radical, is that it builds a space which stops it just being about short term self-interest. And it says actually this is about a broader, common thing.

Manny argues that empowered citizenship is an inherently collective phenomenon rather than an individual one. He reflects on the teachings of seminal community organiser Saul Alinsky,[3] who

> tried to take to very poor white communities and black communities in Chicago the teaching of this idea: that you must organise your own lives, you must build leaders from within your communities. Do not depend on others. Educate your own children, build power in your communities and the form of the power is relational power.

He adds that Alinsky's model of community organising had

> a very strong stress on relationships, a very strong stress that building relationships is the basis of keeping, of maintaining power and tradition; a very strong stress on leadership development, on having people from within your community who can – not external to your community but from within your community – who can represent your interests and negotiate on your behalf.

For several interviewees, strong relationships between different faith groups is an important component of a healthy civil society. Craig notes that for him, engaging Jewish schools in bridging programmes with other faith schools was a way of propagating a form of Jewish identity which was outward-looking, relational and focused on universal, social justice issues. Joe shares this open conception of Judaism, arguing that 'Jewishness functions as a spectrum; people are completely in flux', and that Jewish status should be a matter for individual self-definition. His organisation models this by being 'very open to non-Jews, we always have been. We advertise in the non-Jewish press our events and that's been a big part of our vibe I think, like it's non-parochial. There was always a large contingent of non-Jewish radicals or hipsters or just friends.'

Strong interfaith relations are an important element of the society Calley aspires to create. The ideal church, mosque or synagogue is one which is embedded in deep relationships with its neighbours and the surrounding community:

> My personal interest in this work is I want to change how the Jewish community see themselves. So I want them to be able to be in relationship in public as Jews with diverse groups in their neighbourhoods. I want them to reclaim a sense

of being Jewish as acting in this way. I want them to feel that their life inside the synagogue and their life outside the synagogue don't have to be completely separate in this kind of sphere. I want them to feel that their tradition is something that speaks to them about this.

For Calley, these relationships have to be grounded in compelling, effective political work:

> For a lot of rabbis, they meet imams, they know what that looks like. They do nice text study and they do it with their congregations. But they haven't even seen an experience of sitting in an assembly with this weird multi-faith partnership, with a politician up on stage responding to their asks, and them winning a change. That is out of their experience, that is out of their imagination.

In addition to their role in mobilising religious institutions for social action work that meets the genuine needs of the wider community, interfaith relationships are seen to be an important way of enabling the secure coexistence of diverse groups within a potentially divided, multicultural society. Calley expresses this as follows:

> You know people can be very nervous about things like wearing a *kippah* [head covering] in non-Jewish majority areas of London, and that is painful for them, do you know what I mean? The real question is am I ok to be here, would I be accepted if I'm part of this group? And what I hope they get a sense of is that they're part of a bigger group than just the Jewish community, even though it's really important they get that sense. But what does it mean to be part of your neighbourhood outside of the five streets around you?

Covenantal Relationships

The vision of a strengthened civil society implies a belief in the importance of interpersonal relationships. Orthodox-feminist educator Francesca emphasises the importance of community, which she understands as

> a group of people who have a common goal, a common idea. You don't always agree on the same principles, but basic values and principles you are trying to promote. There should be within that a kind of outward looking as well, that if you are going to be a healthy community that you look around you as well

as look inside to what you are doing, and try to kind of think about the world around you as well.

The connection between relationships and social action is illustrated by Calley. She talks about

> a synagogue … which hosted [a local Muslim community] when their centre burnt down, which was very powerful for the synagogue but which was clearly much more about solving the [Muslim community's] immediate needs. And in the recent spate of antisemitism, this synagogue got an email from the two local Muslim institutions saying we really want to help, we want to be on your side, and can we do anything? We're willing to come and just be a ring of peace for your congregants this Shabbat because we don't know if you've got security, and we'll come and we'll be supportive.

An additional example Calley mentions involves the issue of social care, where unexpected alliances have been created between middle-class children of care home residents and the poor, mainly immigrant carers who work in those homes. Both groups have a direct, personal interest in improved pay and conditions for care workers yet, in Calley's experience, the middle-class group only truly begins to understand the care workers' needs when they are brought face to face with them and are able to hear stories about the concrete challenges they face in their professional and home lives.

Calley's stories involve some tension between a transactional or utilitarian view that relationships are a means to the end of mutually beneficial social change, and an alternative understanding that relationships are inherently valuable. This tension is summed up by Manny in a distinction he makes between contractual and covenantal relationships. At one level, Manny argues that the rich have an interest in a relationship with the poor, on whose labour they depend, because 'we live in a polity and come election time they become a little bit concerned with the poor going to threaten them'. He makes the case that the nature of this relationship must be constructive and covenantal rather than purely legal and contractual. He fleshes out this distinction by saying,

> So contract is an exchange between parties and the problem with contract is that it is immediate and favours the richer side. A covenant is inter-generational, it involves a notion of participating in the political community through time and it involves institutions that mediate between them, and it involves a sense of status for everyone involved in that covenant. So it involves a sense of mutual sacrifice. And what we need now in politics is that the rich have got to make sacrifices and the poor as well, so that's the nature of trying to find a common life. *MP: What*

sacrifices do the poor have to make? Manny: Well I would say to respect the life and integrity and property of the wealthy, so not to be involved in crime, violence, threat, but to have some meaningful hope of a genuine participation in the good life of the community. … So a covenant is a common inheritance and that can't just be conceptual or legal, there also has to be come element of having a home in the world and the possibility of work.

The motifs of sacrifice, common inheritance and having a home in the world imply that the value of covenantal relationships transcends the immediate utility either party might derive from their transactions. Relationships in this view are not just means to the end of social change: they are also an end in themselves which must never be compromised in pursuit of a political goal, even when that political goal involves the very strengthening of relationships. Anti-racist activist Emma articulates a similar idea in the framework of the 'gift relationship':

> When I was in Philadelphia, and we came across an Amish community, and heard a wonderful story where … the Mennonites … there was an arson attack in their barn, set on fire and destroyed, and the next day a group of Amish men who lived next door, or you know, in the same community, arrived. Nobody asked them, they came with their ladders, and the men, they rebuilt the barn in two days. And I thought that's what society. … But that sort of thing about your problem is my problem. And without fanfare, without huge fuss, we're going to … you know. And it's like giving blood, how it used to be: you give it not because you get anything, like in America, twenty bucks or something for doing it, but you give it because it's [a] gift relationship.

If Manny and Emma believe relationships should not be reduced to a tactic in the pursuit of social change, Annie goes one step further by claiming that her educational and social change work for LGBT+ inclusion is above all a means to the end of a more relational society:

> Burial plots was something that we worked on … to have same-sex burial plots for couples, and those kinds of things that you know, the thought that when I die I wouldn't be able to be buried with my partner feels very sad and strange, that that would be something I'd have to think about, or in an old age home, it not be an automatic that if both my partner and I were entering an old age home together, that there would be a question whether we could share a room, and be treated as a couple. … God and Jewish tradition [want] us to find relationships, be in relationships.

Annie is not the only interviewee to discuss the importance of relationships alongside a conception of God and the place of the divine in human interactions.

Calley, for example, recounts a conversation with a politically active, white, Methodist bishop who lives in Soweto, in which she asked him,

> What are you doing? You're a nice, white Afrikaner man and you live in Soweto and you have this call to the Church – what is this about? And he said to me, my mission is to show that God loves people who don't feel that they are loved by God. Who don't feel loved in this world. They are told they don't matter and my mission is this, and this is the mission of the Church.

Similarly, student rabbi Rachel articulates her commitment to social justice based on covenantal relationships in theological terms:

> That is for me the verse that sums it up: that it's about me being made in the divine image. And through that, kind of linking it back to again being in relationships with each other, is that you should love your stranger as yourself, is because you know what it's like to be a stranger, *yad'a* ['knew'], you're in a relationship with the stranger. You know what it is to be that person.

Rachel refers to the well-known image of Abraham Joshua Heschel marching with Martin Luther King at Selma and to Heschel's statement that he was 'praying with his feet'. For her, this connotes 'a sacred duty to do social justice. It kind of almost like makes it feel too small saying social justice … but being there for people, being with each other, and … acting for each other. Being with, holding them, or whatever it is. Like it's sacred work, that relationship work. And social justice is part of that.' She expands on the conception of God that underlies this conviction:

> Knowing God, or knowing the Divine, or the source of everything, or whatever it is, something higher, a higher power, is through relationships with people, and is being able to see the Divine in each other. … But for me knowing God is basically through relationships, and through getting to know the other, and being able to break down some of the boundaries.

For some interviewees, the centrality of God to their justice commitments does not necessarily imply a theistic position. Annie, for example, says,

> I'm never sure if I believe in God. The traditional agnostic position. Sometimes I do, sometimes I don't. If I do it's not a kind of person or … a singular being, it's some sort of … you know, God is the goodness that we do in the world, and the goodness at the core of each of us, and maybe that goodness communicates. And when my goodness speaks to your goodness maybe that creates God.

In contrast, when asked if God 'is something beyond the human relationship, or is it in the human relationship?' Rachel responds,

> For me there's something beyond it as well, like it taps into that bigger picture. ... I don't believe that ... God is only in the immanent, or only in the relationship with the other person. I definitely think that there is something ... My understanding of God is quite kabbalistic. ... What really works for me is the divine sparks being lodged in everything, but yet there's *Ein Sof* [literally 'without end' or 'infinite' – a traditional mystical appellation for the divine], like there's the unknowable, you know, there's no end. That big thing that we're talking about, that God. So I have both of those in mind. But I feel like you access it through relationships.

This statement echoes the sense articulated by Masorti rabbi Jacob that the divine is not only a metaphor but a 'real, lived experience'.

Judaism: Pluralism, Justice and Cultural Autonomy

As we saw earlier in the chapter, many of the interviewees demonstrate a resistance to setting out a concrete ideological vision, at times articulated under the banner of pluralism. However, pluralism is also presented by several interviewees as a concrete, distinct vision for a healthier Jewish community. Shalom, an Orthodox rabbi, bemoans the disconnection between Orthodox and Progressive Jewish educators and rabbis and the consequent weaknesses he sees in each sector of the community: while the Orthodox are strong on textual Jewish knowledge and ritual life, their commitment to a social justice agenda is weak. Conversely, many Progressive leaders are fully on board with social activism but their members tend to be far less Jewishly literate.

> It's like the Orthodox could learn a lot about what's happening from those [Progressive] schools and their passion. By the same token, I'd love for those schools to have a richer environment in terms of text. What does the Talmud say about this issue? So they can sometimes ... they're very action rich but sort of knowledge poor at times. So if you could get those worlds a little bit more united, somewhere in the middle, so people could work together, from education to clergy, that would be a dream.

Shalom's vision encompasses both a celebration of diversity within the community and a call for collaboration across denominational divides in order for every stream of Judaism to benefit from each other's strengths.

Alongside her picture of the individual ideal Jewish school-leaver as someone who has internalised the values of diversity and engaging constructively with the views and experiences of other people, Sally's description of how Jewish life operates at her school implies a wider vision of how a pluralistic Jewish community might look. Pluralism, she says,

> is so embedded in everything that we do. ... [E]verything that we teach and the way that we frame everything, in what we do in school and how we run. ... You know so how do we run *tefilah* [prayer services] on Rosh Hodesh [the new month]; they get to choose a service. They get to choose from explanatory, spiritual, Reform, Masorti, Orthodox, Chabad [a Hasidic group] come in. So when Rosh Hodesh happens, when prayer happens in the school, it happens across the board. You know when we have services on Shabbat they get to choose what service they go to. And then we push them a little bit harder, when they are in Israel we say 'try the other service'. Talk about it, let's see what that other service is like. Go to that talk. ... This year we had someone from each of the major streams of Judaism who spoke to Key Stage 4 assembly for Rosh Hodesh. So listen to the people you agree with and you are now forced in Key Stage 4 to also listen to the people that you disagree with as well. Or whose voice you haven't heard. ... And actually to see us disagreeing, like hear us disagreeing on stuff, but know that we can still co-exist. Like hear the voices and know that you can co-exist.

Jewish pluralism in this account is more than an objective recognition or even an active acceptance of diversity; engagement with diverse views and position is seen as a moral imperative and a vital part of the individual's Jewish experience. Given Sally's sense that large sections of the Jewish community are currently rather insular, closed-minded and intolerant, her vision implies the need for radical communal change.

As we have seen, Joe frames his commitment to difference and subversion within the Jewish community in even more provocative terms. His organisation runs events that exemplify this idea and which are purposefully challenging of many of the accepted norms within the established Jewish community. For example,

> Our first event was called Punk Purim. It happened in a squat in Whitechapel [in East London]. It was in association with Heeb magazine and it had a klezmer band. It was like rammed, absolutely rammed party with a klezmer band. A room of radical Torah talks, where power cuts kept happening. ... [Another] event ['Protocols of the Elephants of Zion'] was looking at a sideways take on Anglo-Jewish history, so it was celebrating 350 years since the re-admission

to England of Jews under Cromwell. But we were trying to look at the dark side; the kind of criminals, the gangsters, like the non-establishment side of it. And we had DAM, a Palestinian hip-hop band performing at that, which is also controversial. We then also had a couple of events called 'Rootless Cosmopolitan Yeshivas' which were basically quite serious events which tried to have a *yeshivah* type atmosphere in which ten different teachers talked in a very loud room, and you had to gather round them. But all the subjects were radical, Jewish, quite often non-Zionist or anti-Zionist … gay and lesbian, feminist. So a broad sweep of kind of non-mainstream Jewishness, and that happened a couple of times and very successfully. We've had a Jewish tent at Glastonbury when I did mass conversions, taught Talmud to non-Jews. They thought I was a rabbi and I didn't decide to correct them.

Joe's account of these events implies a particular, ideological vision of a Jewish community which is radically different from that which currently exists. At the same time, he implicitly assigns value to the principles of diversity and openness in their own right.

Several interviewees argue that there is an intimate, intrinsic connection between Judaism and social justice. Emma, for example, says,

I want Jewish identity to be absolutely bound up in the whole understanding about social justice, so the two are linked. … I want us to be proud of us trying to make the world a better place. I want us to be proud of our past history of trying to do that. And I want us to be committed to a future where we're doing this. … And I want those who talk about Jewish prophets to externalise their commitment. Well, you know, what are the prophets saying to us? … So I want people who call themselves Jewish to have this commitment to social justice, to have it as central to their identity.

Along the same lines, Jodie adds,

As a community we should be making a response [to social justice issues] because this is what Judaism is about. We are supposed to be perfecting the world. We are supposed to be part of the mission that makes the world more perfect. If there is going to be a *mashiah* [messiah], if there is going to be some of redemption then the world needs to be perfected; … actually this is what being Jewish is about, there is a mission here – that we are mission driven.

Calley expresses a similar sentiment in relation to Jews' involvement in social activism: 'I want them to feel that their life inside the synagogue and their life outside the synagogue don't have to be completely separate in this kind of sphere. I want them to feel that their tradition is something that speaks to them about this.'

Calley's reference to a feeling of separation between life within and outside the synagogue relates to a sense among other interviewees that the relationship between Judaism and social justice cannot be taken for granted but rather needs to be negotiated. Jodie, for example, articulates a complex understanding of the relationship between personal, historical and textually derived narratives as illustrated by the following example, which is worth quoting at length:

> So I am in Ghana in a rural setting and I am having lunch. Lunch takes about three hours to prepare, you are just basically sitting there waiting for it because it is on a wood burning fire. It is a very rural setting. There are lots of children milling around because it is sports day. There is a big competition, they are coming and going from school. So, we are just watching that with a guy called Karamu. We are working with schools because we are doing this big project on education in Northern Ghana. Lunch comes. It is once again a fried fish, deep fried, with fried rice and salad. I am not allowed to eat the salad because it might have been washed in regular water and I might get cholera from it. So, I don't eat the salad, I eat the rice, I've had enough of the fish. I am ultimately, a middle class, middle-aged Jewish woman from London. I have had enough of the fish after two weeks. So I leave half of it and Karamu looks at me and gives me a bit of a nudge. I understand at that moment, that it is unacceptable that I don't finish my food in the context in which we are in. He sort of motions, looking at the kids. So I pick at my plate and get eye contact with a kid who is walking past and sort of look sideways and sort of with my eyes, um do you want this. He comes over and sits down, nobody says a thing, on the floor next to me, he takes my knife and fork, he takes the plate, he has a little box with a couple of mismatched crocs in it. He sits down and finishes everything on my plate, he puts the plate back on the table and off he goes. So I am sitting there very close to tears and I am transported to the fact that my parents, my father's parents were in Belsen and his parents died of hunger. They died of starvation in Belsen. A couple of months later I am in front of [my rabbi], it's Yom Kippur, I've prepped for Yom Kippur. He's talking about Isaiah and 'don't give me your sack cloth, you need to feed the poor'. Oof my God, everything suddenly all makes sense, wow, the Holocaust happened to us and we died but we survived and what is our purpose in the world? I have fed the poor literally in such a real way, it's heart breaking, and there is still poverty, and all that stuff made sense. For me it also helped in what is this Holocaust thing? You can feel, certainly, as a second generation [survivor], very sort of persecuted and very afraid of the world and everybody who isn't you. And it translated it, it just sort of said – it's not that it's a moment and it could never happen again; that is a possibility. But there is another possibility as well, another reality. So that is what I took so I can as I said

weave between these different things in order to find a more important, more traditional sense of what is our purpose.

Jacob goes one step further, arguing that uniting the worlds of Judaism and social justice requires us to overcome the tensions – and sometimes the outright conflicts – that exist between them:

> For myself, why is there a link between being a Masorti Jew and compassion and social action? It's somehow taking texts which are often … well some of them, quite inwardly directed at the Jewish community, and wanting to universalise them; to take them beyond their context, to push them into the widest dimension of meaning. … One can always mercifully find Jewish sources that do that. To feel free to rethink what Judaism has to say about the relationship between men and women, about war, about who you're for and who you're against, to be able to understand those boundaries as politically and historically conditioned and not as essential to Judaism, and therefore find a universal vision.

Rachel acknowledges a similar conflict between her conception of the essence of Judaism as a 'Torah of human rights' and the empirical observation that the Torah includes an injunction to commit genocide (e.g. Deuteronomy 7:1-5). She reflects that she has 'red lines where I think what Torah is and what Torah isn't. Like to me, Torah doesn't instigate violence.' At the same time, she acknowledges that rabbinic tradition is a culture of controversy in which conflicting opinions are preserved. Citing a well-known talmudic discussion about a debate between the schools of Hillel and Shammai[4] she comments that while the text accepts both schools' teachings as authentic 'words of the living God', it regards the school of Hillel's legal rulings as authoritative or 'true'. She adds, 'I think there's something in … the way that I view Judaism is what I think is a true Judaism, *the* true Judaism, but yet everything else is authentic'. Rachel implies that 'authentic' traditions are those which are empirically part of Jewish literary culture, regardless of the truth value of their content, whereas 'true' Judaism is restricted to those aspects of the tradition which accord with certain theological or ethical criteria. When asked how she 'reads out' those aspects of Torah which she considers to be 'authentic' but 'untrue' (i.e. they are in the text but do not accord with her conception of Judaism), she responds by talking about one of her teachers:

> He's got quite a specific understanding of God, but that he knows what God is, and what Torah is, and through that he knows that that can't be part of Torah. As in the principles that he has, or that the Torah has, or that God is, which is love

and justice and compassion … when you read the text through that you know it can't be that.

While this statement implies that the truth of Torah is to be understood by filtering the text through a set of extrinsic criteria, Rachel muddies this position somewhat through a subsequent comment:

> If there are two things that conflict in the Torah, and you're stuck with them, you realise that one has to be the right way. So you just wrestle with it, basically, until you get to an understanding of it. So that's what I feel, you know, Israel being the struggler with God, that kind of thing. It's about testing what the red lines are as well, it's a good exercise.

The suggestion here seems to be that the truth of Torah is to be worked out not through the prism of clear, extrinsic criteria but by struggling with the internal tensions between contradictory passages, all of which must be taken into account but only some of which will eventually be judged to be true, presumably on the basis of values and intuitions which emerge from the interpretive process.

Joe expresses the relationship between Jewishness and social justice through a vision of non-statist, Jewish national and cultural autonomy:

> I think on the ground the British Jewish community looks much more like a sort of quasi-autonomist national group within Britain. It's got its own institutions, it's got its schools, community institutions, its own politics even though it's not yet democratic, it's oligarchic. It's got institutions, it's got welfare. It's actually perhaps one of the most successful groups in that … minority groups in the UK for doing that, because of wealth primarily. But I think since the 1970s with the growth of multi-culturalism, there's been more tolerance of that and that has become possible. The traditional British assimilatory discourse has slightly subsided and privileged groups like Jews will be able to take advantage of that by creating institutions. And I think the Jewish community is not a religious community, even though that's the discourse, that's the artifice. So the artifice, the claim, is we're either a religious community or we're kind of a nation only in Israel, so we're a nation in waiting to go to Israel. But I think neither has described what's really going on. I think we have become a national unit kind of here.

However, the existing framework falls short of Joe's vision of a democratic, autonomous Jewish community:

> Well looking historically I think the Bund, and left wing Jewish thinking has always been positive about autonomy, but wanting to make them more left wing,

so they were talking about democratising the Jewish community. And that was a big thing in Eastern European progressive Jewish writers, democracy, having Jewish income tax for example, that would be an amazing thing! ... So in order to have that progressive side we have to have some institutions to work with. I'm particularly in favour of Jewish schools, I would be in favour of a certain type of Jewish school. ... Something progressive, cultural, very open to anyone who wants to enter, who is interested in Jewish culture. So not particularly religious, democratic, progressive. And there are such schools like that in Israel but I want to be able to do that without having the State. *MP: And what would be Jewish about that school?* Joe: Language. Yiddish, Hebrew, Jewish songs, Jewish history. Very much like Workingmen's Circle schools in the States, and there are a few examples left where they kind of talk progressive values through biblical and midrashic stories.

Joe's vision not only relates to Jewish schools but also, somewhat surprisingly, emphasises the role of synagogues:

I think the East End synagogues ... you have to remember that they started off as *shtiebels* [small Hasidic synagogues], right? They were community centres and only later did they get forced into the Anglo-Jewish prism of a faith centre. It was much more a social centre with meals. We'd like to return it to that kind of base where prayer is just like one thing that happens.

Manny echoes this position and believes that the Jews' heritage of Diasporic, autonomous communal life is potentially an important resource for wider society:

And then there's very amazing traditions within Judaism of how to broker difficulties. How to reach out. I noticed ... For example something I've been involved with lately is solidarity with Christians who are being killed in Iraq and beheaded and slaughtered. And what I noticed was, is that the bishops and the Christians didn't have really the interminable experience of how to deal with fellow believers who were abandoned and threatened. But we do have systems of being in solidarity with the captives and the hostages and you know no greater obligation than to free the prisoners and the captives. So the exilic imagination is deeply implanted within us, and we do have wisdom of dealing with that.

Without articulating this explicitly, Manny seems to suggest that the traditions of exilic Jewish community life are an important model for other faith communities and possibly for society as a whole, providing a compelling answer to the question of how it might be possible to negotiate the tensions between participation in general society on the one hand and retaining solidarity with a particular cultural group on the other.

* * *

In the dimension of vision, then, the interviewees explore a number of interconnected themes. Their starting point is a suspicion of utopianism combined with a preference for ideological pluralism, complexity and personal autonomy. They are committed to the moral imperative of equality but combine this with a pragmatic or sceptical attitude to the possibility of radical economic change. Some interviewees note the importance of the State in implementing redistributive policies, but most are more enthusiastic about the role of a strong civil society. Similarly, they exhibit a tension between the importance of individual moral virtues and personal growth – either as a vehicle for social change or as inherently constitutive of a just society – and the importance of community, civic relationships and collective action. If relationships in general are important, relationships across diversity – between different faith and ethnic groups, between rich and poor – are even more significant. These relationships are ideally not transactional but covenantal, involving an element of sacrifice for the common good, and holding religious value; a place where one meets God. The interviewees' vision of the Jewish community itself is characterised in a similar way. The ideal community is diverse, inclusive and dialogical, committed to Judaism as a justice tradition in which social action is of spiritual value. However, the progressive social meaning of Judaism is not held to be innate to the tradition in a naïve sense but has to be worked out hermeneutically. Finally, Jewish communal and cultural autonomy is held up as a value, both as a vehicle for politically progressive Jewish values, and as a manifestation of a healthy, democratic, multicultural society.

Having surveyed the critique and vision expressed by the interviewees, in the next chapter I explore the strategies they advocate to transform the world as it is into the world as it should be.

6

Strategy – Education, Activism and Community Organising

The strategic dimension of the Jewish social justice ideologies articulated by the interviewees can be broken down into four core, overlapping, approaches: teaching and learning; activism and campaigning; community organising and relationship-building; and speaking out, embodying values and personal transformation.

Teaching and Learning

The interviewees who emphasise strategies of teaching and learning aim to shape their students' attitudes and develop them as moral agents or social activists in a wide range of ways.

Sally, the head of informal education at a Jewish secondary school, emphasises the centrality to the teaching and learning process of giving students a particular set of experiences. Thinking about her school's charity and volunteering projects, for example, taking students to visit elderly residents of care homes, she reflects that the school's aim is for them

> to have that experience in their bank of experiences. … So the experience of giving time to others; feeling valued or appreciated for giving the time; being … like being not about themselves; being not about … You know? And also valuing people for being … not for being … you know, it's… not for getting the best grade, or not for not getting detentions. You know, we don't … we take the naughty kids, we take whoever wants to come. And often it is, it's a different kind of demographic from the ones who get valued at school. So you know, I want them to feel valued, but I want them to have the experience as well, to have the same experience that I have, which is like, 'Oh, this is really nice. This is really nice. And I've done something valuable today'.

It is noteworthy that Sally's notion of a 'bank' of experiences gels, at least linguistically, with an educational model that Paulo Freire and other critical pedagogues consider to be oppressive. However, here, the subject of 'banking' is experiences rather than knowledge and, as we will see below, Sally demonstrates a commitment to the dialogical unpacking of these experiences with her students as a means of developing their own, inherent identities and potential. At the same time, Sally's comments imply something of an Aristotelian, habituative approach to the moral development of her students: involving them in particular experiences or behaviours seems to be a means to the end of embedding these habits in them as they emerge into adulthood.

This tension between a habituative or socialisation-type model and a person-centred approach focused on realising the unique potential of each individual is also evident in relation to a charity fundraising project where students researched charities and 'pitched' them to their friends with the aim of securing cash prizes for the winning causes. On the one hand, Sally suggests that the goal of this activity was to induct students into the habits of charitable giving and fundraising, but at the same time she emphasises the importance of the intimate connections between the programme and the biographies and inner worlds of the participants:

> One kid in particular came in to my office in a break time, and he was like, 'I really need your help', he was like, 'I'm trying to research charities that deal with domestic abuse, but I can only find ones that deal with domestic abuse for women, and I want a charity that looks after domestic abuse for men'. And it was just like he … something he'd really … I don't know if there was like a personal connection, but he'd really thought about, and thought about why he wanted to do it, and then he like … we gave him the tools really, and the opportunity to find out about it, and then to talk about that to his peers. … So I guess because it's like student led, and it's following their interests, it's following their passions.

This focus on the genuineness of the students' response is matched by an emphasis on the authenticity of the experience itself. Sally comments,

> I think they really, really felt like they underwent a connection with the real world. There was something … in it, and I'm not sure what it was, but there was something in it that took them out of the classroom and into the real world. Maybe it was the cash… There was a lot of web based research. … We let them come into the office and phone the charities. … You know, it was really about them reaching out and touching the outside world. … But there was something

in that process when they realised it wasn't an exercise. ... They were trying to get that money for something that they felt passionate about.

Yet despite the importance of the authentic, real-world nature of the experience, there is also a managed, perhaps even somewhat manipulative, aspect to the process Sally describes. She reflects that the students' passion for the project came partly from a genuine connection with the causes they were advocating but also because

> it spoke to them culturally. You know, it was like it was The Apprentice, it was Dragon's Den, it was the X Factor, it was like ... I think it spoke to them on a cultural level. ... Like ... it's about meeting them ... where they're at really. But then the agenda was very ... very not where they're at. And I think there was a point at which they realised that this kind of, you know, grown up charity stuff could be as much a part of their world as, you know, as watching what happens on The Apprentice.

Shalom, an Orthodox rabbi, employs a similar educational strategy in a different context. When working with secular or progressive Jewish students, he builds on their existing commitments to social justice to show them the value of Jewish tradition which, unbeknownst to them, also contains these principles:

> What's my aim by going in there? I would like to say that they're hearing something unique about a Torah perspective on responsibility. It's not just why Fairtrade is good but why as Jews they should take Fairtrade seriously. So they're proud about their Judaism, they're now ingrained with something about their Judaism. I'm proud to be a Jew because it says something meaningful about eating Fairtrade chocolate. ... So for that one it was all about just using a couple of quotes from Isaiah, you know, just in case you though Judaism was all about ritual, small ritual acts, prophetic voices say feed the poor and clothe the naked man kind of thing, and that's a really important piece, and yet you probably don't know about this so let's have an educational session about Isaiah.

Sid Schwarz formulates the relationship between experiential and textual Jewish education somewhat differently.[1] He describes an unplanned meeting between young people on a Jewish social justice educational programme and a group of homeless people who had organised themselves into a community on the streets of Washington, DC. Having heard the homeless people's stories, the students articulated for themselves the justice values that happen to lie at the heart of Judaism. Schwarz, as the group facilitator, supplied the students with biblical and rabbinic concepts to match, and the young people were amazed at how these ancient texts spoke directly to their situation. Schwarz describes this process as 'street Torah' and reports that it burst the young people's bubble and propelled them into social action. In other words, the kind of real-world experience employed by Sally helped students shape or clarify their own values, which the educator – echoing Shalom's manoeuvre – was then able to root in Jewish tradition.

Conversely, when teaching in an Orthodox framework where students have a prior commitment to traditional Jewish law and practice, Shalom leverages this in order to convince them that it is important, for example, to recycle.

> You can do a whole class on *bal tashhit* [the commandment 'do not destroy'], from the Torah to the Gemorah [Talmud], the *Shutim* [Responsa literature], and just begin to explore what the rabbis had to say about this important issue, about not wasting. And then you hold a plastic bottle at the end and you say 'what shall we do with this, *le-fi halakhah* [according to Jewish law]?' And hopefully that whole sense has led them on this journey where they're caring about a plastic bottle that would have not been an issue now becoming a Torah issue. It can't go in the rubbish because *bal tashhit* would say not to.

This learning strategy combines the provision of a partially managed set of experiences combined with a process of relationship-building between students and teachers. The nature of this relationship is twofold: on the one hand, the teachers' role is to engage students in critical, reflective dialogue in which they unpack their experiences, and on the other they function as role models whose behaviour is to be emulated. For Sally, the tension between these two aspects of the pedagogical relationship is resolved by the pluralistic nature of the educational setting and goals. Rather than serving as role models for a particular kind of Jewish practice, the school's staff collectively seek to embody the values of Jewish pluralism, which itself demands critical, reflective behaviour. This is achieved not only through role modelling but by engaging students in critical, reflective discussion based on their experiences – with the important proviso that the experience is as vital a part of the educational process as the discussion. For example, Sally comments on the experience of visiting elderly people with dementia in a care home:

> Like it is pretty interactive. And the kids always come away talking about them, talking about the characters, asking about … you know, asking about people's stories. And we talk about the … like the uncomfortableness of it as well. You know? And you can tell by looking at them who's uncomfortable, and who's not enjoying it, and whatever. And you say, 'It's difficult isn't it? Why do you think it's difficult?'

Similarly, in the context of a meeting with a group of Muslim students from another school,

> Kids refusing to go to the *mifgash* [meeting] and saying 'Why bring terrorists into our school?' that is a position. It was challenged. But the challenge was: have the experience and then have your position. Like we will listen to your position once you've had the experience, don't take position before you have been in the room. Go in the room and then take a position.

Just as Sally aims to induct her students into a culture of Jewish pluralism by exposing them to and enabling them to reflect on complex, novel experiences, Tamar, director of a 'pro-Israel, pro-peace' organisation, seeks to challenge the political views of the participants on the trips she runs to Israel and the West Bank. Echoing the Ignatian see–judge–act pastoral cycle, Tamar sums this up as a three-stage process: exposure to new facts and *experiences* stimulates *reflection* and intellectual or ideological change which leads to political *action*:

> So the educational stuff is giving people the opportunity to actually look at the complexity, more broadly, speak to people, and meet with people they wouldn't normally get to hear. That might be everything from Palestinian and Israeli human rights activists to former heads of the Shin Bet inside Israel, the security services, and have a critique of the direction of travel of the country, and we are keen to mobilise people to be more vocal about that. And to actually physically get people out on the ground to see things, and take people beyond the Green Line that everyone talks about to actually into the field and actually see for themselves.

This educational process means helping learners replace what Tamar sees as their incomplete or biased perspectives on the Israeli-Palestinian conflict with more complete ones. For example, she reflects on the reaction of two teenagers to a day-trip organised by her organisation which took place in the context of a month-long Israel tour:

> There were a couple of kids who took real exception to the content of the programme, and in the end the guide said to them 'did you go to Tzfat [Safed]?' Yeah, yeah, we learned about the kabbalists, we learned about the sixteenth century, we learned about the Inquisition. He said 'did you talk about the Palestinian population though, that existed before 1948?' Blank faces. 'Did you talk about the fact that Mahmoud Abbas, the Palestinian president came from Tzfat?' Blank faces. 'Did you talk about the fact that he went on television a few months ago to say "I know I can't return to this place as anything other than a tourist even though it was my family home?"' Blank faces. He turned round to

the kids and said, 'look I'm not going to pretend that what I am trying to teach you does not come from a specific perspective, that it has its own biases and its own subjectivity in it but what I am trying to explain to you is that everything else you have done on this tour has brought bias in another direction. I'm just asking you to expand your possibilities.' What he was saying is it's not that what you learned in Tzfat is not true, all of it is true, but there is more to that story than the bit you learned.

Tamar does not naively assume that there is an inadequate, biased view of reality which needs to be replaced with an objectively true one (although her use of terminology such as 'myth-busting' reveals some ambivalence on this score). When asked 'do you think there are more and less true ways of seeing reality? Or is everything narratives basically?' she responds,

I think it is all narratives. I think the challenge is how do you hold multiple narratives. So the narrative of 'this country is deeply insecure and we need to protect our borders and these people hate us and want to kill us' is not untrue. I mean I would question the validity of those big phrases in particular. But existing alongside that narrative is one that is equally true which says 'we've occupied a people for forty-seven years, we've denied them their basic human and political rights, we're making our world and probably the wider world unsafe because of it, we're making it impossible to build different regional alliances in the Middle East, which can dramatically change the status quo, and we are destroying the moral fibre of Israeli society'. That is equally true. The problem that I think we have is that everyone wants their version and their narrative to win.

Alongside this strong, cognitive thrust, the educational process Tamar describes also involves an emotional journey. While emotional baggage can hold back the planned process of intellectual change, emotion also plays an important role in personal transformation. Tamar implies that experiencing feelings of distress in response to their encounters with abuses of Palestinians' rights and the harsh facts of the Occupation is a vital part of her participants' learning journey: 'Actually I saw … a tangible sense of emotional breakdown over everything they were seeing, and then a twenty-four-hour period where we saw some good positive stuff and people built their world view back up a little.' She comments on the feelings of shock and embarrassment experienced by one family who, after participating in her organisation's programmes, became deeply involved as activists:

I suspect they were always sympathetic-ish but they have gone from being sympathetic-ish to being 'this is not something we can stand back from and we are going to do everything we can to help … and to expose the voices of the people we met to more of our friends, we're going to host events in our homes and going to get more people on these trips'. I think that came down to 'I can't believe I've never seen this before, I can't believe in all my life, all the times I've spent in Israel …' – interestingly it has happened to people who have homes and spend a lot of time there – 'that nobody ever showed me this'. Sometime that is about a slight element of personal embarrassment and am I really that person that is so blinkered. I can't believe that I have lived here all of these years of my life and there is a bit of, I want to compensate for that.

When does emotion stop being an obstacle to transformation and become a positive part of the learning process? Reflecting on the experiences of a women's trip she organised, she reports,

> The thing that changed their lives is that I took them to meet a group of women who are big activists in this new organisation Women Wage Peace. They were Tel Avivian middle class, met them in a nice art gallery in Tel Aviv and I think our women looked at them and went 'you are like me, I could be you,' whereas there was an element of everyone else they had met were not like them. … But they were like these nice middle class women who were saying it's not really okay to occupy people and we are going to march from Jerusalem to tell people that. They [the participants] thought 'oh I could do that'.

The transition from a situation of discomfort and danger to one of familiarity and safety supported the movement to a sense of optimism and activism within the participants.

The ability to identify with a group of not-too-different role models also seems to have been an important aspect of the learning process. Tamar makes this explicit when she reports on a visit she arranged for the women's group to hearings involving teenage Palestinian defendants at an Israeli military court in the West Bank:

> With the women there was a lot of 'as a mother' and there was an element of imagining what it would be like as a mother for your fifteen-year-old son to be arrested in the middle of the night by someone you don't know and taken away from you. I think they did identify with that narrative even though these women couldn't be more different from them. *MP: What do you think that did to them?* Tamar: I think it really screwed with them. They found it traumatic because they could imagine it. They were thinking about the idea of your children being taken in the middle of the night, tied up and blindfolded and that you wouldn't be able to locate them because they are in some police station that you can't get

to and they are not allowed to call you. The terror, there was a sense of 'I can imagine the terror you would feel as I would feel that same terror'. ... *MP: What do you think the impact of that is on the people?* Tamar: On our people? I think it is massive because it becomes about being a human being and it takes away ... back to the subjectivity/objectivity thing which is you see it for what it is. Whether this kid has thrown a stone or a knife they are still a kid and he will be traumatised for the rest of his childhood as a result of that experience and I wouldn't want my child to go through that.

While Tamar connects this experience to the transition she is attempting to facilitate from a subjective or incomplete perspective to an objective or complete one, her use of the words 'objective' and 'subjective' is somewhat confusing. It might be more helpful to describe this process as one in which participants become able to ignore irrelevant, particularistic distinctions between people (e.g. Jewish versus Palestinian identity) and to focus on universal commonalities which unite them. Rather than encouraging her learners to adopt an objective viewpoint, Tamar hopes, perhaps, to displace one partisan view of the conflict and its protagonists with another, more universalist but equally ideological one.

Tamar argues that the learning process discussed above tends to draw the participants towards nuanced, moderate political positions. Just as many people who are immersed in what she sees as uncritical, right-wing Zionist positions move to the Left, so too people from the anti-Zionist far Left have developed a more nuanced view of the conflict and a more sympathetic approach to Israel as the result of their learning experiences. This kind of political education relates to Tamar's belief in the importance of holding multiple, complex narratives. When asked whether the ability to hold multiple narratives leads to a particular political orientation, she responds, 'I don't know. My hunch, and it's only a hunch, but it probably leads to a more compassionate way of being in the world. Whether that is compassionate left or compassionate right I'm not sure. I suspect it probably leads to less extremist, absolutist positions.' It is worth noting, of course, that while Tamar sees her own positions as moderate, her political opponents on both the Zionist Right and the anti-Zionist Left would criticise her as an extremist.

Rather than focusing on politics, LGBT+ inclusion activist Annie's social change strategy emphasises that individual attitudinal and behavioural improvement is both an end in itself and the foundation for organisational transformation. Engendering this attitudinal or behavioural change itself requires a two-stage, training-based method: an affective, experiential process that enables participants to clarify and explore their own feelings and attitudes serves as a preparation for the crux of the learning, which Annie describes as cognitive or intellectual in character. The focus on pre-existing feelings and motivations is clear from Annie's account of her initial meetings with organisational leaders:

> So individuals that might be willing to start thinking about [LGBT+ inclusion], perhaps they've faced a difficult scenario in their own role, but aren't yet necessarily ready to tell anyone that this is something they want to get better at, because they're worried about how other people in their community might react. So that's a big part of it. … Those conversations are educational … but they're done in a very one to one consultation, very led by the person I'm meeting, and what their concerns are…, why they've met with us. What's got them interested, what's got them motivated, because it's almost always them having approached us, and not the other way round. So it's people that already have an interest, but there's also some concern, fear, resistance. And so trying to work with that.

Similarly, Annie relates that her training sessions always begin with a compulsory section focusing on the experiences and motivations that the participants are bringing to the table:

> We'll often do what's your journey, … what got you here? So I ask people two or three key moments, draw it, write it, however you like, and then share them. And one of the things I've done is as people are sharing them help people think through some of those really horrible situations that we don't want to put more in the Jewish community, but we might want to tell those stories in ways that make other people care. And some of those are positive things, like a great session at summer camp, is something that made you think about this more, or … made you believe that Judaism cared about this, or a sermon your rabbi gave. You know? Some of those things are really positive. Or a friend that intervened, or you know, whatever it is. Some of those experiences are really positive, and what can we do to make those more common. And some of the really negative, what can we do to reduce them?

Conversely, when asked what comprises the crux of the learning (as opposed to this experiential phase which is characterised as merely preparatory, albeit vital) Annie refers to a piece of training that deals with language:

> Creating shared language I think is essential. I think a lot of hurt is created by just careless use of language. … *MP: Are you suggesting the kind of language that should and shouldn't be used?* Annie: Yeah. We usually … we'll go through a glossary often … And allow people to ask what the different questi- … you

know, what the different words they've heard that they're not sure how to use: is 'queer' okay to use? Is it not?

She adds,

So some learners respond more to statistics, so we'll often include some statistics. I don't respond to statistics very much, but I know lots of people do. So we'll include it because for some people that's like crucial evidence, and that's what changes their mind. Stories are really important, testimonies can have a huge impact.

Both these comments imply that a 'banking-style' provision of authoritative information (statistics, rules about acceptable language, testimonies) is an important way of changing people's perspectives and commitments. Whether the impact of this material is purely cognitive or has an additional affective component, the process as described here seems to be one in which the educator marshals pre-packaged knowledge in order to pursue a desired learning outcome.

However, it would be an oversimplification to present this learning model as one in which the preparatory emotional–experiential phase simply enables the participants to absorb the information presented in the core, cognitive stage. Annie describes a more nuanced process by which she attempts to bring learners to the point at which they are able to make the attitudinal changes which will lead to more inclusive individual and organisational behaviour. For example,

I mean this has never happened, but if … you know, if that came up that actually everyone in the room genuinely believed that it [homosexuality] was a perversion that could be fixed, and was something you know, terribly wrong with a person, that's crucial information. If I don't know that everything I say is going to be totally like water off a duck's back, it's not going to have any impact, because I don't have a clue who I'm speaking to. So if that were the case I need to know that, because I need to change what I'm doing. … I would go much more into listening and questioning, rather than direct challenge. More trying to get people to see the inconsistencies in their own thinking by following it through, rather than me just telling them they're wrong, because they're not going to learn by me telling them they're wrong, they're going to learn if they start thinking it through. And you know, who … how do you think that affects … you know, how do you think if there was somebody in this room who was gay hearing this, what do you think they would make of it?

The assumption here is that the transition from an 'incorrect' to a 'correct' perspective can be achieved not simply through an encounter with authoritative information (or an authoritative educator for that matter) but by allowing people to take the time to think through the issues systematically for themselves, in Socratic dialogue with the facilitator. Annie makes this assumption explicit:

> I want somebody in that sort of moment to slightly re-think ... you know, take what they've said, and unpick the assumptions underneath it, and be able to think more critically about where those assumptions come from, so that next time they are faced with an equivalent, or a similar situation, they can approach it more thoughtfully, and sensitively.

This 'thinking through' or deliberation has specific characteristics. Annie shares the following incident from a training session:

> We showed a clip that was an example of bullying, of a gay young person, a video clip, which we've used in numerous education sessions, and one of the participants kind of gave a bit of a 'shouldn't they just toughen up' type approach, as ... you know, that was their response. And being able to tease out where does that response come from, like why ... you know, whose responsibility is it to create an environment where young people aren't bullied for being gay? And kind of pushing and pushing on that point, gently, but also in such a way that we are thinking about 'well if teachers have that response, or youth workers, or educators have the response of "well it's kind of the responsibility of the individual to just toughen up and deal with it" – who do you think that that person who's being bullied can go to? Who is a safe person for them to tell, if it's not only the other students making them feel rubbish, but when they tell someone they're told to toughen up, do you think they'll go to that person again? What happens next time?'

The seminar participants are encouraged to consider the practical consequences of their stated position for the young person involved. Once this has been achieved, alternative practical courses of action (not, interestingly, alternative theoretical positions) can then be considered:

> If we're thinking more on the kind of bullying type example, where do you need to intervene if there's some sort of issue of bullying? So do you intervene with an individual? Do you intervene with a class group? Do you ... or a group of friends. Do you need to intervene with parents, or do something with the parents? What about your donors, or what about your shul [synagogue] leadership if this is a shul, or head teacher? What about wider community? What about press? ... So is there something you need to do right now?

The process of 'rethinking' as described thus far involves two elements: first, participants are encouraged to develop empathy by hypothetically considering the likely subjective reactions of young gay people to incidents of bullying or to oppressive remarks. The second component is perhaps more important. While the aim of Annie's practical, action-orientated questioning might be taken as helping learners explore possible courses of action based on a pre-existing, principled commitment to inclusion, in fact the process seems to aim at building this very commitment by proceeding as if it already exists. In other words, by tacitly assuming a commitment to inclusion and helping participants work through how they might behave as if they had this commitment, the commitment itself hopefully becomes second nature.[2]

It is worth noting that several writers and interviewees advocate an educational process which uses Jewish texts to facilitate a similar process of deliberation. In his book *Justice in the City*, Aryeh Cohen seeks to ground a conception of justice in rabbinic discourse by using a process of close reading of entire talmudic *sugiyot* (discussions), reading within the tradition, following in the footsteps of the text and according it some normative force.[3] He aims to enrich this further by bringing classical rabbinic perspectives into dialogue not only with the issues that spring from contemporary urban reality but with the ethical framework provided by the philosophy of Emmanuel Levinas. The tension between these discourses enables deliberation not only about how to improve society (as Annie suggests) but about how we are to understand justice itself.

Finally, the process of facilitating attitudinal change relies on group dynamics. Annie notes,

> One of the methods I often use ... particularly in a larger group, is rather than me challenging as the educator, because I have a certain kind of power, and it can get into confrontation, I'll just ask the group. If somebody said something ... I was in a session, and somebody made a comment like 'I actually think white people are discriminated against more than black people', and so I just kind of opened it to the group: you know, 'Does anyone else have a comment to make about this?', or 'What do other people think about this?', rather than me challenging.

Similarly, in the event that learners resist the message of the training, 'Hopefully somebody else in the group might chime in at that moment, and give a different frame, because otherwise you can get into a bit of a battle, which is not helpful, which is part of the reason I don't like doing training with very, very small numbers.' For this reason, the initial, experiential, ostensibly preparatory phase of the training work is actually vital:

> You can't miss that introduction. You have to be there. If somebody needs to leave early, we're a lot more flexible. Right? Because then what they miss out on is the more action focused practical bit, which I want, but actually from

my perspective is the least important part, because that's the part they can do on their own. The part that they can't do on their own, I think, is that group-learning, values-based education.

For Annie, then, attitudinal change arises partly out of an internal, individual process which combines (1) a cognitive identification of the inconsistencies and misunderstandings implied by one's original position with (2) working through the practical consequences of a more inclusive position until that position becomes second nature and (3) the development of empathy for those who are subject to exclusion and oppression. This process, however, needs to take place in a group setting so that the trainer can enlist those participants who are already 'on board' with the training message to challenge those who are more resistant. This reaffirms Annie's implication that one of the sources of attitudinal change is confrontation with authoritative information or people – in this case other participants or the group as a whole.

Activism and Campaigning

The strategy of activism and campaigning is encapsulated as organising people around a specific cause and mobilising them to create political or social change, where organising and mobilising are seen as instrumental means to an end. Tamar, for example, describes her organisation as one

> which was set up ... to build support in the British Jewish community for a two state solution and end to the Occupation. So basically to try and galvanise the support and energy of Jews, and in our case specifically British Jews, to get behind a resolution to the conflict.

Jodie characterises the work of her organisation as 'inspiring the Jewish community to get involved in development and then we are doing international development work on the ground'. Similarly, Seth says, 'In a nutshell I guess my role is to mobilise the UK Jewish community to get more involved with wider human rights issues.' Andrew frames his work using a series of questions: 'How do we engage people in social change in Israel? And how do we convince them to support it? And then the secondary question is what are the routes through which someone can engage in and support social change in Israel?' Joe is slightly less specific but nonetheless committed to mobilising people for political change:

> Okay, in relation to British politics I want to make people more left wing. I'm not a sort of left winger that wants to retreat into my own little club. I want to

win, and to win I think you have to build a tent and think of creative ways of doing that. So you could say just part of wanting to have left wing governments in Britain, I want to do my part in creating more left wing society.

We have seen how Annie and Tamar both discuss the importance of the group for generating dialogue and enabling participants to acquire the knowledge and understanding which underpins the attitudes and behaviours they seek to inculcate. Joe argues in a different way for the importance of community and relationships in generating commitment to radical, explicitly political change. His organisation is involved not only in bringing Jewish delegations to protests on issues such as austerity, climate change, anti-fascism and Palestinian rights but also with organising communal events such as Friday night dinners: 'It's a real kind of network for left and radical Jews to gather and make plans together and organise.' Community is an important catalyst for activism in two senses. First, it provides a safe environment and enables people to participate who otherwise might have been reluctant to get involved: 'People who will be scared to go on demos otherwise, because there's a Jewish group they feel safer going'. Second, building relationships encourages people to undergo a process of attitudinal change:

> Well I've definitely witnessed quite a few people who started out as liberal Zionist move to a non-Zionist position through engagement with us, and I've seen people who have come from much more Zionist or right position move to an acceptance that we're alright, that we have kind of got some interesting ideas, if not like completely right. So a kind of softening up maybe rather than a full moving.

This insight into the importance of relationships connects with Joe's aim of establishing a communal infrastructure for his work. He aspires to

> start our own youth club, *heder* [Sunday school], demonstrations, concerts, films, a cultural centre basically. An East End Jewish cultural centre I think, which everyone would know had progressive politics but didn't have to be left wing to come. Doing with left wing politics what Chabad does with religion, right?[4] It creates a very open and welcoming space, and you know that there's an agenda but you can still go.

Joe's agenda of converting British Jews to left-wing politics depends on involving people in a communal network of relationships and, in this context, presenting them with a rational, political case: 'We have to talk to each other more. Basically we have to build up social circles ... We have to break down mistrust and I think that's the big barrier basically. People won't want more egalitarian politics unless they trust each other and unless they talk to each other, so that's the kind of stuff that we do.'

How does the successful organisation of people around an ideological agenda lead to mobilisation for concrete social justice outcomes?

Some interviewees see mobilisation as a way of aggregating and scaling up positive personal behaviours in order to achieve broader social change. This approach is evident among some of the interviewees who focus on teaching and learning. Annie and Francesca aim to change the attitudes and behaviours of Jewish teachers and communal professionals around the issues of LGBT+ inclusion and gender equality in order to influence their organisations and the people – students, parents, service users, volunteers and other employees – who operate within them. A slightly different approach is to enable individuals to take small, concrete steps which, if adopted en masse, might lead to concrete social justice outcomes. Danny, for example, says,

> And then I guess if you can take complex or global or difficult challenges, and find a way to cut through them, where you give someone an easy way, or an … a small action that they can see actually can make a difference, that would be helpful. It's also challenging though, because like Fairtrade, for example, I'm very happy to say that if you're making a choice between Fairtrade and non-Fairtrade sugar, in a supermarket, if you buy the Fairtrade sugar it will definitely do more benefit to those people, to some people than if you just buy the non-Fairtrade sugars.

He continues,

> And the other is that thing of, well if my work is able to reach, I don't know for argument's sake over the last few years, three or four thousand people, and those three or four thousand people have been more informed, more engaged, found a personal connection, thought about an issue, are taking more action on their issues, then if lots of other people are doing that then the ripple effect is obviously very big.

Andrew is interested not only in replicating simple, individual actions but in developing and then replicating more complex, interpersonal and organisational behaviours. He reflects on a project he has been involved with in a personal capacity:

> So one of the things I have been involved in, in the last number of years is furniture reuse. Where we have created a model where you are creating direct

environmental benefit, in this case furniture reuse and removing an amount of waste to landfill of fridges and furniture and stuff but at the same time you are also providing a good service to a poor community in terms of access to high quality furniture that they wouldn't be able to receive. That for me is a very neat solution. Is it going to resolve global climate change? No! But a) it is improving the environment and situation in that community and b) it is actually a model that can be replicated and learnt from elsewhere.

Andrew believes that this kind of action also has the capacity to stimulate the intellectual analysis on which any profound social transformation has to be based:

Changing concepts of consumerism, changing concepts of our relationship to material goods. (I'm going back to being Marxist now) It's very much about. … one of the biggest challenges in the voluntary re-use sector has been Ikea. … So there are some really interesting questions here about value, worth, re-use, this is the value circulating in our economy. How does that work?

Funding social change projects and capacity-building are important motifs which run through the interviews. On a simple level, providing money is a tactical way of bringing about immediate, small-scale change. Tamar comments,

I think there are tangible changes you can make that are short term which are not necessarily political change. So for example: our student activists who just raised £30,000 pounds for a lawyer to defend Palestinian minors that are being tried in military courts in the West Bank. That is a practical, tangible thing that will change stuff on the ground.

While other interviewees posit a more complex relationship between the educational and fundraising aspects of their campaigning work, they also ultimately concede that the primary means for achieving social change is through funding. Jodie exemplifies this tendency. On the one hand, she believes in inculcating among UK Jews a commitment to international development work as an end in itself. On the other, it is clear that her ultimate goal is funding this work in developing countries. She comments,

My KPI [key performance indicator] really needs to be about who does what. Not 'we stood in front of 2,000 kids', but '25 kids did fundraising events'. That would be a much better marker for me because they were acting, they did something around development and enabled the organisation to really invest in people. I have a virtuous circle of education, action, leading to doing development and investing in people and you can tell that story back through our Jewish values. And then that goes on and on. But the impact needs to be more than we have educated some people. They can spit back at me the facts and the figures or even give me an emotive story but I don't need that. I need them to have done something.

Jodie believes that funding not only leads to economic development but has the potential to catalyse progressive social and political change:

> I'll start within the developing world. Say in Ghana, or India's even better actually, in both those places, they are middle income countries. They have pretty stable governments and have a fair amount of democracy. They have local government and they've got some resources and all that kind of stuff. So what are we doing giving out micro grants? Is that really still worthwhile? I definitely think so. There are people who are stuck in all sorts of money lending situations or bad agricultural work because they don't have the skills or the education. There is training and resources that you can give to people and it changes their reality and they have a sustainable income. However, something else that happened. If you give a woman a $100 over eighteen months and some training and a cow she will create a sustainable income for her family. When she had done that, her status within the community changes. Totally.

She goes on to argue that the empowerment of women and the emergence of a local middle class in developing countries are important elements in the building and safeguarding of democratic institutions.

A final theory of change which explains the need to organise Jews centres on the notion of leveraging certain kinds of influence which the UK Jewish community is held to possess, particularly for the purposes of lobbying government. Danny, for example, argues that the mobilisation of certain sections of the community was an important element of a campaign to convince the government to live up to its promises on overseas aid targets. He claims that in concert with other community groups, 'we showed them there was a groundswell of general public support for it across a different section of British society'. The implication is that a show of support for a particular issue among UK Jews and their allies carries more weight than if the same argument were to be articulated, for example, by development charities and NGOs in isolation. Seth, education director of a human rights charity, expands on this assumption in the context of a campaign to restrict the detention of asylum seekers, conducted by a coalition of human rights organisations who formed a Detention Forum. His organisation's specific contribution was to work with its 'Jewish hat' on. They

> approached Jewish MPs, and MPs in Jewish areas, and you know, and this is always a process of … you know, we go to the Jewish community and we say …

we go and talk, build a relationship with a rabbi in a community, and say, 'This is your MP in your local area, will you come with us to go and see this MP?' And you know, we want to show these MPs that there's not just a human rights NGO that's coming to talk to them, but a rabbi in the community … coming to talk to them.

Tamar has a somewhat different understanding of the need to leverage the UK Jewish community's influence. She believes there is a moral imperative for Diaspora Jews to speak out against Israel's occupation of the Palestinian territories. She explains why it is important to mobilise large numbers of people in this cause:

MP: Could that mass mobilisation in the Diaspora change Israeli policy? Tamar: I think it would make people think twice. How that translates in reality I'm not sure. I think at the moment it's very easy to say, oh there are a few annoyed Jews that think they have a right to an opinion about what we do in this country and they don't live here and they are arrogant blah blah blah. It's very different when there are millions of people saying it's really not okay and we are telling you as your closest friends and allies and the world is not going to stick with you and we are not going to stick with you either.

Joe makes a similar argument but is clearer about the channels through which the Jewish community's influence can be felt:

Also, a big reason governments around the world aren't … tearing into Israel more and being willing to put more pressure on Israel is because of Diaspora Jewish activism, because the feeling that it would be … potentially antisemitic, or potentially threatening to Jewish interests. That's a really big reason why we haven't got justice, so I think that's… It's the American Jewish community that's obviously the big one, but I think we influence the American Jewish community, it's probably most likely to go that way round than it is any other way round.

He continues,

I know that apparently when David Miliband, when he was Foreign Secretary, met some Jewish leaders and they put the standard line [defending Israeli government policy] and he pointed to the existence of Independent Jewish Voices[5] and said 'Look, not everyone thinks like you!' Well, that's quite important, that a Jewish Foreign Secretary is able to be aware of the diversity of Jewish opinion in the country.

The issue of Israel-focused activism raises interesting questions about social change strategy in particular and Jewish social justice work in general. What considerations come into play when attempting to mobilise a Diaspora community in support of social change elsewhere, and via which mechanisms can the community exercise its influence? The interviewees in this study answer the practical aspect of this question in two ways. The thrust of Tamar's and Joe's work is to enable Diaspora Jews to wield political influence, either by lobbying their own governments or by exercising direct, moral – and perhaps financial – pressure on the Israeli authorities. Against this, Andrew's work enables Diaspora Jews to fund the Israeli NGOs which are working locally for social and political change.

These practical positions highlight a more fundamental question: how is it possible to engage people in a meaningful way in social change which is going on at a distance, and what might be the rationale for doing so? Andrew, for example, reflects on the aims of the educational work carried out by his organisation: 'One of [our] great insights in the UK years ago was the need to do education work that does not directly lead to fundraising. So, work with younger people etc. ... It's about answering the question, what does it mean to be involved? What does it mean to be committed?' He adds,

> I think it is about, moving away from a very static ... a consumption model of ... how to engage people. How we engage people is 'come to an event or let's have some sort of voluntary transaction'. ... Actually what we are trying to model is much more about getting people to help us co-create. What it means to be engaged.

Andrew's comments emphasise the importance of involving Diaspora Jews on a personal level in Israeli social and political issues, even as they reveal a lack of certainty as to how this can be achieved. The controversial idea that Diaspora Jews can and should be practically and emotionally involved in questions of Israeli policy is accepted by all the interviewees whose work touches on this area.[6] This perhaps reflects a view that a Jewish activist's positions on social justice issues cannot be separated neatly from her relationship with Israel; Israeli society and politics are at the heart of any Diaspora Jewish social justice agenda.[7] The assumption that activism should involve something more personal than money also hints that the means/ends distinction is not as clear as previously suggested. Perhaps involvement in justice work is not only a tactical means to the end of concrete social change but is also a moral imperative, a source of personal meaning and transformation, and an end in itself.

Community Organising and Relationship-Building

Community organising involves informal educational work and campaigning, but sees both as elements within a broader process of building power for social change by strengthening relationships and institutions. In this sense it departs from the paradigm which conceptualises organising people as a means to the end of mobilising them to actually create change. For community organisers, building powerful communities is an intrinsic element of the social change they aim to achieve.

Calley, a broad-based community organiser, emphasises the importance of political transformation as opposed to the mere amelioration of social ills:

> I think synagogues in the UK have become very good at building charitable service projects. So we do loads of homeless shelters, loads of asylum seeker services, drop in centres, and they're brilliant. It's a good thing that they exist. But it's fundamentally selfish, because we use the power of our communities to service what is ultimately only ever going to be a very small number of people in a way that we can never be criticised. Can you imagine if we really organised the power of those synagogues to go and change it for everyone? ... I was influenced as a person in my early twenties by liberation theology and [Hélder] Câmara's comment – when I give food to the poor they call me a saint, when I ask why the poor have no food they call me a Communist[8] – has run in my head. ... I think we got very good at organising models of service that help a small number of people [and] make synagogues feel really, really good about what they do, but never ask the question '*why* are people in the Borough of Barnet relying on a homeless shelter?'.

Stuart, the co-founder of a Jewish international development charity, adds to this the importance of combining political change with hands-on work and relationship-building in the developing world:

> If we're creating a new organisation with integrity we should just be focusing on that end game. What can we do to influence the end game? And to me that was what became our education/activism side. But I really believed then, and I still believe now, that if you're doing that by itself it's kind of sterile, and you're in that kind of sterile purist political world, where it's all about theory, and ... and the relationship is really important. So I really believed then, and now, that that had no credibility unless we were also rooted in real experience and real relationships, so we had to get our hands dirty in the really complicated issue of how change happens on the ground. ... [B]oth I think are mutually reinforcing, and they are each I think, indefensible by themselves.

For Stuart, some of the tension between strategic, political change work and hands-on service provision was resolved through a focus on educational projects which sought to increase people's life chances in developing countries by improving the school system. Here, even the relational, hands-on aspect of the work has a long-term, transformative aspect.

Calley describes the work of nurturing this kind of commitment to social justice as a process of building people's 'mental landscape':

> I would say about a third of my work is building in people's imagination a sense of what this could look like, a sense of it to be appealing and Jewish. … My experience is that anyone doesn't just wake up one day and decide I'm going to go and get involved with social justice. They have a series of experiences that help them build the mental landscape to even be able to imagine what that might look like. … And I do it mainly through stories, I tell stories about in South Africa something we did, or I refer to Jewish stories, things like Heschel and Eisendrath marching on Selma, as old as they are and as used as they are, allow people to imagine a way of being Jewish that is specific and different to what they do. If I just said to them, guys, why don't we go and take on HSBC over the Living Wage, at the moment that's out of their mental landscape, for most people. It was out of my mental landscape.

Stuart agrees with Calley that effective action is born of a meaningful learning process. While he concedes that it is possible to engage in superficially beneficial actions – he terms these 'easy *mitzvot*' (commandments, often translated as good deeds) – he argues that learning is an essential foundation for more profound work:

> I'd like to think that it might be more sustainable in the sense of if you're going on a Jewish educational journey it's very rare you're doing that by yourself. You're doing that in an institutional setting. You know, in a synagogue, community, group of friends, or whatever, who are equally connected to that Jewish journey … and that you can sustain each other. … So for me I think it's sometimes quite hard to engage in social justice work for all kinds of … sometimes practically, because it's just very hard; sometimes because the stories are very painful; and … so you need, I think, inner resources. For me as a Jew I get those inner resources from my Jewish tradition.

Within organising, then, learning and relationship-building are two aspects of the same process. Manny talks about the connection between bringing people together and developing narratives which articulate common self-interest. He reflects on the experience of a campaign to prevent the privatisation of the Port of Dover:

> I'm very conscious that what I bring to bear is ... and this is partly the Jewish thing, is not just a personal experience, but a long experience of how to bring people together to make community life function effectively when it is threatened, really threatened by a real lack of leadership and energy from within that community. ... So the first thing was to bring a very important sense of agency and to get people together and do ... leadership training. ... Okay so in Dover you had to have Queen Elizabeth I, Sir Water Raleigh, you know you would have the whole history of the port, it's defence against the Spanish, defence against the French, you have the whole Second World War thing, White Cliffs of Dover symbolising resistance. So the first thing was to get a sense of common ownership of the place and that you have some power.

For Manny, the forging of relationships and the development of agency and power are intimately connected with the building of what Calley calls mental landscape; storytelling is central to this process.

Manny seeks to tap into a history of social activism. This idea of heritage or legacy is important for community organisers in the sense that even while working on specific campaigns or issues, their real focus is on the long-term project of building power which is based on strong, relational institutions. Calley comments,

> So when I go to my classic dinner party and say I'm an organiser people go, oh yeah, my friend does something like that, she works for X charity, and often I try to distinguish ... I try to delineate that there's something about trying to win systemic change in what I do, and there's also something that it's not about the specific changes we win, that we try and build alliances that can last throughout civil society, so where one change happens and it's won, and you move on to the next one.

She goes on to emphasise the centrality of the long-term perspective to organising: the goal is never simply to win the current campaign but always to build a firm foundation or heritage of institutional power for the next one. Sometimes this becomes evident only in retrospect. For example,

> In South Africa, my partner ... was involved in the Treatment Action Campaign which was the big campaign to force the government to roll out antiretrovirals. And what I saw there was something totally different because first of all I saw poor, black communities organised for power. ... But also I saw these church

leaders, I saw Archbishop Tutu stand up and call on the government, take on the government, to roll out these antiretrovirals. And there was this heritage – and I didn't understand this at the time – for the last 45 years the Church had been organising around Apartheid, and it was phenomenal to me, it was an idea of living your theology in the street in a way I'd never experienced.

Community organisers typically prioritise relationship-building which cuts across boundaries of faith, ethnicity and class as the most important way of developing powerful institutions. Calley and Manny both believe that effective social action is entirely dependent on the existence of strong, relational institutions and that, therefore, relationship-building has to take precedence over any ideological commitment to social justice per se. Moreover, community organisers prefer to engage people on the basis of self-interest rather than idealism. Manny reflects,

> I am very suspicious about altruism. I think the only durable relationships can be built if it is of mutual benefit and that's a particularly strong thing amongst Jews, who ... do have a tendency to be motivated entirely by a principle. You can see that with the whole historic engagement with Marxism, where Jews were prepared to essentially sacrifice themselves for the proletariat, and led to massive violence and destruction, not only of other people but of Jewish life. ... But you see it with human rights and people motivated entirely by abstract principle, but unless you can bring people with you into the engagement with other people then it [tends] not to last, not to be a genuine civic encounter.

This pragmatic prioritisation of relationships over principles inevitably shapes the social justice agendas of community organisers. For example, Calley reflects on the difficulty of working on certain issues in the context of a coalition of largely faith-based, often quite conservative, institutions:

> There are things I just can't work on because of the level of conflict around them. So [my organisation] I think is unlikely to ever work on a lot of issues around homophobia, around abortion. There are some things that the level of conflict would be unsustainable for us to hold. ... [S]ome organisations we work with are structurally homophobic, or structurally discriminate against women. ... That is their position on things. *MP: And you're happy to work with those people on issues of common concern.* Calley: Yes. Because I think – again this is Jews who like talking about organising but don't like organising – you can wait a long time waiting for your perfect organisation.

Calley draws together the elements of community organising discussed thus far – change-orientated action, building mental landscape and the strengthening of relationships and institutions – into a coherent, mutually reinforcing structure in which relationship-building supports personal transformation and enables collective action. For example,

> This guy was asking how do I get involved in my neighbourhood, I really want to but I feel so disconnected. And part of me was like, you're just going to have to swallow your pride to come to Grahame Park [a council estate in north London] and meet some people. You're going to have to come with us, you're going to have to say hi to the mums and get to know them and let them get to know you for a bit. *MP: And what's going to happen as a result? What's going to happen to that person?* ... Calley: I hope that they get a sense of how to be effective in action and win, and a sense of relationship that means they don't think that they can go and solve it as a white middle class person. They don't think they're just going to set up a project and go and solve, but they are going to go on a journey where at times they're going to listen to other people and let them lead, and at times they're going to use their own power to act.

The first step on this journey, for Calley, is for people from privileged backgrounds to realise that the conversation should not be centred on them:

> Normally the first step is to kick out white liberal guilt. *MP: What does that mean?* Calley: As in, normally people want to spend hours and hours wringing their hands about how they know everything's really unequal and they feel really bad about it. I guess the first thing I want to do is prepare them to work with people who are different, because we can have these conversations for like fifteen hours and on some level you're going to have to get over your white liberal guilt, and do something and meet someone and get over your assumptions. *MP: You have to get over the guilt, or you have to ...?* Calley: It's not about denying your privilege. I think it's just about ... Privilege in its own way can re-centre things around a powerful group. So I think interrogating whiteness is really important. But I also worry that basically these people just want to share their guilt about how they feel about the privilege, in a way that a poor kid from Grahame Park Estate does not need to have to deal with you and your own guilt, they just want to sort out the doors on their flat.

Calley describes this emotional transition from guilt to anger as a necessary preliminary to collective action with poor people. This position taps into a distinction between 'education for organising' and 'organising as education' and is ambiguous in two senses.

First, it is unclear whether the emotional change is a precondition for or the result of a meaningful engagement with poor people; in other words, to what extent is the encounter with the poor an educational technique for the personal transformation of the privileged? Are the poor a means to this essentially educational end, or do the privileged have an obligation to prepare themselves adequately to ensure that the ensuing encounter is genuinely dialogical rather than a way of meeting their own emotional and ideological needs? Alternatively, the encounter with the poor could be conceptualised as a form of *praxis* which erases this means–ends distinction, as well as the dichotomy between transformed consciousness and action: we learn to build relationships by building relationships.

Second, Calley indicates that the goal of the encounter is to create a collective agenda which is centred on the needs and the agenda of the poor (implying perhaps that the privileged are no more than a means to this end). However, in other comments she implies that strong relationships cannot be formed other than on the basis of equality and mutual benefit. For example, discussing the process as it affects the privileged participants, she comments,

> And what I hope they get a sense of is that they're part of a bigger group than just the Jewish community, even though it's really important they get that sense. But what does it mean to be part of your neighbourhood outside of the five streets around you? What does it mean to be part of … to go to Grahame Park Estate and be like, well, I vote in councillors just like these guys vote in councillors, to the same Council, and that means we have mutual responsibility for each other. And that means actually if they want change or if I want change I'm going to need to build alliances with them because on our own we only have three councillors.

In this conception, the relationship between rich and poor rests on the fact that both have equal political rights and the same ability to exert political pressure through voting; the exigencies of electoral maths means both parties need each other. When asked how she feels about this tension between helping the poor and forming equal partnerships with them, Calley says,

> Right, because if it's only going to be one-way, then it is really patronising. But actually when you don't have secure doors and you need thicker doors, you actually just want to know can you help me get these councillors to get thicker doors. What I hope they also understand through the training is that it's not always this way for ever and that at times that relationship is built on the idea that sometimes they're going to have to come and help people from West Hampstead [an affluent neighbourhood] or whatever.

The potential mutuality or equality of the relationship manifests itself in benefits that accrue to both rich and poor as a result of the learning and the partnerships that emerge from their encounter with each other. This is evident in Calley's account of house meetings in which people are encouraged to name and explore the issues that affect their lives:

> My experience in middle-class Jewish communities has been, first of all, that's it's even radical to name what your issue is, in public, like to admit you have an issue and to admit that. So that's the first thing. Whereas in poor communities people live really closely together and often it's just much harder to keep certain kinds of secrets. So for some people it's really radical to even name it. For other people it is radical to be listened to and cared about. And I want them to get a sense that this isn't just private to them. This is a public, broader issue, which various kinds of public spaces therefore have something to say about.

Acknowledging private problems as public issues which require collective, political solutions is equally relevant, in different ways, to both rich and poor. The encounter between them is a way of generating this insight for both groups. Calley illustrates this by discussing an action led by the members of a suburban synagogue to get justice for a nearby Muslim community in the wake of an arson attack on their community centre. This had, according to Calley, a profound impact on the people who were motivated by an altruistic desire to help their less privileged neighbours:

> So one thing that tends to be an experience for middle class people is they experience the system working for them. They experience the police responding to them. White people don't tend to be racially profiled, they don't have these experiences. So when for example the police promised the [Muslim community] a meeting and nine months later still hadn't, and the synagogue that led the work with the [Muslim community] were like, oh I don't know maybe we should give them another chance. We've written to them four times, we've called their offices, nothing. And eventually we convene a meeting and I say, look, it's your decision, but my proposal is we go into action. And the [Muslim community] were ready for this four months ago, I mean they were frustrated and pissed off four months ago. But the Jewish community wanted to check that the police haven't had a bad day. … And we end up doing this action where 120 children from the synagogue write a note to explain to the borough commander why it's rude to not keep your promises. … And the kids, the younger, the little kids, are up for the conflict, they are outraged that the borough commander, and they write in notes going no one will play with you if you carry on breaking your promises. They have such a sense of right and wrong. And we basically patch them together and we dress them up as a fake Christmas present, and we deliver them as an ironic

Christmas present from the Jews and Muslims of the borough. But that ability to sustain tension … I mean it's uncomfortable for very powerless communities as well, because they're terrified. It is scary for random churches to take on the immigration authorities. But I think it's very uncomfortable for middle class communities, particularly Jewish communities who have both all the experience of the system working for them plus a deep anxiety about challenging too much, stepping out of place, losing.

While the primary beneficiaries of this action were ostensibly the members of the Muslim community, Calley claims that the experience of dialogue and action was also transformative for their middle-class, Jewish partners. It helped them confront their own nebulous sense of marginality and vulnerability, encouraged them to cut through the veil of middle-class privilege to understand something of the oppressive reality of British society, and simultaneously pushed them into a more radical form of action than that with which they would previously have been comfortable.

Speaking Out, Embodying Values and Personal Transformation

Elliot Dorff writes that speech is a way of destroying or repairing the world, it gains moral character in the way we use it and has a concrete impact on other human beings.[9] In the same spirit, several interviewees report that their preferred social change strategy is to influence others to act by means of speaking or writing. The strategies outlined in this section bring to mind the notion of 'coming to voice' as an important process in the emancipatory struggles of oppressed groups such as women and people of colour. Bell hooks writes,

> Moving from silence into speech is for the oppressed, the colonized, the exploited, and those who stand and struggle side by side a gesture of defiance that heals, that makes new life and new growth possible. It is that act of speech, of 'talking back', that is no mere gesture of empty words, that is the expression of our movement from object to subject – the liberated voice.[10]

However, most of the interviewees cited here emphasise the process of speaking out not as part of a personal process of liberation but as a way of advocating for oppressed others, and coming to voice as a process of spiritual development as a moral agent.

Among the interviewees, Jacob comments that while as a rabbi he has 'hands-on' involvement in certain projects, 'the other thing is the use of pulpit because I think sermons are primarily an expression of values, and I would say the spiritual and the ethical are the dominant sort of motifs of the sermons that I'm trying to give'. This kind of influence can also be exercised by embodying or representing values rather than by talking about them. Jacob articulates this position as follows:

> I don't think it's possible to [support people on an ethical and spiritual journey] without caring about that oneself. It's not a proxy thing. I think in some respects one of my most successful activities is doing the synagogue garden when the children come out of preschool, because they see me with my hands dirty and they ask questions, and they will I hope link rabbi, being Jewish, growing things, environment, these things are interrelated, they're not a separate box. I hope so.

While Jacob emphasises the importance of representation and embodiment as methods for developing potential social change agents, Annie focuses on the impact of role models on people who are themselves marginalised or excluded:

> So why is role modelling important? It's important for people to see themselves represented. You know, all male panels bother me, because I don't see myself in them. The fact that the majority of the world leadership is male bothers me. I don't see myself in it. So I think role modelling matters, and I've seen it for myself. Not seeing people like me affects my ability to see myself in those positions, and in that ... in those communities, worlds, whatever it is. I also think particularly for somebody who is really struggling to believe that they will be accepted. Me saying, 'You will be' is easier to dismiss than somebody saying, 'I have been'.

At the same time, Annie recognises that the direct, first-person experience presented by role models can be dismissed by people who are resistant to their message. In fact, the uniqueness and personal nature of the experiences they communicate render their testimony vulnerable to the charge that it is not transferrable to other people and situations. Sometimes, Annie suggests, this needs to be complemented by testimony from an ally rather than someone who has encountered the specific form of marginalisation themselves.

> I still hear it dismissed all the time, like, 'Yeah, but you're not Sephardi', or 'Yeah, but your parents ... blah blah', or 'You didn't grow up in this', and ... you know, so there are limits to that role modelling as well, whereas what I can offer is saying, 'No there are people in the Jewish community who aren't L, G, B or T who care a

lot, and who are committed to making the community more inclusive. And this is a Jewish community issue, not an LGBT issue'.

For some interviewees, the exercise of influence through speaking, writing and role modelling is dialogical rather than exclusively unidirectional. Jacob, for example, understands his role partly as an amplifier, turning his community into an echo chamber for the positive actions individual members are already carrying out:

> To my mind possibly the single most important thing about sermons is having listened to one's community beforehand, because a lot of what they are is hearing the inspiring things that people are doing or the challenges they are facing, and some of them are not social justice, some of them are just growth and compassion issues, and framing them within the Jewish and wider context. But quite often people who are not opinion formers are nevertheless doing very basic and amazing things, and although social justice and compassion are big concepts they actually realised by something somebody does in the next hour of their time for a person near them, so they're very practical. ... So those small things that are happening all the time ... and I think to be aware of what people are doing already and highlight them is really important.

Rather than influencing people to act on his agenda, Jacob describes his role as enabling people to act on their own deeply held commitments. 'How does one work against a culture of individual autonomy and "I do what I want" towards a culture of compassion and moral imagination and obligation? And how does one do that in a way which enables people to find their fulfilment in that way?' This perspective casts the 'influencer' not as a hierarchical leader or as the owner of an ideological agenda but rather as a facilitator for a collectively held set of values. Similarly, Rachel, while seeking to influence others through her sermons, sees herself neither as an ideological authority nor as the originator of the principles she is attempting to communicate. Rather, she understands herself as a conduit for insights she has received from her own teachers and, more broadly, from Jewish tradition.

Speaking and representation as ways of influencing and enabling social activism are related to the idea that speaking out or giving voice are valuable social justice strategies in their own right. Some interviewees imply, albeit with some ambivalence, that this can be the case even in the absence of any concrete action. This implies a politics in which utility is not the only criterion and in which protest is a categorical imperative: a way of refusing to be complicit in injustice.[11] Emma introduces the activities of her anti-racist organisation in this spirit:

> Well, our overall thing is to provide a Jewish voice. And the voice, it isn't just the voice, but it's Jewish action as well, on race and asylum issues. ... So that's why I was involved in starting a rabbinic social justice network, because I've been desperate, if I could use that word, to have rabbis speak out on social issues, because I'm very aware that many people within the Church speak out, and again I wanted, as we come from the same place so to speak, in terms of an understanding of responsibility, I wanted to see the Jewish voices.

Just as Emma believes that making statements is a valuable activity in itself, Annie argues that her decisions to participate in or opt out of various non-egalitarian or exclusionary institutions are important in their own right, even in the absence of a clear road map as to how opting out might lead to concrete transformation. This position reveals the important role that notions of moral principle, integrity and complicity with injustice play in her thinking. Annie's perspective echoes the idea that statements (whether verbal or behavioural) have inherent, and not only instrumental, value: 'So there is a conflict there doing things that I know I'm only able to access because of certain privileges that I have, created by structural inequality. Right ... it's not that I am personally responsible, and yet I am in some way perpetuating that system by taking part.'

Jacob and Rachel both identify an additional way in which they are able to exercise influence: providing inspiration and enabling the spiritual growth which they believe to be preconditions for social activism. Jacob reflects on the experiences of his father, who escaped from Nazi Germany before serving in the Haganah (the pre-State Jewish defence force) in Israel's War of Independence:

> But he said I think there was always outstanding music. I'm sure he's talking about classical music. He said, without that we wouldn't have managed, and as I thought about that, you know 'why music?', and I think what he was saying is if there isn't some level of spiritual and artistic inspiration and some vision, some place of solace, refuge and inner inspiration, you'll run out of the _koah_ [power], the inner force to do stuff in the world, and so I think a synagogue also needs to provide a religious community to be a place of inner healing and re-grouping and re-strengthening, and that's Shabbat to go out and do your work whatever it is in the world.

Rachel continues this line of thought with the insight that an individual's practical commitment to social action is necessarily shaped by her spiritual discipline and personal theology. She explains the connection between empathy (developed through relationships with others) and the theological insight that all human beings are created in the image of God as the twin roots of her commitment to just, compassionate behaviour towards the weak and vulnerable. When asked how this theological position affects her behaviour, Rachel responds that

> it kind of flavours how I want to campaign. Especially as a Jew. … I don't want it to be tokenistic, I don't want it to be about advocacy, solely, or service provision. It has to be something that is addressing root problems, and that you're doing with the people who it's being affected by, and that you're listening to them and you're hearing them. … And but also on lots of different levels: like it affects how I talk to my husband, and it affects how I am with people in the street; how I am with congregants. … [I]t's like a spiritual discipline for me, with *tzelem elohim* [the image of God], you're trying to see that people have the divine within them, and that everybody's equal.

However, the relationship between spiritual growth and social action is not unidirectional. Jacob comments that while *tikkun ha-nefesh* [repair of the soul] leads to *tikkun ha-olam* [repair of the world], sometimes the process is reversed: actions in the world lead back to motivations, feelings and meaning.

The idea that personal, spiritual transformation is a precondition of social action bleeds easily into the notion that personal change is a legitimate, or more accessible, alternative to social change. In this spirit, Rachel comments,

> *Tikkun atzmi* [repairing the self] … transforming myself and working on myself and healing myself, which is all part of the spiritual practice stuff, enables me to do *tikkun olam* [repairing the world]. Like it's the other side of the coin. There's an amazing quote that I've only just read recently by the Kotzker Rebbe,[12] was it? 'I tried to change my world, but I realised I couldn't. I tried to change my country, but I couldn't. And then I thought, well I'll just try and change myself'. … I don't think campaigning works, I don't think I'll ever be able to affect change, if I haven't gone through like a spiritual process myself.

If activism is not only a means to the end of social change but also aims at moral and spiritual transformation, the function of speaking out and embodying one's values becomes clearer: they are vital components of being (or becoming) a moral agent, a decent human being and a good Jew. This sense explains why speaking, listening, testimony and dialogue are sometimes described by the interviewees as no less important than concrete action and change. Note, for example, this emphasis in Rachel's account of a rabbinic campaign against the detention of people seeking asylum:

> One of the first things was we heard from someone who's been in detention … He came and spoke to a bunch of rabbis, and told them his story. … And then we had an inter-faith tent that was at Harmondsworth [the site of a detention centre] … where people came together to talk about it, and again share testimony about it. And we're working towards a Hanukah action to do with indefinite immigration detention, where we're hoping … again, for it to be through stories, and rabbis telling people stories, or bringing their own stories into it.

Rachel reports that she hopes to anchor these stories around what she sees as the foundational Jewish narrative – the story of Abraham *ha-ivri* – a word which is translated as 'the Hebrew' but whose etymology connotes 'border-crosser' – someone who embodies the biblical injunction to empathise with and love the stranger. Creating and retelling narratives is thus a way of constructing one's own identity as a certain kind of human being and Jew. The same principle also applies to the Jewish community as a whole: speaking out collectively against injustice becomes a marker of identity and a moral imperative. Emma, similarly, reports on her feelings of pride when she reads about Jews who have set up human rights and social justice organisations such as the Child Poverty Action Group, Amnesty International and the Medical Foundation for the Care of Victims of Torture. She wants people – both Jews and non-Jews – to be aware of this, 'because I want Jews to understand that more of us should be doing this sort of thing. … And I want the non-Jewish world to see that the Jewish community does care.' She adds,

> I want Jewish identity to be absolutely bound up in the whole understanding about social justice, so the two are linked. … I want people who call themselves Jewish to have this commitment to social justice, to have it as central to their identity … alongside other things they do as Jewish, but I want that to be in their centre stage.

* * *

In her article 'From a language to a theory of resistance: critical pedagogy, the limits of "framing," and social change', Rebecca Tarlau notes that social movement theorists have tended to use the concept of 'framing' to characterise the ways in which social activists assign meaning to their activities in order to mobilise participation.[13] Tarlau claims that framing theory emphasises the active role of movement leaders, 'not the ways in which a community's collective consciousness can transform through engagement with alternative educational spaces'.[14] Against this, she argues that Freirean critical pedagogy provides a framework for understanding the bottom-up or dialogical process, neglected by many social movement theorists, in which 'marginalized groups go through a process of cognitive liberation, develop an oppositional consciousness, and learn that they have the ability to take action'.[15] Tarlau also draws on a debate between seminal community organisers Myles Horton and Saul Alinsky[16] to distinguish between the Freirean notion that a discrete process of education is a precondition of organising, and the idea, associated with Alinsky and his disciples, that organising is an inherently educative phenomenon.

In terms of these distinctions, teaching and learning approaches emphasise 'cognitive liberation', the processes of attitudinal change in which students come to critique unjust reality, develop the desire to create change and learn that they have the ability to do so. Similarly, while advocates of speaking out, embodying values and personal transformation tend to articulate a clearer social vision, they share the teacher-learners' focus on attitudinal and personal–behavioural change. In contrast to these approaches, some of which neglect almost entirely questions of 'organising' or movement-building (and, arguably, any coherent, strategic understanding of social or political change), the interviewees who articulate a community organising approach emphasise the processes of capacity-building and civic engagement and tend to see these phenomena as inherently educational: learning is not a means to the end of organising, but rather organising is seen as a form of education. As against this, the activism and campaigning approach sees the nurturing of agency among individuals and groups as no more than a means to the end of political action. Inasmuch as activist-campaigners discuss education, they tend to view it in purely instrumental terms.

The relationship between education, personal change, community building and social transformation will be discussed in more depth below, as I begin to explore questions of *praxis*, dialogue and the Jewish complexion of social justice pedagogies (see Chapters 8 and 9). These strategic issues also touch on the identities of the people involved in the social justice enterprise and their roles and experiences as agents and objects of social change. In the next chapter, I turn to this final dimension of Jewish social justice practice: people.

7

People – Agents and Beneficiaries of Social Change

The interviewees' approaches to the fourth component of ideology, people, can be analysed in terms of the relationship they posit between agents of – or obstacles to – social change, and the beneficiaries thereof (who can sometimes also be thought of as victims of current reality). While most of the interviewees are somewhat inconsistent in their approach, they all tend to be preoccupied with the identity and role of agents rather than the beneficiaries. This is at least in part the product of the interviewees' primary aim of mobilising members of the Jewish community as change agents. However, it also illustrates a tendency towards a values-driven or ostensibly altruistic understanding of social justice which echoes themes from Catholic social teaching rather than the more class-conflictual models of liberation theology or critical pedagogy. The interviewees' approaches fall into three broad categories:

1. Change agents and beneficiaries of change are seen as two distinct groups. This parallels Freire's division of society into oppressors and oppressed but differs from his analysis in two important respects: first, it shies away from a conflictual class analysis and tends to identify these groups less in terms of their position within the world as it currently exists and more in relation to the process of progressive change itself. Second, in direct contrast with Freire's insistence that the emancipatory educator must work *with* the oppressed, not *for* them, this implies that change agents emerge from the privileged class and that beneficiaries tend to be passive recipients of their generosity.
2. Change agents and beneficiaries are distinct but overlapping groups, in that change agents stand to benefit from the results of their own work, albeit usually in different ways from the primary beneficiaries. This is connected to the view that change agents are working for the common good or a

universally better society, which promises to benefit both groups. This model originates partly out of a reluctance to invoke a conflictual model of society. It also echoes the Freirean notion that while oppression is a zero-sum game in which one group prospers at the expense of another, the phenomenon of dehumanisation affects both oppressors and oppressed and, as such, even oppressors stand to benefit from the process of humanisation.
3. Beneficiaries are the change agents; in Freirean terms, the oppressed are the agents of their own liberation. This emphasises the humanity and agency of disadvantaged people as subjects, not objects, of social change and stresses that change agents must emerge from the beneficiary group. However, this picture is complicated by two factors: the role of non-oppressed change agents as partners in the creation of social justice, and the complex relationship between privilege and disadvantage in an intersectional context. In a society affected by economic inequality, racism and antisemitism, the liminal social position of UK Jews and their role in the change process brings this complexity to the fore. In the view of some interviewees, this serves to collapse the distinctions between agents and beneficiaries, oppressors and oppressed.

Change Agents and Beneficiaries as Distinct Groups

Several interviewees identify politically progressive, religious Jewish leaders and organisations as important social change agents.[1] For Shalom, rabbis – specifically Orthodox rabbis – are an important group because of their influence over religiously observant Jews. Jacob discusses the importance of faith leaders such as Pope Francis and the Dalai Lama who are able to articulate a vision of justice and morality in dialogue with the community. He alludes to a rabbinic teaching about three crowns[2] – the crown of Torah, the crown of priesthood and the crown of kingship – and applies the lessons of this text to non-Jewish spiritual leaders no less than to Jewish ones:

> The crown of Torah seems to me about Jewish learning and Jewish leadership. It's about the whole rabbinic method, it's about the discourse and debate about what God wants of us. And the crown of kingship is about political power, and they're never in the same hands but they're always in discourse, and it seems to me that's what one needs: a discourse between ethics, religion, politics. And the Pope! That's exactly what Pope Francis really asks for in his encyclical.[3]

For Jacob, the current political climate makes faith leadership even more important:

> I also think that will grow because I think … how shall I put it? What feels like a crueller government which isn't going to go away in a hurry and that's likely to be the case across significant parts of Europe and the world. … [R]eligions and alternative sectors of society will be more responsible for social justice and compassion. They're not going to be things that the government consider part of their concern. They will need to be things which religious organisations consider part of their concern, more and more so. The obligation will deepen.

Seth attaches importance to faith leaders for tactical reasons – both because of their moral authority and because they are seen as representative, community leaders:

> I think faith voices are for some reason very strong in the UK. … Even just let's say in the media, when faith voices say 'this is wrong' … there still seems to be some kind of moral weight attached to what bishops think … bishops, rabbis, imams. … And you know, we want to show these MPs that there's not just a human rights NGO that's coming to talk to them, but a rabbi in the community.

Many interviewees assign responsibility for social justice to powerful or privileged groups. Former foundation director Craig is particularly interested in the role of wealthy philanthropists in advancing social change and has been intimately involved in pioneering this kind of work in the UK Jewish community. At the same time, he is ambivalent about the connection between philanthropy and justice:

> Charity or philanthropy on the other hand is voluntary, it is preference based, it is individualised and it is not about fairness or justice. It is about preferences that individuals have projected into the public realm. So one person's notion of what philanthropy is will be very different to another. So some would support effort to combat climate change, whereas others would use philanthropy to support efforts to deny climate change. Both are philanthropic. … So my idea that would follow that therefore there's a tension between philanthropy and justice.

In contrast, Craig emphasises the role of the State as a powerful institution whose contribution to achieving social justice is indispensable. Tamar agrees that disparities of wealth and privilege can't be changed 'without sufficient, organised, state intervention. It can't. It doesn't mean we have to live in a nanny state but unless you have a state which is helping to – that is what taxes are for – redistribute wealth and create infrastructure where people are given opportunity, then that can't change.' She applies this insight to the State of Israel as both a cause of oppression and as a potential instrument of transformation: 'The more I work in this conflict the more it seems to me that unless you can mobilise as many of the state policies as possible then nothing is going to change.' At the same time, Tamar attributes ultimate responsibility for social change to individual citizens, as democratic governments are in the end subordinate to the will of the electorate.

References to professional or highly committed social change agents – charities, NGOs, activist-campaigners, human rights lawyers, community organisers and teachers – are scattered throughout the interviews. Student rabbi Rachel, for example, takes as a source of inspiration a senior human rights lawyer with whom she worked:

> She was absolutely fearless and tireless in her like quest to help people, to help the clients that she'd … you know, she kind of had a track record of getting … I don't know, it was one family, as in multigenerational, I think they were Kurds, and she'd just got the whole lot over. And she would basically almost not sleep. She'd spend like the evenings in the firm working, and just devoted her entire life to it. … Like it wasn't just a job, it was who she was as well.

Most interviewees, however, express reservations about the effectiveness of full-time professionals in the change process. Seth recognises the role of NGOs in lobbying to improve government policy but, at the same time, acknowledges that

> the government … expects NGOs to complain … you know, that's the sole purpose of NGOs in many ways, and [it] expects that … to come into contention. But they certainly take more notice when it's coming from civil society, and perhaps get slightly more worried because it's mobilising beyond just the kind of specialist NGO sector, and starting to build … broad civil society support, and community leaders can bring communities with them, and that's when we start getting change I guess.

Feminist educator Francesca sees huge potential in teachers as facilitators of individual opportunity and social justice. At the same time, her reflections on her work within schools demonstrate that teachers often take on conservative or reactionary roles and that more often than not, the catalysts for change in a school setting are students and their parents. Sally also believes in the transformative potential of teaching, but similarly points out a drawback of teachers as change agents. She discusses the importance of

> holding your nerve, but holding that knowledge that you might not see the impact of what you are doing for a generation. You really might not. Certainly

with my year sevens, I am doing feedback, and it is so dispiriting in so many ways, because they are not ready to feed back on those experiences. They won't be ready to feed back on those experiences for another ten, fifteen years, some of them.

The ambivalence surrounding the place of social change professionals is well illustrated by Calley's discussion of the role of community organisers, which draws on the tradition of broad-based organising as initiated by Saul Alinsky in 1940s Chicago. Calley's reflections highlight two areas of ambiguity: to what extent do professional organisers – as opposed to leaders embedded in their communities and organisations – drive and direct the process of change? And what degree of personal, as opposed to detached, professional, involvement do organisers bring to their role? She argues that while the organiser has a vital, permanent role ('Alinsky thought you built your organisation and you could move on, and all Alinsky's organisations collapsed') the relationship between organiser and institution is nuanced:

> I think partly it's about agitation. It's about having someone that is outside of those groups to say, hey, what about this, or that commitment, that thing you said was really important to you, or you claim to be interested in X but you're not doing Y. And I think it's partly to have someone to stay up at night worrying about this stuff, and will devote that much energy and time to thinking and building and be able to … Because by definition, people are really busy in their own organisations, and that means for a lot of them organising is a real passion, it really matters to them, but they don't necessarily want to go in and run a … And I think a lot of what an organiser does, most of what I do, really good leaders could do. But what an organiser's about is agitating from the outside, and building a journey for people to go on, that people can't think about their own journey in that way.

While organisers are indispensable, their role here is only to facilitate and bring professional rigour to the agendas of organic community leaders, while helping to build alliances between communities. However, Calley makes clear that in fact the organiser takes on more of a leadership and an agenda-setting role than this implies:

> I don't want to pretend it's completely clean, because there are aspects of me in almost every campaign. I took on [a campaign about social] care because I care about women and organising women and that's a particular interest. I took on a [Muslim community's campaign to rebuild their community centre following an arson attack] because I met … and he reminded me of my grandfather who

was this migrant. I just felt what it was like and I felt what the Jewish community, how people were emailing each other finding out what was going on. But it's definitely not built in my image in that way. So if it was left to me we'd all be organising on left wing socialist feminist issues. But I like that it's not because I like that actually even for me it's a passport into different worlds.

Who are the intended beneficiaries of social change? Several interviewees identify the poor in general, and poor people in the UK or in developing countries in particular. Others focus on victims of human rights abuse: Seth identifies the targets of his work as victims of genocide, modern-day slavery, the Gypsy–Roma–traveller community and asylum detainees. These two threads come together in the leitmotif of concern for refugees which runs through the interviews. Non-Jews feature as a specific beneficiary group. Emma says,

> It's interesting: when I tell people about my organisation, the question that both the Jewish and non-Jewish people ask me is, 'Do you do anything for non-Jewish refugees?' And it's ironic because I don't know any Jewish refugees. And I find that sad, that in both the Jewish and the non-Jewish world they think our focus is on Jewish refugees.

Similarly, Craig reflects on his foundation's aim, unlike that of many other Jewish charities, of working with both Jewish and non-Jewish beneficiaries:

> So notions of the Jewish contribution to society became very important to the Foundation. It really became a kind of calling card for the kind of values and vision of the Foundation, that you can be concerned about social justice, because you are a Jew and not in spite of it. And it was because you were a Jew you had concerns both for fellow Jews and for others, and it shouldn't be an either/or. And that meant that distribution of support philanthropically to causes that had Jewish beneficiaries and non-Jewish beneficiaries. The notion that there was such a thing as a Jewish cause and a non-Jewish cause was completely rejected by [our founder] and I think very persuasively in that all causes to him were Jewish, because they came from a place of his Jewish values and beliefs.

Andrew describes the beneficiaries of his work as marginalised Israelis, irrespective of national and religious identity; indeed, his priorities include work with non-Jewish refugees and Palestinian citizens of Israel. Tamar's activities focus on Palestinians whose rights are being denied by the Occupation. This Israel-orientated work goes one step further than simply identifying non-Jewish beneficiaries; it aims to improve the situation of non-Jews who have been marginalised or oppressed in, or by, the Jewish State.

Finally, various interviewees identify beneficiaries on the basis of gender identity or sexual orientation. Francesca's work is designed primarily to benefit women but also men and families, who would gain from increased gender role flexibility and inclusivity:

> So I think the total vision is that we have a more inclusive Jewish world which is healthier for women and men to operate within. That they are not forced into specific gender roles and gender identities. That they have many more opportunities to choose from what kind of Jewish person they want to be, and how they want to be active.

Francesca believes that people in the Orthodox community suffer particularly from issues like rigid gender roles, stereotyping, exclusion of women from leadership roles and the hyper-sexualisation of women.

Agents as Beneficiaries of Social Change

Some interviewees blur the distinction between agents and beneficiaries, arguing that social change activists benefit in some way from the processes they engender. Craig and Jacob, for example, both make the case that many young Jews get involved in social justice initiatives partly in order to address issues surrounding their own Jewish identities. Craig reports that this insight led him and his colleagues to explore 'creating a Jewish service corps, where Jews could go off into the developing world to both learn and study, but also put those values into practice through volunteering work'. Similarly, Jacob argues that social action is a way for non-observant young Jews to express both their modern, secular political values and their (sometimes inchoate) commitment to Judaism. Stuart agrees that the primary aim of his early Jewish justice work was to deepen the Jewish identity and cultural literacy of the change agents themselves: 'For me the main agenda was shifting the Jewish community. ... But it was about could we shift synagogues, could we shift the Jewish mind-set?' While assisting the non-Jewish poor and oppressed is clearly important to Stuart, his work was also intended to generate personal or spiritual change for the Jewish activists themselves. He uses the concept of *'tikkun'* (repair) to refer to both social change and personal transformation. Helping victims of injustice and finding individual, spiritual fulfilment are complementary aspects of the same process.

Sally believes that her school-based educational work has the potential to transform young people into moral agents, involved in charitable giving and volunteering, and initiators of progressive change within the Jewish community. This transformation is intended to benefit the young people no less than the ultimate beneficiaries of their communal and charitable work.

> I think we do think about who are we sending out into the world. Like who are we sending out into the Jewish community? And beyond. You know? … I think you meet someone who's been in Noam and you can kind of tell that they've been … you can kind of tell they've been in Noam. When you meet someone who's been in Bnei Akiva, and you can tell they've been in Bnei Akiva [Noam and Bnei Akiva are Jewish youth movements]. Like I'd like people to meet graduates of my school and kind of be able to tell that they've been in that school in some way, that they've got a certain understanding of the world, or way of looking at the world. And that actually that whole kind of being a good person, *mensch*, whatever it is, is a part of that.

Sally's assumption is that developing young people as moral change agents is not only good for the world, but it is good for the young people themselves. In particular, this work has transformative potential for young people who suffer from marginalisation and exclusion, as it provides them opportunities for involvement, learning and growth. This approach blurs the boundaries between agents and beneficiaries and conceptualises marginalisation in individualistic terms. The fact that the young people she works with come mainly from socially and economically privileged backgrounds has no bearing on their susceptibility to being excluded on a personal level.

Joe's notion of social change disrupts the boundary between agents/oppressors and beneficiaries/oppressed in a different way. His stated aim is to create the most egalitarian society possible with the greatest degree of freedom. This requires the development of social circles, communities and relationships that can build trust and win people over to a progressive agenda. Joe's strategy is to connect members of the privileged classes, particularly the predominantly middle-class Jewish community, with radical politics. This implies involving people in political and social change which, in terms of a Marxist, purely class-conflictual social model, would be seen to contradict their economic interests. Instead, Joe implies that the ideal of social justice is either an expression of altruism or a concept of the common good from which both oppressors and oppressed ultimately stand to gain. One aspect of this conception is the benefit that Joe believes accrues to Jews through their participation in radical politics.

> Look, I think all of us in [my organisation] are people with a strong non-Jewish social network. … We want to be part of a broader left and broader radical

politics, we just want to not have to dissolve our identity in order to do that. We just want to have our bloc that can be on a wider march, and … I think we always enjoy the dialogue. … When it comes to issues of antisemitism and Israel we're the ones who've got the connections, we're the ones that are friends with all the left wing groups, so we're on the front line of some of that dialogue actually.

This quotation touches on several important themes. First, Joe argues, contrary to deep-rooted, assimilatory trends on the Jewish Left, that involvement in radical politics should not require the sacrifice of one's Jewish identity. Specifically, radical groups should prioritise the struggle against antisemitism, not only because antisemitism is itself a form of injustice but because the resulting vulnerability experienced by many Jews often leads the community to close ranks and avoid speaking out against what Joe sees as oppressive phenomena, such as Israeli policy in the occupied territories. Second, Joe is committed to building up autonomous Jewish institutions which are able to function as part of a broader progressive coalition, both as an empowering process for a community which suffers from certain forms of marginalisation, and as part of his wider multicultural, communitarian social vision. Emancipatory work by the Jewish community on its own behalf, therefore, also serves as a means to the end of the common good. As such, radical Jews have the potential to advance social change and simultaneously benefit from its results.

The Oppressed as Social Change Agents

Several interviewees argue that potential beneficiaries must play an active role in the process of social change. Annie emphasises the centrality of members of the LGBT+ community as role models for inclusion and equality and goes on to explain the importance of LGBT+ leadership in terms of the power dynamics of oppression:

> Well in any group the facilitator has a certain amount of power that has to be acknowledged. … That's slightly harder for me in an LGBT group because actually a straight cis person holding a position of power in a predominantly LGBT group is kind of replicating problematic power dynamics that are happening in the rest of the world all the time. … *MP: I'm interested that you'll put yourself in a training session as a facilitator with a predominantly LGBT group.* Annie: Never on my own. So I won't train without at least one of the other trainers being an out LGBT person.

In her efforts to promote egalitarian gender role modelling within Orthodox schools, Francesca focuses primarily on the teachers as agents of, or obstacles to, change. However, she comments that an effective way of overcoming resistance from educators is when female students who take on non-traditional roles in Jewish ritual within their families and synagogues relate these experiences to their teachers upon their return to the classroom. This approach collapses the distinction between beneficiaries and primary change agents.

The role of partnerships between rich and poor is an important theme for several interviewees. Calley reflects on her experiences as an organiser in South Africa, where she saw 'poor, black communities organised for power' and began to question the assumption that the oppressed need the help or leadership of privileged groups. At the same time, she came to recognise the important role of the Church in South Africa's political conflicts and, by inference, the importance of the role played by professional, educated leaders. Calley argues that while those from privileged backgrounds are often motivated to improve society and do have a role to play in effective community organising, this requires them to develop genuine relationships with disadvantaged people and to acknowledge that their problems can only be solved in partnership. Calley holds that 'people are broader than their class interest' and sees community organising as a way of enabling people from different social backgrounds to work together in a way that enables all of them to address their own needs. Manny adds that the partnership between rich and poor (or other diverse, potentially antagonistic groups) requires the identification of genuine leaders who emerge from the community and are in relationship with their people, rather than an unrepresentative elite:

> So I always ask; Is the person I am talking to a genuine leader? Do they actually have difficulties here bringing people with them? Are they in some ways externally funded, self-appointed, representatives? I mean that's a particularly huge issue with the Muslim community where I come across a load of people who want to build a better world, a better life and to build relationships between Christians and Muslims and Jews, who don't have any Muslim followers.

The distinction between agents and beneficiaries of change tends to collapse when the interviewees discuss the role of Jews as such in social change movements, principally due to the ambivalent position of Jews in relation to concepts of power and oppression. Student leader Danny, for example, notes that Jews in the contemporary world face a tension between experiences of power and powerlessness, both historically thanks to the dramatically changing circumstances of the Jewish people during the twentieth century, and in contemporary society due to the complexities of Jews' social position in an intersectional context. Calley agrees that Jews in the UK occupy a fragile position, experiencing a tension between white, middle-class privilege, a history of oppression, and ongoing, contemporary marginality and vulnerability. For some interviewees, this delicate social position and sense of self means that Jews are able to play two simultaneous roles: as privileged change agents and marginalised beneficiaries. Manny reflects on the fragile nature of this position as follows:

> I'm certainly much more concerned now than I ever thought I was with the continued conditions of Jewish life in England, in exile, you know, for which I see as fundamentally much more precarious than I ever thought it was. …
>
> And I found myself involved in putting together an anti-usury campaign, essentially led by Muslims and by Christians, and the alarm bells starting ringing about the lack of Jewish engagement. That's where I really tried to re-engage with the Jewish community, that's where we met. Where I was, at that moment, just absolutely concerned that this had to be Jewish led, not just Jewish participants, otherwise it would be a classic antisemitic, anti-usury campaign.

Manny recalls feeling that involvement in a social justice campaign which ostensibly aimed to improve the lot of economically marginalised groups was, for a community which was economically secure but vulnerable as an ethnic and religious minority, a vital means of self-preservation.

* * *

In the dimension of people, then, many interviewees emphasise the role of implicitly privileged social change agents. One important group is rabbis and non-Jewish religious leaders who are able to articulate a religious vision of justice and use this to mobilise their communities. At the same time, the interviewees are ambivalent about the role of full-time, professional social activists and educators. They tend to put more faith in community members, volunteer leaders, parents and young people. At the same time, they recognise the need for focused professionals, organisers and teachers to support the development of voluntary organisations and activists.

While some practitioners are focused exclusively on supporting vulnerable, non-Jewish beneficiaries such as refugees, genocide survivors and victims of discrimination in Israel, most interviewees blur the boundaries between privileged and oppressed, agent and beneficiary groups. Privileged activists are held to benefit from the process of social change in terms of Jewish learning and personal, moral and spiritual growth. More fundamentally, most interviewees recognise that privileged people can suffer from forms of disadvantage, and insist that people are broader than their class interest. This conviction stems from an intersectional perspective, from a person-focused, almost apolitical concern with individual well-being, or from a notion of the common good – a social model that focuses on the confluence of interests rather than antagonism between different groups.

Finally, these sensitivities are both triggered and illustrated by the ambivalent status of Jews within the matrix of agency, privilege and oppression. The powerful sense that Jewish people occupy a simultaneously privileged and fragile position is a source of insight into the complexities of social injustice and an important resource for developing a sophisticated social justice pedagogy.

Part 3

Towards a Jewish Critical Pedagogy

I have now surveyed the approaches to social justice education associated with Freirean critical pedagogy, Catholic social teaching and liberation theology, Jewish social justice literature, and interviews with UK-based Jewish practitioners. In the next two chapters, I explore the important philosophical, theological, political and educational issues which emerge from this survey. Rather than isolating the positions of particular thinkers and practitioners, my aim is to identify and analyse the broader questions that emerge from the interplay of all these sources. While fundamental philosophical issues are not necessarily made explicit by all the Jewish interviewees, their implicit preoccupation with them comes into focus when their narratives are contextualised against critical pedagogy, Catholic thought and Jewish social justice literature. As well as developing a dialogue between the interview narratives and these theoretical frameworks, the ensuing discussion will add philosophical depth by drawing on secondary sources suggested thematically by the interviewees; thinkers introduced in this way include Hannah Arendt, Martin Buber, Emmanuel Levinas, Alasdair MacIntyre and Nel Noddings. This is an example of the power of a hermeneutical approach to create depth of meaning through dialogue between different kinds of discourse.

8

Philosophical, Theological and Political Themes

The question at the core of most of the approaches I have surveyed is: what does it mean to be a human being? Freirean critical pedagogy is structured around the goal of humanisation. Catholic social teaching and liberation theology seek to eradicate poverty so as to recover the humanity of the poor. And Jewish social justice educators are preoccupied with inclusion, relationship-building and personal transformation. The narratives we have been exploring collectively suggest that being a human being has three essential elements: involvement in *praxis*, being in relationship and community, and engagement in the spiritual aspects of life. As explained in more depth below, the intersection of these dimensions of human meaning generates three further issues: attitudes to pluralism and multiculturalism, the nature and role of dialogue and encounter, and the relationship between faith and politics.

Involvement in *Praxis*

All the thinkers and practitioners I have surveyed agree, whether explicitly or implicitly, that involvement in *praxis* is an incontestable ingredient of what it means to be human. Most often, this means a Freirean or Marxist concept of *praxis*, defined as a dialectical cycle of interpreting and critiquing the world, acting on the basis of this critique so as to transform reality, and taking transformed reality as the subject of further interpretation and critique: 'men's activity consists of action and reflection: it is *praxis*; it is transformation of the world. And as *praxis*, it requires theory to illuminate it. Men's activity is theory and practice; it is reflection and action.'[1] For Freire, participating in this cycle is what makes us human, in that it provides us with subjectivity and agency and enables us to act on the material world, rather than being objects which are submerged in it. This idea is the foundation of Freirean critical pedagogy, the Ignatian pastoral cycle ('see–judge–act') that underlies many of the Catholic approaches to social justice education, and many of the Jewish activism and campaigning approaches which see education as a means to the end of the attitudinal and behavioural changes that lead to social action. It should be noted that some of these approaches fall short of Freire's conception of *praxis* in that they are not necessarily fully committed to the agency and subjectivity of the learners, sometimes tending to see them in instrumental or objectified terms as means to the end of social change and occasionally, as a result, resorting to non-dialogical, arguably manipulative pedagogies. Other approaches neglect the dialectical nature of Freirean *praxis*, seeing the transition from learning to action as a one-off process rather than a cycle in which a transformed reality is always subjected to further reflection and critique.

In parallel to the centrality of *praxis* to being human, some of the interviewees understand it as part of a Jewish vocation. In the same way that Freirean political involvement both requires the humanity of its agents and simultaneously contributes to their humanisation, the vocation of being Jewish can only be achieved through social action which itself flows from Jewish identity or values. And just as Freire acknowledges that certain kinds of left-wing politics can themselves be dehumanising, several interviewees note that radicalism has often been destructive rather than constitutive of Jewish identity. Similarly, in the same way that humanity in the Freirean sense is not an inevitable biological fact but rather takes the form of an ideal to work towards or a potential to be realised, so too being Jewish does not lead automatically to a commitment to Judaism's values of social justice; this is a commitment in relation to which many Jews and Jewish tradition itself often fall short.

At times, involvement in *praxis* is understood in Aristotelian rather than Marxist terms. In this sense, and as articulated by Hannah Arendt,[2] *praxis* – as opposed to *poiesis* or production – refers to action in a complex, human network of relationships in which the distinctions between means and ends, processes and outcomes, and subjects and objects collapse. Whereas the process of *poiesis* and its outcome (*poieton*) are distinct, no such distinction can be drawn between *praxis* and its outcome (*prakton*). Unlike *poiesis*, *praxis* is not about making something external to oneself; it is about being a particular kind of person, community or society. Freire's conflation of pre-revolutionary strategy and his vision of the post-revolutionary society reflects this idea, as do Catholic and Jewish notions that community- and relationship-building are both vehicles for, and constitutive of, social justice. Here, there is no distinction between the actions required to create a good society (e.g. building relationships between rich and poor) and the practices which such a society are held to embody. This understanding of *praxis* marks the approach of those who adopt community organising strategies, for whom powerful civil society and relational community organisations are both means and ends, and who reject any attempt to instrumentalise human subjects in pursuit of predetermined social justice goals. It characterises educators motivated by the values of pluralism, for whom diversity and debate are both educational means and societal ends. This attitude to *praxis* is also in evidence among those interviewees who emphasise the importance of voice and speaking out, of being a just person rather than seeking to realise an extrinsic concept of justice. It can also be discerned in the dissatisfaction of some interviewees with the idea of fundraising, which implies a desire for a more personal involvement in social change.

Just as Freirean/Marxist *praxis* has echoes within Jewish culture, so too the Aristotelian understanding of *praxis* evokes a distinction drawn from rabbinic Judaism between two modes of ritual and ethical observance: *lishmah* (literally, 'for its own sake') and not-*lishmah*.[3] These two modalities of faith apply to all the ritual and ethical precepts of Jewish law, each of which may be observed *lishmah*, for its own sake, or not-*lishmah*, for an ulterior purpose. *Lishmah*-observance echoes aspects of *praxis*. It conflates means and ends in that religious practice is not a path towards faith but rather constitutes faith and cannot be separated from it. For Jewish social justice practitioners, the privileging of *lishmah* over not-*lishmah* echoes the commitment to Aristotelian *praxis* in that it rejects any instrumentalised conception of social action and insists that we adopt actions which not only lead to the extrinsic good of a just society but which themselves intrinsically embody justice.

What is the relationship between Freirean/Marxist and Aristotelian varieties of *praxis*? Freire presents *praxis* as a dialectical process, where learning leads to action and action shapes the world which, in turn, becomes the subject of renewed learning. Stepping back from action in order to reflect on the world enables the production of a body of theoretical knowledge and this knowledge then suggests or even determines the forms of action to be taken. In an Aristotelian context, however, this kind of theory-based action is reminiscent not of *praxis* but of *poiesis*, a mode of making or production informed by *techne*, defined by Joseph Dunne as the kind of knowledge possessed by a craftsperson: the capacity to realise a form in material in line with a given *telos*.[4] In contrast, Aristotelian *praxis* is guided by practical knowledge (*phronesis*) which is generated inductively through experience. Dunne notes that *praxis* is so complex that it cannot be derived straightforwardly from theory, but instead has to be worked out in situ on the basis of the practitioner's character and resourcefulness. Theories are never more than schemata which are shaped only upon application, where application refers not to the imposition of a fully articulated set of ideas on an inert reality but to the very articulation of those ideas as a result of the encounter between theory and a particular situation. In Aristotelian *praxis*, then, action does not flow in a linear fashion from learning, rather both are part of one integrated process.

These differences imply that each model is applicable to different social change strategies. Freirean *praxis* sits more comfortably with the campaigning/activism model, in which ideas formed on the basis of research, reflection and pre-existing ideological commitment are harnessed in order to develop social critique, attitudinal change and transformative political action. The Aristotelian approach, conversely, underlies motifs from the strategies of community organising and speaking out/embodying values: the conflation of processes and outcomes, the priority of people and relationships over issues, and perhaps more willingness to recognise the constraints of the world as it is over the imperatives of a vision for change.

However, it would be a mistake to over-emphasise the differences between Marxist/Freirean and Aristotelian conceptions of *praxis*, as in fact they share two core elements. First, each insists on the dialogical nature of both learning and action. This reflects the centrality of human subjectivity and agency and the fact that for both, *praxis* fulfils a function within the broader enterprise of humanisation. In this respect, the Aristotelian approach forms a corrective to a potential danger which stems from the Freirean model's Marxist roots. Habermas has pointed out that the emancipatory potential of Marxism is undermined by Marx's exclusive focus on production and the consequent subordination of his system to the alienating, mechanistic assumptions of modern capitalism; this, for Habermas, is symptomatic of the penetration of modern, scientific, technical rationality into the realm of *praxis*.[5] In our context, this hazard manifests itself in the tendency of some educators and activists to subordinate concrete relationships to abstract causes, to instrumentalise people and to slip into manipulative pedagogical practices. Freire is, in fact, alert to this danger: it underlies his insistence on dialogue and his opposition to banking education and populist political leadership.

Second, while the two approaches differ over how learning leads to action or how theory determines practice, they agree that there is an intimate connection between the two fields. It is possible that some of the differences between the two approaches can be resolved if we recognise that what Freire labels 'theory' is in fact much closer to an Aristotelian conception of *phronesis*. In any case, in both schools of thought, the concepts and processes of action, experience and reflection cannot easily be disentangled. In the Aristotelian model they intersect in *phronesis*, in which reflective practice generates experience and experience simultaneously shapes and enables reflective practice. For Freire, these processes come together even more closely in that the production of knowledge is itself a form of action. These insights into the characteristics which cut across all understandings of *praxis* raise challenging questions about the extent to which various systems of social justice education realise their core goal of humanisation.

Being in Relationship and Community

There is universal agreement across the thinkers and practitioners I have surveyed that humanisation is inextricably connected to being in relationship and community. However, there is less agreement on the nature of these concepts, their function within the process of humanisation and the more general question of the connection between community and social justice.

One widespread approach is to see relationships and community in instrumental terms, as means to the ends of social justice, echoing Freire's insistence that a dialogical, group setting is a necessary precondition for conscientisation and therefore for political action. This instrumental view links community more or less convincingly with the goals of social justice. However, its impact on the individual is indirect: in this context, humanisation is seen either as the long-term result of social and political change where community and relationship-building are a means to this end, or as the result of involvement in social action, that is, *praxis*, as explored above. Certain thinkers argue, against this, that relationships and community are vital for humanisation not in an instrumental sense but as ends in themselves. This idea is connected with a conception of relationships and community not as a means to the end of a good society but as constitutive of it. Two philosophers – Martin Buber and Hannah Arendt – have made this argument in different but equally compelling ways.

The first approach is associated with Martin Buber, who claims that modernity and in particular the global political crises of the twentieth century represent the displacement of the 'social principle', according to which society is a free association of organic, relational communities made up of autonomous but mutually dependent individuals, by the 'political principle', which requires the subordination of individual freedom to a centralised authority in the context of the mass society and the nation state. Societies based on the political principle are characterised by anonymity and alienation; ironically, true community is extinguished at precisely the moment at which the individual surrenders to the illusion of commitment to a perfect community – the nation state.[6]

In his seminal work, *I and Thou*,[7] Buber conceptualises his ideal community within the framework of dialogical philosophy. He posits that the human subject is defined in accordance with two fundamentally different modes of relating to other human beings and the world. The 'I–It' mode is transactional and objectifying, sees the other as a means to an end, and, inasmuch as it expresses itself in terms of experience and use, forms the basis for the entire realm of human enterprise. While 'I–It' is therefore vital for human thriving, its subject (the 'I') is accordingly transactional and objectified. In contrast, 'I–You' encounters are objectless, unmediated, and prior or unrelated to conceptualisation, knowledge or even experience. The 'I' of these encounters is the subject which is able to live 'in the spirit', to relate genuinely to others and, in these relationships, to encounter God (the 'Eternal You' in Buber's parlance). The evolution of modern society is associated for Buber with a decrease in human beings' power to relate – the displacement of the social principle by the political principle. Buber's solution to this malaise is the reconstitution of society as a non-hierarchical commonwealth of independent, organic communities based on the possibility of genuine, dialogical encounters.

For Buber, then, community is constitutive of a just society because it represents the resurgence of the social over the political, that is, the priority of unmediated, intimate relationships among human beings and between human beings and God, over the mechanised, transactional and alienating character of modern life. In terms drawn from the foregoing analysis, Buber's prioritisation of the social over the political represents a preference for a form of *praxis* over *poiesis*.

The second approach to community and relationships, articulated by Hannah Arendt, is based conversely on the priority of the political over the social. Arendt sets out from a fundamental distinction between three modes of activity: labour – the production of consumable goods such as food which are necessary to sustain life; work – the creation of objects such as tools, buildings or works of art which, while they may have use value, are not consumed but rather become permanent parts of the environment; and action – activity which takes place in a pluralistic network of interpersonal relationships among autonomous agents.[8] In ancient times, the private sphere (the home) was the primary site for labour and work, while action was located in the public arena – the *polis*. While the function of the private sphere was to enable families to provide for their own material needs and to guarantee basic social stability under the autocratic rule of the head of each household, the public sphere emerged once these needs had been addressed and involved a process of deliberation among active citizens about all other matters affecting the community. Politics, therefore, as an instance of action, sat firmly in the public sphere and took no interest in questions of labour or material survival.[9]

The advent of modernity, the expansion of the market economy and the consequent dominance of large-scale processes of production, consumption, acquisition and exchange heralded the emergence of 'the social', a category which blurred the distinction between public and private, as politics took on concerns which had previously belonged to the private sphere – the satisfaction of material desires.[10] The social began to colonise the public arena, leading government to focus on economic questions, resulting in levelling, conformist tendencies, recasting politics in bureaucratised and elitist forms, and banishing action and speech to the private realm. Thus both the content and the form of politics took on the character of production (*poiesis*) in which subjects act on objects, rather than a deliberative *praxis* which relies upon and reinforces the plurality and the freedom of its participants. Arendt illustrates her comparative analysis of the political and the social using the examples of the French and American revolutions. The American revolutionaries were preoccupied with establishing a political order that would preserve liberty (an approach that was facilitated by ignoring social problems such as slavery); this focus on creating a genuine public sphere ensured the success of the American revolution and the longevity of the political system it spawned. In contrast, the French revolutionaries' primary aim was to solve social problems, in particular, poverty. The result was tyranny and chronic political instability.[11]

If Buber demands the subordination of the political to the social, Arendt seems to call for the reverse: the resurgence of politics (or at least protection of the political sphere within the modern state). However, Buber's notion of the political is remarkably close to Arendt's conception of the social, and vice versa. Buber's political and Arendt's social are both associated with the inappropriate penetration of *poiesis* into the arena of *praxis*: modernisation, the emergence of mass society, the market economy and the nation state, and the development of bureaucratised, authoritarian forms of government.

While both thinkers argue for the recreation of forms of community based on interpersonal relationships, Buber's 'social' differs from Arendt's 'political' in several important ways. First, for Arendt, the ideal political community is disassociated from economics (questions of work and labour) which tend to objectivise people, and instead focuses solely on action, which enables individuals to emerge as free subjects. Her conception of justice is restricted to the principle of equality before the law; she argues that the role of the State should not extend to solving social problems such as poverty or discrimination so long as they do not infringe this principle.[12] In contrast, Buber, writing as a socialist, has an organic, holistic view of community as a unit of egalitarian economic, social and political life.

Second, Arendt's political community is characterised by the cut and thrust of deliberation, debate and the exchange of views, through which participants bring their innate uniqueness as human beings into the world:

> The presence of others who see what we see and hear what we hear assures us of the reality of the world and of ourselves, and while the intimacy of a fully developed private life ... will always greatly intensify and enrich the whole scale of subjective emotions and private feelings, this intensification will always come to pass at the expense of the assurance of the reality of the world and men.[13]

Buber rejects this speech-dominated conception of public life, instead arguing that community is constituted by the possibility of unmediated I–You dialogue between its members, where the absence of third-party observers is a crucial aspect of true encounter. On Buber's account, Arendt's ideal of action within a network of unique, autonomous human subjects would only be possible if contained within a space which engendered genuine, holistic relationships; in their absence, or in a context where partners to dialogue act merely as witnesses for the emergence of the self, political debate risks slipping into a transactional or instrumental mode of relating. At the same time, Arendt's model is based on the public relationships which characterised the life of the *polis*; in her terms, Buber is guilty of inappropriately attempting to transplant intimate, private, household relationships into the public realm, thereby endangering the freedom and agency of the participants.

Finally, as implied by the foregoing, Arendt's political community is not a means to the end of the common good (a social rather than a political concept) but an arena within which participants are able to assert their freedom and individuality and thereby realise their potential as human beings. While Arendt clearly recognises the interpersonal, relational nature of action and the fact that individuals are unable to control or author their own stories within a complex network of other autonomous agents, she nonetheless implies that the individual as such has unique, innate potential to bring to the world and, accordingly, takes interest primarily in this contribution and in the impact of the community on the individual. For Buber, the use of community as a means to the end of individual self-realisation implies an instrumentalisation of one's partners to dialogue and as such falls into the category of I–It. His aspiration, in contrast, is towards dialogue not as a means to the end of human identity but as constitutive of it and, as such, as an end in itself. If Arendt is primarily concerned with what is within each human being, Buber's interest lies in that which is between them.

This distinction between individualist and collectivist anthropologies resonates in the tensions between notions of individual and structural sin in the Catholic tradition and between communitarian and liberal/multicultural approaches to social justice. In our context, Buber evokes the Catholic thinkers who interpret injustice as the exclusion of the poor from the social and economic life of the community and the denial of their humanity. Their commitment to the common good and social equality stems from a desire to rebuild relationships, to rehumanise the poor (recognised as being created in the image of the divine) and in this way to bring God into the world. Similar concerns occupy Jewish thinkers like Arthur Waskow and Aryeh Cohen and interviewees such as Jodie, Rachel and Shalom, who prioritise relationship-building, particularly with the poor and oppressed.

Arendt's position finds resonance in the pedagogical politics of Paulo Freire and his commitment to critical dialogue and literacy in a collective setting as important mechanisms of conscientisation and humanisation. Crucially, Freire sees dialogue not only in instrumental terms as a means to the end of radical politics but as constitutive of the ideal, post-revolutionary society. The radicalisation of individuals, that is, enabling people to participate in progressive, political action, is no less important than the transformation of society that Freire hopes will flow from this participation. Jewish community organising strategies evoke Arendt's preoccupation with reconstituting the public sphere in the form of a pluralistic civil society built on strong, action-orientated, public relationships. While community organisers also see politics as a means to the end of social change, it is noteworthy that their strategy involves strengthening communities as a counterbalance to the power of the market and the state; this echoes Arendt's call for the subordination of the social to the public. Arendt's vision of a just society embodied in a reconstituted public sphere also finds expression in Sally's aspiration to develop a genuinely pluralistic community, marked by thoughtful deliberation and critical dialogue among its members, and free from prescriptive ideological limitations other than the broadly liberal–democratic values such a community needs to sustain itself.

Involvement in Spiritual Aspects of Life

The third component of humanisation is involvement in spiritual aspects of life. While a minority of interviewees tend implicitly towards a secular, materialist approach, most of the thinkers and practitioners from across the Jewish, Catholic and critical pedagogy traditions – both secular and religious – incorporate spiritual or idealist elements in their systems. These take two main forms: explicitly God-centred approaches, and more secular spiritual and anti-materialist perspectives.

God enters the social justice discourse of both Catholic and Jewish thinkers through the biblical idea that human beings are created in the divine image and are, in consequence, fundamentally equal and of infinite value. Poverty and exclusion are therefore seen as spiritual and communitarian evils in that the oppressed are treated as non-persons, excluded from the community and denied their human dignity, understood to derive from their creation in the image of God. This concept is the foundation for Catholic responses to poverty and also explains the motivation of Jewish interviewees to resist exclusion and discrimination against women and LGBT+ people.

While this notion of injustice as the denial of people's divinely instilled humanity relates primarily, by definition, to the poor and oppressed, creation in the image of God also applies more broadly to the humanisation of the non-poor. The doctrine of *imitatio Dei* (the requirement to imitate or follow in the path of God, that is, to realise the divine potential innate in every human being) leads to a rejection of the narrow anthropologies of both capitalism and Marxism and an insistence that people should aspire to be more than *Homo faber* or economic man; using Arendt's terminology, this means engaging in action – relationships and *praxis*. More specifically, *imitatio Dei* is connected to the ideal of evangelical poverty as expressed in Catholic thought, understood variously as the obligation to renounce material wealth for the sake of spiritual benefits, the importance of disengaging at least emotionally from one's possessions, or as the imperative to develop a commitment to justice and solidarity with the economically poor. While Jewish thought does not valorise poverty as such, a similar impulse underpins the biblical injunction to love the stranger, putting aside the constraints of kinship to recognise the fundamental humanity of the other.

Alongside the notion that human beings are made in the divine image, several Jewish writers also describe creation as a whole as suffused with God's presence, often understood in abstract, immanent or panentheistic terms. This presence of God in nature is seen as a vital foundation for justice in the world. Jonathan Wittenberg, for example, derives his commitment to environmental justice not only from divine moral imperatives but from a keen sense that nature itself is suffused with the spiritual.[14] Michael Lerner describes the universe as being alive with both physical and spiritual energy (as opposed to the inert physical matter perceived by our senses), a worldview which for him accords with the mystical idea of God 'breathing us' and God's breath permeating us, implying a fundamental oneness of subject and object in which human beings are an organic, interconnected part of a cosmic whole.[15] He claims that Western political movements are unable to achieve the transformation they seek because they are not rooted in this kind of transcendent vision of the universe where God, understood as the power that makes for transformation, has a stake in human life.[16] If, as these writers claim, the presence of God in the world is an indispensable constituent of or impetus to justice, this raises a fundamental question: how are we to react in times of crisis when God appears to be absent? Several writers have addressed this challenge by alluding to Abraham Joshua Heschel's insistence that the role of human beings is not to search out or accuse the Divine but to take responsibility for serving God through action. In contrast to the intuition that the divine presence is constitutive of our ability to work for transformation, some Hasidic traditions have understood God's hiddenness as the condition under which human beings are able to receive Torah and function autonomously in the world.[17]

The concept of creation in the divine image is closely connected in both Jewish and Catholic traditions with the importance of entering into a relationship with God. Recognising the divine imprint in others mandates us to relate to them in certain ways. Similarly, in an apophatic theological context which assumes the unknowability and absolute uniqueness of God, *imitatio Dei* pushes into the realm of ethics as the only way of following in God's path. Thus a relationship with God is both a means to the end of justice work, and the *telos* of social action. Following Buber, interpersonal relationships are often described as an arena for encountering God (where God is understood either as a metaphor for the absolute humanity which is revealed in the act of dialogue, or as a transcendent reality which is glimpsed through the encounter with the other). However, Buber argues that while the encounter with God is transformative, the outcome of genuine dialogue cannot be predicted or even identified retrospectively, such that the relationship with the divine does not give rise in any straightforward way to ethics or social action. For other thinkers, conversely, creation in the image of God is connected with a moral imperative to know the stranger and to be in relationship; as Levinas argues, a sacred duty to do justice flows from this meeting with the divine in human form.[18] Similarly for Catholics, the ability to transform the world depends on God's grace. At the same time, the ethical treatment of the oppressed and the elimination of poverty are seen as steps along the path to spiritual goals. For Catholics, justice work leads to the eradication of sin and bringing God into the world, that is, salvation. For Jewish thinkers, social justice work itself constitutes the fulfilment of religious obligations or the realisation of values emanating from the tradition.

Involvement in spiritual aspects of life does not apply only to explicitly theistic belief systems and even committed religious thinkers do not always articulate their approaches using God language. 'Non-God' spiritual and anti-materialist approaches touch on two main issues: a focus on personal transformation and spiritual growth, and the indispensability of culture and tradition.

Ideals of personal transformation, the development of subjectivity and spiritual growth form the backbone of all varieties of thought surveyed in this research. Even secular interviewees who focus on collective, political questions believe that injustice is caused in part by psychological trauma and envisage a therapeutic process towards individual emotional health as a vital ingredient of social transformation. For these practitioners, personal transformation is a means to the end of social change. Others prioritise spiritual and emotional growth as ends in themselves, seeing the purpose of their work as personal transformation and development of students into human beings or moral agents. The concept of *tikkun* (repair) is applied not only to social change but also to personal growth, where ethics represents a *tikkun* of the outside world while spirituality is a *tikkun* of one's being. This internal *tikkun* facilitates the development of a sense of duty; enables individuals to find their personal passion, commitment and authenticity; and gives them the energy to act in the world. Conversely, ethics ensures that spirituality does not become a form of empty narcissism. Freire similarly emphasises both social change and personal development – formulated in terms of humanisation, conscientisation, class suicide or, in tellingly Christian terminology, a 'personal Easter'[19] – and argues that one is impossible without the other. While these approaches either prioritise moral–spiritual development over political change or posit a mutually reinforcing relationship between the two, they also echo the convictions of Catholic theologians for whom combatting material injustice is a step on the path towards spiritual goals: the eradication of sin and religious salvation for individuals and for humanity as a whole.

The process of personal transformation illustrates an additional sense in which spiritual concerns are important to social justice educators: the centrality of culture. Both Catholic and Jewish educators describe the transformative impact of genuine encounters with poor people in the context of service programmes in developing countries. While the unmediated experience of poverty and the accompanying emotional reaction are undoubtedly important catalysts for attitudinal and behavioural change, the true power and meaning of these encounters is realised only when set in a cultural or religious context. This insight resonates with the work of Zygmunt Bauman and Alasdair MacIntyre. Bauman claims that modernity is destructive of identity and meaning in that it dislocates and alienates people from their clear, pre-modern sense of place and social role. It demands on the one hand that we create our own identity but on the other eliminates the very grounding structures which would have rendered this possible.[20] MacIntyre argues similarly that in conditions of post-Enlightenment modernity, commitment to one set of virtues rather than another inevitably becomes a matter of arbitrary choice. His antidote to this is the Aristotelian view that virtues make sense only in the context of a teleological anthropology, and that a *telos* which constitutes the good of a whole human life can only be derived from the tradition in which that life is fundamentally embedded.[21]

Pluralism: Politics of Redistribution and Recognition

The intersection of the first two ingredients of humanisation (involvement in *praxis* and being in relationship or community) raises issues of pluralism, multiculturalism and inclusion. If just societies are built on relational community life and the creation of justice involves *praxis* (critical thinking, dialogue and common action), this presents the challenge of building relationships in the absence of uniformity and authority – that is, in a pluralist, multicultural environment. However, the nature and status of pluralism in the approaches to social justice education under discussion require some clarification.

A pertinent theoretical framework is the distinction between the politics of redistribution and the politics of recognition. In her essay 'Social justice in the age of identity politics', Nancy Fraser sets out to attack what she sees as the false dichotomy between these two modes of progressive politics, arguing that many oppressed groups are in fact affected by economic inequality and by cultural domination or non-recognition and are therefore in need of both redistributive and recognition-based political solutions.[22] She weaves these two modes into one, bivalent conception of social justice in which economic and cultural oppression are seen as twin barriers to parity of participation in society. This parity of participation requires not only legal equality but two additional factors: an adequately egalitarian distribution of resources to ensure participants' independence and 'voice', and the enforcement of institutional cultural patterns which express equal respect and guarantee equal opportunities for all to participate. Ensuring both conditions are met requires policies of redistribution and/or recognition, depending on context. Fraser goes on to distinguish between universal/egalitarian and difference-based approaches to recognition. Where misrecognition results in oppression by denying some people's common humanity, the remedy is universalist – minimising difference and recognising them as human beings; where it involves denying people's specificity, the remedy could be the recognition and valorisation of difference.

Fraser's analysis raises a number of questions which are pertinent to the issue of pluralism. To translate these questions into terms which emerge from the present study: is pluralism seen as constitutive of a just society and if so what is the philosophical or ideological basis for this position? Or is pluralism a means to the end of justice understood in economic terms? Thinkers who take this latter view are divided between those who see culture as a battleground for political and economic power struggles (who tend to prioritise the recognition of difference), those who see social and ideological pluralism in educational terms as a mechanism for the inculcation of the values associated with social justice, and (overlapping with this group) those who argue that epistemological pluralism is a condition for the development of justice-orientated attitudes.

In this framework, four broad positions emerge: a liberal identity politics which sees cultural pluralism and diversity as constitutive of a just society; a Marxist or postcolonialist position in which questions of cultural difference mask underlying issues of political and economic oppression; the approach of community organisers and thinkers in the Catholic social teaching tradition who prioritise social harmony and the common good and who seek to bridge difference; and finally, the idea of cultural, ideological or epistemological pluralism as a necessary foundation for social justice, which is understood in social and economic terms.

Liberal identity politics: Pluralism as justice. The first position is a liberal, identity-politics approach which conceptualises justice in terms of pluralism, social inclusion and diversity.[23] This applies to interviewees whose work is motivated by the ideal of a community which welcomes people regardless of gender identity and sexual orientation, who celebrate ideological and cultural diversity within the Jewish community and whose educational projects aims to inculcate attitudes and behaviours which reinforce this pluralism. Some of the Catholic writers surveyed tacitly apply a similar, identity-politics lens to poverty; while arguing for the eradication, or at least the amelioration, of poverty, they also valorise the poor as a distinct group with their own valuable identity and press for the inclusion of the poor in community life. The approach of most interviewees who adopt liberal identity politics is fundamentally universalist. They claim, for example, that an excessive focus on sectional identities has discriminatory potential in that it risks excluding people (such as Jews) from progressive politics if their identities do not coincide with agreed racial, gender or sexuality markers of oppression. While they are undoubtedly committed to diversity and pluralism, several interviewees frame their arguments for inclusion and equality in terms of a belief in the common humanity of all individuals, phrased in the religious language of creation in the divine image. This universal humanism provides a powerful, non-contestable foundation for these interviewees' commitment to diversity.

Marxism and postcolonialism. Advocates of a liberal identity politics are preoccupied primarily with culture and identity and, in general, fail to connect their recognition-based positions with social and economic issues and questions of redistribution. In contrast, writers who are influenced by Marxism and postcolonialism tend to critique the liberal and multicultural assumptions of these perspectives which, they argue, reduce race and ethnicity (and, by extension, gender and sexuality) to cultural categories and therefore ignore or underplay power relations, especially in their essentially economic or redistributive dimension. In this view, pluralism and diversity are not constitutive of justice; rather a robust understanding of difference and misrecognition as manifestations of underlying inequities of cultural and economic power is a vital ingredient of any move towards social justice, which is understood primarily in redistributive terms.

Freire, for example, sees culture as a field for social oppression, within which the dominant class preserves its power by strengthening national and class differences and denigrating the cultures of oppressed groups. This creates a culture of silence which prevents the oppressed from correctly analysing their situation, encourages self-blame and neutralises potentially emancipatory social movements.[24] This critique, developed in the context of neocolonialism in Latin America, has been applied by Macedo and Giroux to what they see as the conservative, anti-multicultural positions of academics such as Allan Bloom and E. D. Hirsch and has been employed by Giroux in his discussion of North American racism which, while expressed in cultural terms (e.g. the normalisation of whiteness), has social and economic roots and effects.[25] The Freirean ideal is therefore not to promote diversity as such but to enable the oppressed to reclaim their marginalised languages and cultures as a necessary step on the path to political and economic emancipation. Similarly, Freire is not a vulgar Marxist who understands oppression and liberation in binary, class terms. He acknowledges the existence of hierarchies of oppression and welcomes the diversity of contemporary, identity-based radical movements, but calls for solidarity and a broad-based struggle, rather than setting marginalised groups against each other and thereby colluding with the interests of the oppressors.[26] For Giroux, this form of collaboration requires the deconstruction of binary polarities of identity and the creation of 'borderlands' where multiple, interpenetrating identities can coexist and cross; he sees this not as an end in itself but as part of a wider, solidary struggle for justice.[27] Peter McLaren is also concerned about the conservative potential of postmodern multiculturalism and argues that while identity-based oppression needs to be understood on its own terms, it must also be conceptualised through the central category of class; the ultimate solution to identity-based oppression is the transformation of capitalism.[28] These critical pedagogues see cultural and identity-based marginalisation as a support structure for political oppression and economic inequality but also argue that this kind of misrecognition cannot be remedied without redistribution – a class-based, materialist politics.

This insight is shared in various ways by Jewish social justice educators. Several interviewees trace a connection between cultural and material oppressive structures: a lack of pluralism within the Jewish community, underpinned by an overly dominant communal establishment which does not recognise the legitimacy of diverse forms of Jewishness, buttresses concrete instances of injustice by silencing protest against discrimination or by facilitating financial and political support for oppressive policies. This phenomenon reflects the relationship between cultural and political–economic injustice in an additional way, in that UK Jews' experience and fear of antisemitism tend to act as a catalyst: the perceived need for Jewish unity in the face of misrecognition militates against the legitimisation of dissenting views and therefore, according to some interviewees, tends to perpetuate the community's acquiescence in instances of oppression.

A progressive antidote to this situation (not proposed explicitly by any of the interviewees but implied by this critique) is suggested by Fraser's principle of identifying the correct balance between differentiating and universalist recognition strategies and by the Freirean call for a solidary alliance of class- and identity-based social movements to combat the oppression which affects them all. This kind of solution would involve recasting antisemitism not as a particularistic problem which isolates the Jewish community but as one target of a broader anti-racist struggle to be conducted in partnership with non-Jewish allies, many of whom face parallel issues of marginalisation which often spill over into social and economic discrimination. This approach would remove some of the incentives towards the defensive homogenisation of discourse within the Jewish community and therefore allow for the emergence of narratives which, rejecting the tension between Jewish self-interest and progressive political commitment, could simultaneously and coherently address antisemitism, other forms of racism and discriminatory government policies, both in the UK and Israel.

Social harmony and the common good. In contrast to the conflictual social models assumed by these Marxist and postcolonial approaches, community organisers, writers in the Catholic social teaching tradition and faith-based service learning practitioners tend to emphasise the goals of social harmony and the common good, understood primarily in material, socio-economic terms. While none of these thinkers advocates the suppression of diversity (and many implicitly or explicitly celebrate it), they also see pluralism as a challenge to be overcome if diverse groups are to work together in the pursuit of common goals.

In Catholic social teaching, social justice is conceptualised in socially harmonious, non-conflictual terms under the banner of the 'common good'. This is reflected by the fact that the relevant papal encyclicals are addressed to the entire Church or 'all people of good will', in the idea that love and care for other people is a basic religious duty, and through the principle that private property rights are subordinate to and must be used to promote the common good – the state therefore taking responsibility for redistributing resources and safeguarding the rights of the poor. Educational writers in this tradition favour service learning programmes in which non-poor activists develop relationships with poor or marginalised people in order to build solidarity and create incremental social change around this common set of values. However, Catholic social teaching reflects some tension between this vision of interclass cooperation in pursuit of the common good, and a view of the poor as passive victims or recipients of religiously motivated charity.

Community organisers similarly advocate bringing people together on the basis of common self-interest to work for justice, understood in terms of the common good. They discuss the need to build the capacity of the community for political action by weaving narratives which bring together diverse groups (e.g. local businesses and trade unions; Muslims, Christians and Jews; working-class men and middle-class women) and enable them to find common ground. They also emphasise the covenantal nature of society and the need for both rich and poor to make sacrifices in order to achieve coexistence and social peace. While this perspective recognises the social and cultural differences and the power differentials which exist between people, it emphasises the need to leave these differences at the door and to concentrate on finding areas of common self-interest. This involves an effort to overcome social and cultural pluralism and, in Fraser's terms, represents a de-differentiating, universalising approach to recognition in the service of a redistributive agenda.

However, while various writers attest to successes in overcoming difference, this enterprise involves significant challenges. Bergman's account of service learning programmes for American students in the Dominican Republic, for example, reveals that while cultural barriers can be overcome such that volunteers do succeed in developing feelings of solidarity for the poor people with whom they are working, this solidarity cannot resolve the fundamental economic differences between poor and non-poor groups.[29] The volunteers are left with the realisation not only that they can do nothing significant to help their Dominican friends but that their privilege is inextricably linked with the global inequality and poverty from which their counterparts suffer. This insight highlights a fundamental weakness of the 'common good' idea, in that it is unable to deal with situations where an absence of common self-interest or agreed values prevents joint action. This weakness is further illustrated by Calley's description of her failure to engender cooperation between Jewish shopkeepers and non-Jewish pupils from a local school on the issue of crime and street safety. Here, the absence of common self-interest was underpinned by a failure to overcome cultural difference and the efforts to do so actually exacerbated the problems of misrecognition on both sides. This dynamic can be diagnosed in Fraser's terms as a problem of over-differentiation leading to misrecognition, which becomes an obstacle to solving concrete social problems. The implied solution is de-differentiation: this means encouraging the shopkeepers to step inside the social and cultural world of the students and to take up a more universal conception of community. However, the fact that one party to this relationship is expected to accommodate itself to the other evokes the view that any attempt to value all cultures equally cannot be sustained because we inevitably end up judging one from the (privileged) point of view of the other.³⁰

Jodie's description of Jewish service learning programmes highlights similar problems of misrecognition and failing to overcome the fundamental differences caused by economic inequality. Her account suggests that these differences can be overcome and that self-interest can be established on the basis of a connection between one party's internal, cultural narrative and the other's objective reality. Jodie experienced this kind of connection between herself and a hungry, African child on the basis of her family narratives about the Holocaust (other interviewees expressed similar sentiments in relation to refugees and traditional Jewish narratives or family history). In this sense, combatting poverty becomes a matter of common self-interest because both parties understand themselves – in different ways – to be suffering from it. However, it is possible that this manoeuvre denies the agency or subjectivity of the poor person, since the alignment of identity and self-interest only exists from the point of view of the non-poor partner. While a British, Jewish volunteer might see herself as similar to and sharing self-interest with an African child, the child almost certainly does not see her in the same way.

Another potential solution draws on the tension between two views of relationship and dialogue as espoused by Martin Buber and Emmanuel Levinas. Both Buber and Levinas ground their philosophy in notions of dialogue or relationship as the defining category of human existence. One of the characteristics of Buber's I–It transactions is the tendency of the subject ('I') to assimilate other people to itself. In contrast, while I–You encounters preserve the independence of both parties, they also imply an aspiration to ever-deepening, intimate relationships which in some way overcome difference. Levinas, while similarly preoccupied with relationships, rejects this idea.³¹ Following the Cartesian tradition and in terms reminiscent of Buber, he argues that since ideas are inventions of the mind, any idea of the other is no more than an interpretation and cannot be taken to refer directly to an independently existing person. Knowledge ('ontology' in Levinas's terms) closes off contact with the real person to whom it ostensibly points. He characterises this imposition of rational categories as a totalising, violent denial of the other's autonomy and essential otherness. The alternative is to retreat back to a pre-conceptual or pre-rational stage of consciousness, in which life consists of sensations to be enjoyed. In this state, the encounter with the face of the other is the first interaction with something that cannot be assimilated; something which is genuinely other and as such resists consumption. The presence of the other is not known, but rather felt as a resisting force and, as such, has power and exerts an immediate, pre-conceptual ethical claim of infinite responsibility towards the other person. Levinas therefore sees ethics, understood as this primal obligation towards a concrete other, as 'first philosophy'. This balancing act between the attempt to encounter or recognise the other and the awareness that any knowledge of that other inevitably involves misrecognition provides a possible basis for genuine dialogue and the identification of commonalities without subsuming difference. It points to the possibility of ethics (working for the good) independent, or in the absence, of any attempt to bridge difference.

Epistemology and education: Pluralism as a foundation for justice. A final group of thinkers posit that cultural, ideological or epistemological pluralism is a necessary foundation for social justice, understood in social and economic terms. Jacob, for example, notes that religious fundamentalism – understood as a monistic approach to religious truth – tends to be associated with racism, sexism and other forms of chauvinism. By implication, pluralism is associated with progressive, egalitarian values. Why should this be the case? The thinkers surveyed here provide a range of answers to this question.

Some thinkers see social or ideological pluralism as a mechanism for character education in the service of values such as good citizenship, spirituality and *menschlichkeit*. This is articulated by interviewees who aim to develop young people as tolerant, thoughtful human beings by confronting them with and encouraging them to develop open-mindedness towards unfamiliar views in a diverse social setting. Similarly, the dialectical, pluralistic nature of traditional rabbinic thought is conceptualised as an antidote to linear, dichotomous Western culture; exposure to this mode of thinking has the power to undermine consumerist, transactional approaches to life and to inculcate a spiritual alternative that puts a premium on relationships, people and their narratives and which provides a motivation for engagement with social justice work.

While this approach supplies a rationale for the connection between pluralism and morality or good citizenship, it does not necessarily translate into an egalitarian social and economic agenda; it is equally applicable to those approaches which conceptualise justice in purely cultural, recognition-based terms or which see pluralism in itself as constitutive of a just society. However, some practitioners argue that exposure to the kind of pluralism reflected in rabbinic literature can teach people to listen specifically to the voices of the poor and oppressed, to understand their needs and to act on their behalf. It is worth noting in this light that rabbinic literature is indeed characterised by its preservation of minority views; accordingly, pluralism is related to justice because both involve listening to the marginalised other. This position is distinct from the approach of liberation theologians, who contend that studying scripture from the perspective of the poor enables the text's 'true', radical meaning to be drawn out. The Jewish practitioners under discussion here tend to recognise that religious texts are inherently plural, containing both oppressive and emancipatory voices, and that they have the capacity to be enlisted for diverse political agendas. For these thinkers it is the very pluralism of the text which provides its progressive potential. However, it is hard to see how a commitment to an explicitly egalitarian, radical politics might result automatically from this kind of engagement; in order to avoid becoming a purely liberal or identity-politics approach which celebrates diversity without privileging the needs of the poor, a prior sensitivity to inequality and power relations seems to be required.

An alternative understanding of the relationship between pluralism and social justice is that the former is an essential context for encouraging people to develop progressive political positions. In this view, challenging people's pre-existing opinions by exposing them to 'reality' – understood as a holistic aggregation of the perspectives and experiences they encounter – enables them to cope with the complexity generated by multiple, conflicting narratives; to use this complexity to arrive at a correct diagnosis of social problems; and to develop the motivation to take appropriate political action. Rather than seeking to engender particular character traits, this approach presents itself as resolutely intellectual and evidence-based in that it assumes a correlation between access to information and the accuracy of the conclusions inferred from it. This approach rests simultaneously on two contradictory epistemological assumptions: on the one hand, the idea that there are multiple, legitimate ways to experience and understand the world, and on the other that by aggregating these views it is possible to arrive at a perspective which is objectively true and therefore politically correct (with the implication that other positions are only partially true and concomitantly politically misguided).

A subtly different variation of this approach takes the view that exposure to different perspectives engenders centrist political positions not by encouraging the empirical weighing up and analysis of evidence but through a dialectical process in which the clash between radical or one-dimensional ideological theses and antitheses tends to produce complex, relatively moderate syntheses. This approach dispenses with the problematic assumption that progressive politics derives from epistemic objectivity (and the underlying notion that particular political views are in some sense 'true') and also resolves the epistemological inconsistency described above by taking a thoroughgoing constructivist position.

In other words, understandings of reality that derive from an exploration of diverse experiences and perspectives are valuable due to their depth and complexity, not because of an assumed objective verisimilitude; they do not necessarily reflect objective reality any more than the partial perspectives they encompass. Similarly, the political positions which emerge are considered to be valid not as a result of their accuracy or correctness but on the basis of a value judgement that centrism and moderation are inherently desirable (an important caveat here is that centrism and moderation are themselves subjective terms which are likely to be contentious when applied to any given political position). This notion has something in common with character education approaches, in that the generation of complex worldviews and moderate political positions depends not only on exposure to information but on the development of virtues such as compassion, tolerance, sensitivity and deliberativeness.

Dialogue

In several of the approaches surveyed, dialogue is seen as a vital means to the end of relationship-building and personal transformation, both of which are central to the pursuit of social justice. The importance of dialogue and encounter emerges from the understanding that there is a connection between being in community and relationships on the one hand, and engagement in spiritual or idealist aspects of life on the other; dialogue is a framework for describing the micro-process of one-to-one relationship-building and communication and the transformative impact – often described in spiritual terms – this has on the individual. Dialogue is also an indispensable element of *praxis*, in both Freirean/Marxist and Aristotelian understandings, in that dialogue creates the arena for critique and reflection, the development of subjectivity and agency, and for collective action. Finally, the importance of dialogue is magnified in the context of pluralism, where achieving justice necessitates communicating across difference, either as an end in itself or as a means to the end of social action. However, the character and role of dialogue in these processes can be understood in diverse ways, each of which reveals a different approach to social justice on both eschatological and strategic levels. These can be broken down into three main, sometimes overlapping, categories: dialogue as rational discourse, dialogue as a care relationship and dialogue as existential encounter.

The first type of dialogue can be summed up as rational discourse aimed at developing the participants' agency and capacity for critique. As opposed to service learning approaches, for example, which use encounter and relationship-building to generate the emotional impact which forms the background for an academic learning process, here dialogue itself, understood as the cut and thrust of different, contradictory worldviews and opinions, serves to facilitate the intellectual development of the participants. This approach gels with the model of community and politics presented by Hannah Arendt and is associated with worldviews which emphasise the values of humanisation (understood primarily as a process of intellectual development), pluralism and democracy.

In this spirit, Nicholas Burbules defines dialogue as a 'pedagogical communicative relation'.[32] 'Pedagogical' means dialogue is directed towards increasing the participants' knowledge through a non-authoritarian learning process; 'communicative' specifies that language is the medium and the product of dialogue, where reason and morality are shaped by language; and 'relational' emphasises that truth claims are to be negotiated between people and, as such, the quality of the relationship between the participants is paramount. The implication of this approach is that the relationship between interlocutors gives rise to a certain kind of communication which thereby enables a cognitive learning process; the intellectual growth (and consequent attitudinal and behavioural transformation) of the individual is the goal to which the activity of relational communication is directed.

This dichotomy between means (relationships) and ends (personal development) is clouded by a twin distinction Burbules makes between convergent and divergent models of dialogue (the extent to which dialogue aims at or results in arriving at an agreed conclusion) and between inclusive and critical approaches (described by Burbules as the 'believing game' or 'connected knowing' as opposed to the 'doubting game' or 'separate knowing'). While the intellectual development of the individual is important in all these categories, the convergent and inclusive paradigms put more of a premium on the development of mutual understanding, consensus and a connection between the participants as ends in themselves. This is made clear by Burbules's insight that dialogue can lead to any of five outcomes: first, agreement and consensus; second, no agreement but common understanding and a common ground for discussion of differences; third, no common understanding but a shared grasp of the differences between participants, which can be bridged through translation or analogy; fourth, little understanding but mutual respect; and, finally, incommensurable plurality.

A second tension which emerges from this model of dialogue and from Burbules's definition in particular relates to an epistemological question: what is the source of the knowledge that the process of dialogue unveils or constructs? Freire writes that dialogue enables learners to interpret the world by interacting with each other and with a teacher, where the subject matter or 'the world' mediates between the participants. This model of dialogue is egalitarian and non-hierarchical in that all parties – students and teachers – are expected to contribute to the construction of knowledge about a common reality which is the source of the raw material or data on which their reflections are based. The role of the teacher here is to provide structure and discipline to the process, so as to encourage rigorous, critical thinking. In contrast to this Freirean model, other thinkers echo the position of Buber, who writes that the role of the teacher is to choose and manifest the educative world with which students are to interact.[33] Rather than facilitating dialogue between individuals about the world, Buber implies that the teacher becomes a dominant partner to dialogue in that she represents the world, or the source of knowledge, to the students.

In this model of rational discourse, dialogue is seen as an indispensable ingredient of *praxis*; it serves to foster the intellectual development of the participants and create connections between them as a means to the end of collective action. When understood as the development of a care relationship, however, dialogue is seen primarily in terms of affect and action (rather than intellect) and is also understood as part of the fabric of a just society rather than simply as a means to the creation of justice. Several interviewees imply a concern with caring as an end in itself, aiming to nurture the kind of communities in which caring can take place and, in the context of service learning, creating caring relationships as a means to the end of developing agency among their volunteers.

This sense of dialogue as a care relationship is articulated in detail by feminist philosopher Nel Noddings, who provides a critique of liberal individualism and argues for the fundamental connectedness or interdependence of human beings.[34] Noddings discusses caring as a relationship between the 'one-caring' and the 'cared-for', in which the one-caring seeks to resonate with the feelings of the cared-for, to understand his reality (rather than imposing her own reality on him), and to adopt an attitude of engrossment towards him. For Noddings – drawing on Buber – the cared-for 'fills the firmament' in the experience of the one-caring. Caring means being unconditionally present for and accepting the cared-for. This presence prevents the cared-for being 'thrown back' on himself and is just as important as any concrete act of care. Noddings notes that in various biblical narratives, God or a parent (Abraham, for example) demands the attention of a subordinate human being or child, who is required to respond 'here I am'. These stories represent a reversal of a genuine relationship of care in which 'here I am' is the requisite attitude of the one-caring, not the cared-for. At the same time, caring requires a response on the part of the cared-for. This does not mean reciprocation in kind (as assumed, for example, by some community organisers who reject a unidirectional caring relationship in preference for collaborative partnerships from which each party derives benefit) but the ability of the cared-for simply to accept the care being offered and respond appropriately to the one-caring. This ability exists within young children, babies and even animals, and explains our ability and duty to care for them.

The importance of response has two implications. First, Noddings argues that our ability to care is contingent upon the direct response of the cared-for and therefore upon our closeness to and affinity with other individuals, described in terms of 'circles' and 'chains' of caring. She describes a parallel between being 'seized' by the creative impulse and the receptivity which is central to caring; the impulse to care is in some degree dependent on the responsiveness of the cared-for and not fully under the autonomous control of the one-caring. Any attempt to universalise our caring obligations (extending them, for example, to faraway strangers or people with whom we have no direct connection) threatens our basic ability to care. However, natural caring – the innate human inclination to care for those with whom we are in relationship – does provide the foundation for a more universal ethical caring. Noddings argues that the experience of caring results in the construction of an internal image of myself as caring or ethical. She continues that 'caring arises naturally in the inner circles of human intercourse and … it must be summoned by a concern for the ethical self in situations where it does not arise naturally'.[35] This applies both to people in the one-caring's immediate surroundings who are unable to respond appropriately as a cared-for (e.g. as the result of a disability) or people with whom we are not in direct relationship and who are therefore unable to respond to us. An alternative formulation of the same point is that our ability to care *about* people who are outside our circles and chains of caring is based on our ability to care *for* those who are.

Second, the actions of caring are not governed by principles but instead vary depending on the one-caring's response to individuals in concrete situations. This responsiveness is primarily intuitive-affective rather than rational-objective in orientation; while deciding on the appropriate caring actions in a given situation requires rational thinking, any premature switching from the former to the latter mode threatens the fundamental caring orientation. There is a place for norms, but rather than governing ethical decision-making these norms emerge phronetically from the accumulation of concrete caring experiences. This position has implications for social policy which, according to Noddings, should be designed around the principle of enabling caring relationships.[36] Caring is to be understood, like literacy, as something to be spread as widely as possible across society, rather than concentrated in bureaucratic, impersonal institutions. Caring professionals should be enabled to respond to their cared-fors in a non-rule-bound, responsive way.

Noddings's position also has implications for educational dialogue.[37] On the one hand, a caring relationship is a necessary foundation for cognitive or practical educational dialogue. The one-caring's role is to accompanying the cared-for, providing the necessary attention and support to enable him to explore subject matter and take on his own learning projects. On the other, caring is the goal of education. Noddings argues that both parenting and the curriculum of schools should be shaped in line with the ultimate outcome of making children feel cared-for and able to care. Schools should see their role as not only preparing students for public life (citizenship and employment) but primarily for domestic life, teaching them how to establish loving, caring homes. At the same time, Noddings sees value in the verbal–cognitive aspects of educational dialogue. These are important means to the end of caring, in that verbal communication and reflection are required for overcoming problems in and deepening the caring-orientated educational relationship. The centrality of care enables Noddings (unlike exponents of dialogue as rational discourse, such as Burbules) to see that dialogue or relationship can continue even in the presence of incommensurable plurality. I can continue to care for someone even when we do not understand each other. This conception of dialogue might help service learning practitioners overcome the barriers between rich and poor outlined above: people from industrialised and developing countries are able to connect in a caring relationship even in the absence of mutual understanding, common self-interest or the possibility of reciprocation.

Noddings presents her ethics of caring as a form of Buberian dialogue, implying that the cared-for stands in relation to the one-caring as a 'You' to an 'I'. While Buber indeed writes that the encounter with God brings people into a more intimate relationship with the world and therefore makes possible relationships based on kindness, love and responsibility,[38] the form of encounter described in the first part of *I and Thou* seems to be fundamentally incompatible with dialogue understood as a care relationship in Noddings's sense. There are certain parallels between Buber's view of dialogue and Noddings's care relationship, primarily the phenomenon of engrossment in the cared-for and the idea that one has to be 'seized' by the relationship in order to truly care. However, for Noddings, love or caring is a deliberate practice, behaviour or act of will, reflecting a certain stability or consistency of character on the part of the subject. Conversely, Buber sees dialogue as a transformative encounter with a You who is emphatically not an object, and hence not an object of care. While encounter is inherently relational, its unpredictable, unknowable quality means love, caring or any other attribute can never be assumed as constitutive properties or outcomes. There emerges a clear distinction or even dichotomy between dialogue as a relationship of care and dialogue as a transformative, existential encounter.

This understanding of dialogue does not emerge strongly from my interviews, nor from the literature on critical pedagogy and Catholic social justice education. This is due, perhaps, to the potential incompatibility between a fundamentally open, non-directive approach to dialogue and the practices of ideologically motivated, politically focused educators and activists. One exception to this is community organising, which relies on dialogue and relationship-building as processes which lead to personal transformation and thereby to stronger communities and the possibility of collective political action. This model is potentially compatible with Buberian dialogue: it assumes dialogical relationships are partly a means to the end of action for the common good but also emphasises that the relationship-building process has to precede the emergence of any conception of that common good's actual content: 'people before programme' in the language of community organisers.[39]

There are, moreover, other thinkers who have conceptualised dialogue as existential encounter in ways which are more compatible with Jewish practitioners' approaches to social action. Levinas, as noted above, writes that dialogue creates an immediate, pre-conceptual ethical claim of infinite responsibility towards the other person; a sacred duty to do justice therefore flows from the encounter. In his book *The Star of Redemption*, the Jewish philosopher Franz Rosenzweig develops a similar position in a more explicitly theological way. Rosenzweig understands the encounter with God ('revelation' in his terms) as exposure to God's loving, commanding presence.[40] God's love is what gives the divine presence the power to command and to elicit a loving and therefore attentive, even obedient, response. If God can be met in human relationships, then Rosenzweig makes possible a genuinely open-ended, transformative dialogue which has the inherent ability to demand and elicit action.

Faith and Politics

The intersection of two further aspects of humanisation – participation in spiritual life and engagement in *praxis* – raises the question of the relationship between faith and politics. This relationship can be articulated in a number of ways: one proposes the preservation of faith and politics as two unrelated spheres, a second sees faith as a means to the end of politics (or sometimes vice versa), while a third conflates religious faith and political commitment to social justice.

While the idea that religious faith should be apolitical and restrict itself to spiritual and moral matters is commonplace in the UK Jewish community,[41] this approach is roundly rejected by most of the Christian and Jewish writers and interviewees I have surveyed. At the same time, certain Jewish interviewees sometimes imply that personal transformation – while intended to be a precondition for action – can also legitimately serve as a substitute for it; in other words, spiritual growth is important even when it does not lead to political change. The more conservative tendencies within Catholic social teaching also come close to this kind of perspective in their insistence that injustice is a matter of individual sin and is therefore to be remedied through moral and spiritual improvement rather than through politics. This is echoed on the level of strategy by those practitioners who adopt a faith-inspired model of direct service provision rather than politics or campaigning as a path to a more just society (e.g. volunteer-led educational interventions in deprived communities as a way of increasing social mobility for individual students).

This support for the separation of faith and politics resonates with the view described by Yeshayahu Leibowitz that religious norms apply only to individual behaviour and are to be realised within the given framework of the social and political reality in which we happen to find ourselves.[42] However, this position entails two inconsistencies. First, while the thinkers under discussion may adopt individualist, ostensibly apolitical social change strategies, they are usually motivated by an explicitly collectivist, social critique and vision. Faith-driven personal behaviour is not only a matter of private morality but a way of engendering social change; the boundary between this and politics is far from hermetic. The second inconsistency is particularly pronounced in a democratic setting. If it is legitimate for religious norms to govern an individual's behaviour towards a homeless person she encounters in the street, why should the same norms not apply to our collective treatment of the homeless, in other words, to government policy on homelessness, and why should individuals not take these norms into account when they vote or engage in other political activity? It follows that the line between the moral or religious and the political cannot be drawn clearly. Perhaps this ambiguity can be explained with reference to Hannah Arendt's claim that modernity is characterised by the development of the social arena and its displacement of the pre-modern public sphere. The separation of interpersonal morality and politics only makes sense in the context of a clear divide between the private and public realms. The emergence of the social, in which politics becomes preoccupied with debates about previously private economic concerns, goes some way towards unravelling the contradictions which accompany any modern attempt to separate religion and politics.

Several Jewish and Catholic thinkers reflect the view that faith and politics are connected instrumentally – one is a means, the other an end. Writers from both Catholic social teaching and liberation theology traditions, for example, raise the question of whether combatting poverty is a means to the end of eradicating sin and building a relationship with God, or whether a just society is the goal of faith. Most Catholic thinkers argue that faith and justice are both means and ends and this is echoed in the claim made by some liberation theologians that evangelisation and the struggle for social justice are inseparable or even identical. Several Jewish interviewees grapple with similar questions, asking whether it is appropriate to leverage people's Jewish commitments to impel them into social action or to use social action as a means to the end of Jewish education and identity.

The study of scripture is understood by many writers and interviewees not only as an important religious practice but also in instrumental terms as a key educational strategy for developing students' commitment to social justice. None of the thinkers surveyed make the simplistic assumption that the function of religious texts is to provide content (stories, values, norms) for assimilation by students as part of their journey towards political consciousness or social action. This would reflect a 'banking' approach to religious education for social justice. The Catholic writers surveyed here (as well as some Jewish interviewees) largely adopt a hermeneutical approach to Bible study, arguing that in order to play a role in the formation of social activists or in the conscientisation of the poor, texts must be read in the context of the students' pre-existing commitment to social justice or their experience of oppression – either as victims or as observers. This context foregrounds the emancipatory message of the Bible or, in another formulation, enables students to construct this kind of content as they engage in dialogue with the text. This kind of learning, carried out in a faith-based, group setting and accompanied by the experience of social action, enables students to develop social critique, the motivation to create change and a community of colleagues with whom to take action. As above, the purely instrumental role of scriptural study is tempered by the assumption that the values of social justice are intrinsic to the texts and the tradition in which they are read.

Most of the Jewish interviewees who discuss textual study assign it a different role in the development of learners as social change agents. A key motif for these practitioners is the pluralistic, dialectical nature of Jewish – primarily rabbinic – texts, which record all sides of the discussion and preserve minority as well as majority opinions. Engagement with this textual pluralism is put forward as a way of engendering pluralistic behaviours and attitudes among learners: open-mindedness, the capacity for critique and the ability to listen to others, particularly the exponents of minority or marginal views. In this context, the instrumental role of faith is more apparent: texts with no explicit justice content can be used as an educational resource for the inculcation of the character traits necessary for social action.

A final formulation of the means–end relationship between faith and politics comes from thinkers who argue that religion is a vital ingredient of civil society. Jonathan Sacks, for example, claims that faith communities are the antidote to contemporary society's loss of moral and spiritual direction.[43] Sacks bases his claim on the theories of Charles Darwin and Alexis de Tocqueville: 'If Darwin discovered that man is the community-creating animal, Tocqueville discovered that religion in America is the community-building institution. ... Religion creates community, community creates altruism, and altruism turns us away from self and toward the common good.' This perspective resonates with community organisers for whom religion not only acts as this kind of social or communal glue but also provides a resource bank of narratives that can be drawn upon to build 'mental landscape' – developing people's ability to imagine getting involved in effective social change.

The idea that faith and politics are intrinsically connected, that spirituality and social action are empty without each other, is articulated in different ways by the majority of thinkers in this study. Of particular interest here is the detail of the ways in which particular theologies explicitly articulate the argument for the conflation of faith and politics. Apophatic or negative theologies as expressed by both Christian and Jewish writers recognise that God cannot be grasped intellectually and therefore conceptualise faith as service to God, that is, action. In this context, politics driven by religious values can be seen as constitutive of faith. Dialogical theology, as articulated by thinkers such as Buber, Levinas and several Christian writers, suggests that God is to be encountered in dialogue with other human beings and sometimes implies that our interpersonal relationships actually constitute our relationship with God. Building just, inclusive communities where people are able to develop relationships and encounter each other in genuine dialogue is therefore both a religious and a political act. For Christians who are attuned to social exclusion and inequality, dialogical theology comes to be associated with ideas such as seeing the poor as sacraments and models of servant leadership, while for Jewish social justice practitioners it often finds expression in the imperative to welcome and support members of marginalised groups such as refugees.

An alternative way in which faith and politics are conflated stems from the work of Alasdair MacIntyre.[44] We have already encountered MacIntyre's neo-Aristotelian view that modernity threatens to render ethical decision-making entirely arbitrary and that the only antidote to this is to locate moral choices in the context of a teleological anthropology that emerges from a tradition. It is worth clarifying that the construction of or induction into a tradition is not a means to the end of the development of moral identity, much less an educational technique to be adopted in order to rationalise prior ethical positions. Rather, the content of the tradition actually constitutes and determines the meaning of the moral choices which take place within it. To translate this into terms of faith and politics: if political commitment is seen as a subset of moral identity, then the political actions of a person of faith – that is, someone embedded in a religious tradition – are determined and acquire meaning only by virtue of their relationship to that tradition. It could be argued similarly that the form and meaning of a politically committed person's religious actions are determined by the political tradition with which he or she identifies. In any case, for politically engaged people of faith, it emerges that religious and political commitments cannot be separated.

9

The Jewishness of Social Justice Pedagogies

Are there intrinsically Jewish pedagogical approaches to social justice education and, if so, what form might this Jewishness take? This question is of relevance not just to Jewish educators. In the spirit of Thomas Groome's assertion that the 'depth structures' of Catholic Christianity can contribute to a universal, spiritual, humanising education,[1] I hope Jewish pedagogies have the power to inspire and influence a broad array of approaches to social justice education. In order to address this issue, it is necessary to clarify what we mean by the term 'Jewish pedagogy'. While very few researchers have dealt explicitly with this question, scholarly discussions of other topics in Jewish education can be drawn upon for relevant insights. Among the relevant research, two main approaches are in evidence.

Aetiological Approaches – Jewishness by Origin

The first can be labelled as aetiological or 'Jewishness by origin' and assumes that pedagogies acquire Jewish status when they are derived from Jewish texts, culture or traditional practices. Isadore Twersky, for example, presents a vision of Jewish education by drawing on Maimonides' authoritative and systematic depiction of Jewish belief and practice and the pedagogy Maimonides designed to instil them.[2] This pedagogy is considered Jewish because it derives from a canonical, authoritative rabbinic source. Jonathan Cohen, in a variation on this move, focuses on a series of modern Jewish thinkers who deal with philosophical but not explicitly educational matters. He asks how these thinkers might deal with an educational issue (e.g. how to engender spirituality, how to translate and interpret texts) if it were presented to them, in other words, how it might be possible to derive a pedagogical approach from philosophical foundations.[3] This project is motivated by a desire to draw educational conclusions from Jewish philosophical texts and therefore arguably entails the idea that a pedagogy can be defined as Jewish by virtue of its derivation from broader Jewish thought.

This kind of historical or causal approach is not prominent among the practitioners interviewed here. It is, however, possible to discern elements of it in the view that a theory of human rights can be defined as Jewish thanks to its origin in the Torah and in the desire to engender a Jewish commitment to social and environmental justice by revealing to students that these values originate in Jewish texts. It is worth noting that ascribing Jewishness to a pedagogy on the basis of the literature from which it derives in a way begs the question of whether the literature itself is Jewish. While it might seem self-evident that canonical works such as the Talmud or Maimonides's *Mishneh Torah* fit the definition, there are modern thinkers and texts whose Jewish status is more controversial. Is the Jewishness of a piece of writing determined by the identity of its author, by being recognised as part of the canon by the Jewish community (and if so, which Jewish community) or by containing certain types of content?[4] At worst, this line of argument risks becoming circular, in that a pedagogy comes to be defined as Jewish by virtue of its grounding in texts whose Jewish status is also in question.

Teleological or Functional Jewishness

The second approach to the Jewish quality of pedagogy is functional or teleological: a pedagogy can be considered Jewish if its specific characteristics function so as to construct Jewish identity, life or practice. Lee Shulman, in one of the only pieces of research to deal directly with the question of what makes a pedagogy Jewish, builds a case from the perspective of vocational education.[5] He asks how a person learns to 'profess' – to act, for example, as a lawyer or a doctor. While pedagogies for vocational training vary by profession, they all share three features: public performance and visibility on the part of the student (e.g. clinical rounds), interdependence and collaboration between learners, and the need to deliberate and grapple with uncertainty in the pursuit of expertise. Based on these characteristics, Shulman suggests three signature pedagogies for Jewish studies (not vocational training, to be sure, but certainly an educational enterprise which aims to teach people how to 'profess'). The first is *dvar torah* – literally 'a word of Torah', used generally to describe a sermon or teaching moment in which the lessons of Jewish texts are applied hermeneutically to the real-life situation of the audience. This requires the student to build a dialogue between the tradition and contemporary concerns and to share the resulting insights performatively. The second signature pedagogy is *hevruta*, the practice of studying in pairs. *Hevruta* study is characterised by 'mutual and reciprocal coaching, scaffolding, challenge, and debate' but more importantly by the setting in which it takes place: not two students sitting over a page of Talmud but 'dozens of dyads filling a noisy *beit midrash* [study hall]' (p. 11). The third signature pedagogy is *mahloket* (debate or controversy), a value drawn from rabbinic literature which ensures learning processes enable grounded, rational disagreements and arguments, and challenge students with competing interpretations and analyses. For Shulman, a pedagogy based on *dvar torah*, *hevruta* and *mahloket* is a Jewish pedagogy because it develops the habits of mind, practice and heart that in his view construct a coherent and well-integrated Jewish identity.

Other researchers echo this type of functional or teleological argument. Elie Holzer argues that *hevruta* learning is a distinctive cultural practice that functions not only as a method of acquiring knowledge but also as a devotional activity which has a transformative impact on its practitioners in terms of religious practice, beliefs and values.[6] Twersky, cited above as a proponent of the aetiological approach, also advocates a teleological perspective: Maimonides's educational approach is Jewish not only because of the identity of its author and its place in the canon but because it is designed in accordance with certain theological principles and as a way of inducting students into a particular conception of observant Jewish life. Lehman and Kanarek believe that being Jewish in the modern world is defined by the tension between a commitment to the goals of liberal education and devotion to the continuity of a religious tradition. This translates naturally into an educational dilemma: how can our students become critical, active, democratic citizens but also loyal Jews when this involves learning to accept and question authority simultaneously?[7] Lehman and Kanarek concur with Holzer and Twersky that the texts of Jewish tradition exemplify different pedagogical approaches which attempt to answer this question. They argue that a pedagogy which derives from the Talmud (from explicit injunctions about education contained in the text and from the Talmud's broader, implicit approach to learning) embodies both the goals of liberal education – rationalism, critique, pluralism, making space for the reader's voice – and acceptance of traditional authority. Talmudic pedagogy is therefore not only Jewish because of its source but because it embodies or constitutes a relevant conception of what it means to be Jewish.

While the researchers surveyed above tacitly agree that a pedagogy can be defined as Jewish if its effects are to construct or develop Jewish practice, there is no consensus on the nature of this practice or, therefore, on the character of the pedagogy. This is illustrated by Inbar Galili-Schachter, who has identified five different 'pedagogic hermeneutic orientations' (PHOs) commonly adopted by teachers of Jewish thought.[8] She notes that each PHO reflects distinctive ideas about the status of the text, the practice of interpretation, and the role of teachers and students in the learning and interpretive process. It also emerges (although she does not make this point explicitly) that PHOs correspond with specific conceptions of Judaism, as reflected both in their approach to the text and in the kinds of student–teacher relationship they imply. This is illustrated by two examples from Galili-Schachter's research.

The first focuses on teachers who aim to convey moral educational ideas by creating *midrash* (creative, plural interpretations of Torah) and communicating these to receptive, largely passive, students. These teachers consider the text to contain infinite meanings from which ideas relevant to the reader's context can be drawn. This pedagogy implies and serves to construct a conception of Judaism which features a hierarchical relationship between a universally relevant, infinitely meaningful text and an interpreter of that text who is both authoritative and sensitive to her audience on the one hand, and a receptive reader who is expected to act in accordance with the prescriptions of the teacher-mediated text on the other. While this model gels with certain traditional conceptions of revelation and religious authority, it differs from a fundamentalist religiosity in which the text is considered to have one fixed meaning. In this midrashic model, the teacher (and possibly eventually the student, if she internalises and reproduces the methodology) is free to interpret the text and draw out diverse meanings in response to changing contexts.

The second example features teachers who seek to facilitate a dialogue between the students and the text. While the text remains as 'senior partner' in the dialogue, students are encouraged to develop their own worldviews by interpreting and arguing with the teacher, the other students and the text itself. For these teachers, meaning is created in the dialogue between reader and text, each of which has its own voice but where both are enriched or even transformed through the encounter. If in the previous example the content of Judaism was *contained* in the text, communicated to the students and then acted upon, here, Judaism is *created* in an ongoing dialogue among Jews and between Jews and their texts. This vision of Judaism, while according respect to the text, imparts less structure and promises individuals and communities far more autonomy in determining the norms and practices of Jewish life.

* * *

What emerges when we apply the foregoing understandings of Jewish pedagogy to the enterprise of social justice education? Three possible understandings of specifically Jewish social justice pedagogy present themselves: political-Jewish education, Jewish social justice education as *Torah lishmah* and emancipatory cultural education.

Political-Jewish Education

The first possibility is to understand Jewish social justice pedagogy as a form of education that frames Jewish history, texts, practices and values in explicitly political terms and presents political ideas and behaviours (liberalism, socialism, democracy, for example) as inherently Jewish. This requires a hermeneutical pedagogy whose goal is to read political and Jewish narratives in light of each other and to create dialogue between the two. It also echoes Shulman's signature pedagogy of *dvar torah*: the practice of bringing Jewish texts to bear on contemporary concerns (and vice versa) and learning how to communicate these connections.

Clearly, the political and religious impact of the educational process will be shaped by the texts selected and the specific interpretations which are thrown up by the hermeneutical dialogue between them. Among the interviewees, for example, Joe's attempts to find synergies between Jewish culture and left-wing politics have led him away from an essentialist conception of Judaism as a textual tradition which supports progressive ideas to an attempt to find radical potential in historical Jewish political movements such as Diaspora nationalism, Yiddishism and the Bund. He also seeks out and makes a point of exposing people to the intersection of marginalised voices from the tradition and contemporary Jewish culture (akin to Walter Benjamin's notion of 'brushing history against the grain'). Joe is aware that conservative and reactionary narratives exist within – and perhaps dominate – Judaism; his educational practice is predicated on the need to flush out the tradition's radical potential by viewing it through the lens of progressive politics; that is, reading Judaism through a socialist or anarchist prism. Another interviewee, Manny, provides an example of this dynamic in reverse. While he echoes Joe's attempt to construct a politics which is inspired by historical Jewish movements (he appeals to the Bund and the community organising of Saul Alinsky but also to more conservative forces such as nineteenth-century neo-Orthodoxy), he is concerned not only to read Judaism through the lens of radical politics but to use Jewish culture to interrogate and reform contemporary socialism; he describes the left-wing, communitarian movement 'Blue Labour', for example, as originating in models derived from the Bible and the heritage of Diaspora Judaism.

Alongside this dialogue between Jewish and political narratives that operates on the level of subject matter or the formal curriculum, Galili-Schachter's notion of PHOs points to the importance of the relationship and power-balance between student and teacher. In addition to their theological significance, PHOs also have political import in that they imply different conceptions of authority, democracy, autonomy, pluralism and so on. The relationship between student and teacher and the role of each party in the learning process has the potential to act as a hidden curriculum which inducts students not only into a particular set of religious ideas and practices but also, as pointed out by Freire, into a specific and ideologically loaded mode of politics. For instance, a pedagogy such as Shulman's, structured around *dvar torah*, *hevruta* and *mahloket*, reflects the political values of pluralism, personal autonomy and relational community life. The approach of Schachter-Galili's *midrash*-orientated educators, inasmuch as it seeks to habituate students to accepting the textual interpretations of an authoritative teacher, communicates a more hierarchical mode of politics.

Many practitioners place pluralism and difference at the centre of their religious or cultural, political and educational Jewish practice, and therefore advocate for pedagogies (exposure to ideological diversity, developing textual sensitivity, a facilitative rather than a directive role for educators) which reflect these values. This implies an attempt to construct a consistently liberal or multiculturalist conception of Jewish religion and politics. However, it should be noted that this position is far from universal and does not adequately reflect the ideological positions articulated in the interviews. Many of the practitioners express different understandings of Judaism and more radical political views and, in general, are far from consistent in their thinking. Community organiser Calley's pedagogy, for example, combines several disparate elements: (1) a conception of Judaism as a source of inspiring, emancipatory narratives; (2) a directive teaching style (storytelling as a way of creating 'mental landscape' or what might be termed 'political agency'); and (3) an emphasis on unmediated relationship-building and listening across social and cultural divides. Elements (1) and (2) evoke the midrashic PHO with the religious and political implications alluded to above, whereas element (3) resonates with the democratic and pluralistic approaches of *hevruta* and *mahloket*-based pedagogy. It is notable that Calley, unlike other educators who encourage their students to bring these critical, dialogical processes to bear on Jewish texts, does not seek explicitly to relate these aspects: the midrashic moment which connects learners to Torah and Jewish tradition is separate from the more critical, dialogical phase of relationship-building and listening.

Orthodox rabbi Shalom, conversely, adopts a pluralist, non-fundamentalist conception of Judaism as reflected in the form and structure of rabbinic literature, and advocates a twofold educational process. First, he aims to sensitise students to diverse voices (particularly those of the poor or marginalised) through textual study and then encourages them to apply this sensitivity to contemporary social problems. This reflects a functional/teleological understanding of Jewish education: inducting students into a particular conception of Jewish practice. Second, in a move which is both more directive and reflects a conception of 'Jewishness by origin', he encourages students to apply the content of prophetic and halakhic texts to contemporary justice issues. This implies using social analysis and politics as a framework through which to interpret the text (or at least to highlight those aspects of the tradition which speak to social and environmental problems), and applying norms derived from the text to these social and political problems. It is worth noting that there seems to be a discrepancy between Shalom's open, almost deconstructive approach to the text (with the attendant liberal religious and political implications) and his assumption that a hermeneutical pedagogy will inevitably lead to conclusions which conform with particular political and religious positions.

Jewish Social Justice Education as *Torah lishmah*

In its most extreme form, a thoroughgoing political-Jewish education would seek to conform to the model of *Torah lishmah* – Jewish learning conducted for its own sake, not as a means to an end or in pursuit of an external reward. This suggests an approach which refrains from connecting education and social justice in a means–ends relationship but rather seeks to align the internal goods of Jewish education and social action or, in other words, to develop a pedagogy which is constitutive of a Jewish conception of justice. However, in practice this is very difficult. Practitioners seeking to create a relationship between Jewish education and social justice generally face a dilemma. Either they accept the instrumentalisation of Jewish learning by putting it in the service of an extrinsic social or political aim, thereby foregoing the *lishmah* principle, recasting Jewish social justice education as *poiesis* rather than *praxis*, and possibly endangering its humanising potential. Alternatively, they remain committed to the ideal of Torah *lishmah* and relinquish the hope of employing Jewish education in the pursuit of social justice. The contradiction between education as *praxis* and education for social justice is not merely semantic. MacIntyre states that a practice is a

> coherent and complex form of socially established cooperative human activity through which goods internal to that form of activity are realised in the course of trying to achieve those standards of excellence which are appropriate to, and partially definitive of, that form of activity, with the result that human powers to achieve excellence, and human conceptions of the ends and goods involved, are systematically extended.[9]

Since a practice is an activity aimed at realising internal goods, and assuming Jewish education to be such a practice,[10] there is a real danger that the internal goods of Jewish education will be incompatible with the internal goods of the social justice practices in whose service it is ostensibly employed. This risk is exemplified by the potential slippage between education and indoctrination in the service of progressive, political goals.[11] It is also highlighted by Freire who points to the risks associated with 'naïve' educators who attempt to use dehumanising, banking educational methods in the pursuit of social justice.

It might be possible to resolve this conundrum based on a closer analysis of the term *lishmah* – 'for its own sake' – in which the referent of the possessive pronoun 'its' is undefined. Norman Lamm claims that Jewish tradition contains three definitions of *Torah lishmah*.[12] The first is a functional definition which understands the term as 'for the sake of the commandment'; here, *lishmah* study is taken to mean learning which leads to practical observance and is motivated by the desire to perform the commandments. The second, devotional, definition interprets *lishmah* as 'for the sake of love' and refers to those who are motivated to study by their love of God, their desire to serve God or by the goal of attaining a mystical experience of the divine. Finally, the cognitive definition understands *lishmah* as 'for the sake of Torah'; here the goal of study is the intellectual experience or the act of study itself.

Of Lamm's three definitions, the functional and the devotional understand an activity to be *lishmah* if its motivations are acceptable in terms of Jewish practice as a whole; they are intrinsic to Judaism even if not to the act of learning. Study achieves goods which are internal to Torah (religious observance or experience) but potentially external to the practice of study. This matches MacIntyre's understanding of teaching as a way of inducting people into practices rather than as a practice in its own right, and also gels with his idea that practices acquire meaning only when they are contextualised within a tradition. In this context, education can be defined as the induction of people into practices embedded within a tradition, without compromising the praxical or *lishmah* character of the overall enterprise. If so, perhaps Jewish social justice education can be appreciated not as a practice with its own internal goods which stand to be corrupted when harnessed to an outside goal but rather as a method for inducting people into a broader tradition of justice-orientated Judaism and its associated political and philanthropic practices.

However, if we rely on Lamm's third, cognitive, definition and on Dunne's insistence that education is a practice in MacIntyre's sense, then *Torah lishmah* cannot be a means to any end outside of the act of study itself, since the internal goods of Jewish education might clash with those of the practice it is intended to advance. If so, the role of education in social change needs to be conceptualised in a different way. Jewish education must be understood not as leading to but as in some way constitutive of social justice; this requires that the internal goods of Jewish education and social justice coincide. The point is illustrated by various interviewees whose conceptions of educational and political pluralism reflect each other; the educational practice forms a microcosm of the social practice which informs it. Similarly, outside the Jewish world, Freire sees a particular kind of learning as embodying the political and social ideal of humanisation. This explains his attack on naïve educators who pursue justice through anti-dialogical pedagogies: it is impossible to achieve humanisation by dehumanising people.

Emancipatory Cultural Education

A final approach to Jewish social justice pedagogy emerges from the idea that cultural education has emancipatory potential for minority ethnic, diasporic communities. While Diaspora Jews usually have high levels of literacy in their local languages and cultures, they tend to be relatively illiterate in Hebrew, the Jewish textual and literary traditions, and other Jewish languages.[13] Freire has pointed out the oppressive nature of this kind of cultural submergence for indigenous populations in colonial and postcolonial societies, both in terms of its role in broader processes of political and economic discrimination, and due to its dehumanising impact in terms of the identity and self-esteem of its objects. Ahad Ha'am and other nationalist-Jewish thinkers of the late nineteenth and early twentieth centuries made similar comments about the disintegration of Jewish culture and identity under the impact of industrialisation, the rise of European nationalism and the growth of antisemitism.[14]

It is possible to conceptualise a Freirean approach to Jewish literacy education which aims to create a qualitatively Jewish form of political agency by enabling students to 'read the world' while learning to 'read the word' – where reading the word is taken to mean fluency in Hebrew and other Jewish languages and an ability to read and engage in dialogue with the Bible, rabbinics and other texts of the tradition. This kind of pedagogy would involve a programme of language acquisition, informed by Freirean principles. This means avoiding the use of primers which fail to connect language to students' real-world concerns, and instead emphasising the acceleration of learners' ability to engage in dialogue and describe and critique the world around them from the outset. It would then draw on this linguistic foundation to provide students with the skills needed to read Jewish texts (given the dominant place of Hebrew in the tradition and in the contemporary Jewish world, an argument can be made that this should be the language of choice; however, other Jewish languages such as Yiddish, Ladino or Judeo-Arabic with which students feel an affinity could also address the issue of cultural alienation and help them develop a sense of rootedness in the tradition). The talmudic pedagogy proposed by Lehman and Kanarek and in a different form by Aryeh Cohen[15] is a relevant resource here, inasmuch as it seeks to construct meaningful forms of Jewish life, practice and moral identity by teaching students to read Jewish texts in all their particularity. Finally, a Jewish pedagogy of cultural emancipation would involve the study of Jewish history, understood as a resource for combatting the internalised oppression often experienced by members of minority and marginalised groups, and for the development of self-respect, positive Jewish identity and humanisation.

10

Normative Theories of Jewish Social Justice Education

In this final chapter I will attempt to cut through the various philosophical, political and educational questions I have raised in order to propose three coherent suggestions as to what a theory of Jewish social justice education might look like. While the various models of Jewish social justice pedagogy presented in the last chapter focused on questions of curriculum, teaching and learning, the theories outlined below are broader in scope, taking in theological, philosophical and political elements alongside more narrowly defined educational themes. I have entitled these theories 'Jewish politics in a renewed public sphere', 'Jewish education for relational community building' and 'Jewish critical pedagogy for cultural liberation'. These are only three examples of the infinite possibilities thrown up by this research. While I believe that having a coherent normative theory is an important foundation for educational practice, I do not mean to imply that Jewish social justice educators need to choose one of the theories I outline here. Rather, my suggestions are intended to stimulate and enable other thinkers and educators to engage in their own processes of theory formation. Since my goal is to think through the issues raised in the book (and not to offer up a simple menu of options), I have tried to construct three theories which overlap or resemble each other as little as possible, in order to give a maximally diverse illustration of possible approaches to Jewish social justice education.

Jewish Politics in a Renewed Public Sphere

'Jewish politics in a renewed public sphere' rests on liberal, radical-democratic and individualistic foundations, and echoes Jewish traditions of autonomous community life and a culture of *mahloket* – difference and debate. Its diagnosis centres on a form of dehumanisation, understood as people being deprived of the capacity for social critique and political agency and, in particular, the exclusion of marginalised groups from public discourse. This dehumanisation of individuals corresponds with a degradation of the democratic public sphere, manifested in terms of extreme partisanship and lack of complexity in public debate, political discourse dominated by images rather than words, a culture of ubiquitous lying and 'fake news' where truth and evidence cease to be criteria of legitimate discourse, and a manipulative populism. These processes lead to the emergence of harmful policy solutions which do not answer the social problems they purport to address and which fail to serve the common good.

Dehumanisation and the degradation of the public sphere are underpinned by three interlinked phenomena. First: Arendt's notion of the subordination of the political to the social and the displacement of genuine public life and agency by a technocratic, bureaucratic culture that focuses on means not ends. Second: society's failure to sustain a common culture and set of values, which makes rational discussion based on shared assumptions impossible and leads to the replacement of deliberation with relativism and the self-interested exercise of power. This cultural malaise has been reflected in the UK in the form of demands for educational institutions to inculcate 'British values' and the difficulties experienced by educators in articulating what these values are, beyond universalist, liberal–democratic principles. Within Judaism it manifests itself in a different form, as a process of ossification or a radical detachment of Jewish discourse, ideas and practices from contemporary issues that touch people's lives and the resulting inability of the tradition to serve as the ground for public or communal deliberation. Examples of this include the prevalence of unsophisticated or primitive theological ideas and an excessive focus on legalistic or ritual components of the tradition which render religion irrelevant to – and ideologically incompatible with – wide sections of the community. Third: the strengthening of various kinds of chauvinism, that is, an insular attachment to one culture or the interests of a narrow social group, conceptualised in opposition to what is perceived as an empty or alienating multiculturalism or egalitarianism, advanced by a bureaucratic elite.

Educators and the education system as a whole are to be held partly responsible for failing to equip students with the capacity for social and political critique or to construct a common culture of shared values which would strengthen their ability to discuss ends as well as means, engage in rational deliberation and develop a sense of agency. At the same time, this perspective acknowledges the relative weakness of educational institutions in the face of broader cultural shifts, political populism, mass media and, more recently, social media, and acknowledges that while educational reform can support social change, its power to effect political transformation is limited.

The envisioned antidote to this critique is a healthy democratic public sphere, characterised as rational, deliberative, critical and pluralistic. Politics and public debate are to be grounded in a common culture and a set of values which, vitally, must also be amenable to difference and open to critique and negotiation, thereby facilitating the participation of individuals with diverse cultures and identities. This democratic public sphere rests on a foundation of vibrant, grassroots civil society organisations including membership organisations, faith institutions, community groups, charities and NGOs, which serve as a framework for individual human flourishing. This is the context for humanisation and *praxis*, understood in terms of four ingredients: people feeling at home in their culture, having a developed sense of agency (involving reflectiveness, criticality, subjectivity and empowerment), being politically and culturally literate, and being able and willing to communicate and deliberate across difference. This kind of democratic public sphere inevitably shapes the outcome of politics, strengthening a community-based civil society which has the power to hold the State and the market to account and thereby encouraging the development of policies based on a shared conception of the common good – while continuing to recognise and value the diversity of political beliefs in an open society.

In this setting, Jewish communities and organisations function as components of a healthy civil society, while the specific character of Jewish culture and education enables these institutions to perform a particularly valuable role. Judaism provides the Jewish community – and thereby the wider society to which it contributes – with a dialogical, pluralistic cultural and theological foundation that promotes agency by enabling cultural critique (facilitated through hermeneutical dialogue between the Jewish and secular cultures which Jews in Western society simultaneously inhabit), engendering pluralism and debate, and centring discourse around issues of values and justice.

Accordingly, the core strategy associated with this model is the building up of civil society institutions – an array of dialogical spaces for learning, discussion, debate, policy formulation and political action – as the basis for a democratic public sphere, using the tools of community organising. This includes Jewish community organisations (schools, youth movements, synagogues, community centres, charities and political organisations) that meet two criteria: they must accommodate and explicitly encourage the religious and political diversity of their students, and incorporate interfaith or inter-community learning and dialogue, that is, meetings with groups of learners from different faith and cultural backgrounds.

In this context, the function of education is to engender individual and group agency by enabling people to deliberate about and debate issues of common concern and mobilising people, where possible, around a shared agenda which is arrived at through a process of collective learning. This learning process is inherently dialogical, where dialogue is understood as rational discourse leading to the intellectual development of agents and the ability to communicate across difference (critical as opposed to inclusive dialogue in Burbules's terms). The pedagogical processes employed are largely open and cognitive, enabling learners to reach their own, diverse conclusions by grappling intellectually with the issues under discussion. Affect, if employed, is only a basis for cognitive learning, for example, using experiences and encounters with others as subject matter for reflection and analysis rather than as direct catalysts for attitudinal change. This approach is broadly compatible with the methods proposed by Freire and Shor but puts particular emphasis on challenging learners' pre-existing positions, a genuine commitment to pluralism and recognising difference, and taking care to avoid convergent or manipulative approaches.

This kind of open, critical, intellectual dialogue dovetails with what might be termed a Jewish political education: a process of hermeneutical dialogue between learners, Jewish texts and contemporary issues as a way of generating critique and action. In Freirean terms, Judaism can be seen as a source of generative or topical themes which provide a framework for the interrogation of social, political and cultural reality. However, this takes place in the context of a hermeneutical circle in which extra-textual reality and values commitments also shape the meaning of Judaism and facilitate a critical approach to the tradition. This reveals the importance of the signature pedagogies of *dvar torah* and *mahloket* and implies a dialogical pedagogical hermeneutical orientation in which students, teachers and texts are all equally epistemologically authoritative and in which meaning, rather than residing in the text, is understood to be constructed in the process of dialogue. The construction of meaning is linked to the generation of critique and agency and, as such, is more important than attempting to understand the details of the text itself (the *peshat* or plain meaning in rabbinic parlance).

Jewish politics in a renewed public sphere is marked by a characteristically liberal neglect of power analysis. While this approach recognises marginalisation and inequality, it tends to see society as a collection of individuals operating on a reasonably or potentially level playing field rather than in terms of privileged and oppressed groups. As such, it emphasises pluralism and enabling communication across multiple categories of difference and makes little distinction between agents and beneficiaries of social change. The aspiration is to develop everyone as agents in a renewed democratic public sphere. Accordingly, educational leaders in this model can be drawn from any social group, on condition they have the cultural capital, knowledge and skills to engender learning, critique and dialogue.

Jewish Education for Relational Community Building

'Jewish education for relational community building' rejects the individualism of the previous model, adopting instead a collectivist anthropology which claims that human beings are innately social, inherently interconnected and fundamentally incomplete in the absence of community and relationships. This model's diagnosis focuses on the inappropriate penetration of *poiesis* into the domain of *praxis,* understood as the tendency to see society as a collection of objects to be used or acted upon in the manner of making or production, rather than a network of subjects or ends in themselves with whom to develop interactive, mutual, ethical relationships. One important manifestation of this tendency is the dominance of what MacIntyre calls external rather than internal conceptions of the good, a flawed view of the world which leads inevitably to a totalising instrumentalisation. The most visible example of this is commodification or monetisation, the compulsion to pursue profit, to measure success and meaning in terms of financial outcome, and to see any other outcome of human endeavour as a means to this end. Monetisation is particularly revealing of the way instrumentalisation tends to invert healthy priorities: the proper function of money is to measure value, as such it has no inherent value of its own and should only ever serve as a vehicle, not a goal. A *poiesis*-dominated, instrumentalised culture, therefore, undermines any possibility of genuine meaning and value.

This kind of instrumentalisation is also enacted in relation to human beings, giving rise to a form of dehumanisation in which people become objectified, commodified and reduced to their use value; this kind of 'economic man' can never be fully human. This leads to the breakdown of relationships and social bonds (since a relationship between subjects is fatally undermined by the orientation of either partner towards the other purely as an object), exploitation, alienation, mechanisation and oppression. In modern society, we have lost sight of the divine image in other people – that is, their ultimate, infinite, intrinsic value – and are therefore unable genuinely to care for them, love them, relate to them with respect or treat them justly. The tendency to see people as objects through the prism of our narrow subjectivity, combined with the absence of a universal orientation towards others as inherently human, underpins the phenomena of exclusion and discrimination towards minority or other marginalised groups, whose difference renders them unworthy of care and respect as subjects.

These phenomena have concrete outcomes in both the private and the public arenas. In the private sphere they include domestic abuse, sexual harassment, the inability to sustain relationships, loneliness, poor mental health and the absence of meaning and purpose in the lives of individuals. In the public sphere they encompass the breakdown of community and civil society and, more broadly, social injustice: inequality, poverty, discrimination and human rights abuses. They also involve specifically educational issues, in particular the ascendancy of instrumentalised, technical, individualistic pedagogies, which seek to mould students purely in line with the demands of the labour market, are preoccupied with attainment and testing, and focus exclusively on the promotion of economically relevant skills. Conversely, an instrumentalised society tends to devalue the arts and humanities as lacking economic utility – or distorts them into commodified, monetisable forms, thereby destroying them as potential sources of meaning and counterweights to the dominant, dehumanising social trends. This underpins and accelerates the neglect and destruction of religion, tradition and culture, including Judaism.

The antidote to this malaise is a reassertion of Aristotelian *praxis* and a commitment to the Jewish value of *lishmah* – 'for its own sake'. This implies a widescale reaffirmation of internal conceptions of the good and a commitment to practices that seek to realise internal goods and strive to align or conflate means or processes with outcomes wherever possible. It also requires us to see in all people – including ourselves – a reflection of the divine image or, in less religious language, to recognise the infinite value of every human being. This principle inevitably strengthens both our sense of agency and the imperative to treat others ethically. It is rooted in a theology of dialogue or renewal that sees spiritual growth and moral action as two sides of the same coin and, drawing on a collectivist anthropology, understands that ethical relationships actually constitute our humanity.

These principles are associated with a social vision: a bottom-up, egalitarian commonwealth of dialogical communities, in which individuals and communities themselves take on caring responsibility for each other. This web of caring, communal relationships itself constitutes the good society, replaces the top-down, hierarchical state and severely reduces the place and importance of the market. It also provides for an ethos of universal inclusion on the basis of caring that transcends difference and cross-cultural failures of communication or understanding. Work is understood not as a competitive means to the end of profit but as a collaborative or collective venture in pursuit of internal goods and human thriving. This also implies a return to an education which emphasises personal growth, relationships and caring as ends in themselves, grounded in a cultural context which stimulates these values but which does not necessarily have any other utilitarian value.

The strategy associated with this model unifies processes of relationship-building, learning and personal growth, and social change. It centres on using the tools of community organising to build up relational, dialogical, grassroots communities within interlinked neighbourhoods and institutions (including faith, membership and educational organisations). This process facilitates, and is accelerated by, communities taking social action in the form of direct service provision and service learning, allowing individuals to learn and develop while forming caring relationships across difference and making a tangible contribution to the welfare of others. This model steers away from political action as a means of driving structural social change. Instead, it centres on spiritual or moral transformation as the foundation for a healthy society, to be built gradually through caring relationships and ethical personal conduct.

The core educational method employed by this model centres on experiential, relationship-based service learning that engenders affect-driven attitudinal and behavioural change. As people and situations are seen as fundamentally unique and individual, it makes sense to reject formulaic or principle-driven educational approaches and to rely instead on *phronesis*, the incremental development of character through experience, reflection and dialogue. Where this dialogue takes a cognitive form, it tends towards the inclusive and divergent, encouraging learners to share and reflect on their experiences as the foundation for personal growth and transformation. However, the dominant form of dialogue in this paradigm is one of caring and existential encounter. This enables participants to engage with others and establish caring relationships even where communication and understanding are difficult – for example, across differences of class and culture. This learning process is underpinned by two key Jewish pedagogies: <u>h</u>evruta (the development of dialogical relationships through learning in study-pairs) and a *lishmah* ('for its own sake') conception of induction into justice-orientated

Judaism. In this approach, the function of Jewish education is to embody a relational, caring, dialogical society and to socialise students into it. The role of Torah in this context is to enable *phronesis*: adopting a combination of midrashic and dialogical pedagogical hermeneutical orientations, teachers are able to interpret Jewish texts in a way that focuses on social justice issues and present them to students as a focus for inclusive dialogue that enables them to reflect on their experiences of an unjust world and on issues of relationships, caring and community.

This approach resembles the universalism of 'Jewish politics in a renewed public sphere' in that it seeks to bring people together, enable dialogue across difference and to develop the caring virtues among poor people and within poor communities as much as among privileged ones. However, this model features a stronger element of class or power analysis, an understanding of privilege and oppression, and therefore a distinction between agents and beneficiaries of social change. While this form of Jewish social justice education seeks to nurture the caring, relational virtues on a universal basis, it tends implicitly in the direction of privileged educational leaders working to develop agents from within their own communities who are then able to extend caring to poor and marginalised groups and individuals.

Jewish Critical Pedagogy for Cultural Emancipation

Just as the biblical prophets demand justice for the poor, this model starts out from the insight that society is characterised by political and economic oppression or a state of conflict between oppressors and the oppressed: those who have economic, cultural and political power and resources and those who do not. This is primarily a class-based critique, shot through with an intersectional appreciation of the importance of gender, race, culture, disability, sexual orientation and other characteristics as loci of oppression in their own right. 'Hard' political and economic oppression is underpinned by 'softer' cultural privilege and marginalisation in which oppressed groups are stripped of their own cultures, forced to perceive reality through the ideological lens of the oppressors, and thereby prevented from achieving critical literacy, agency and humanisation.

Jews are subject to this process in common with other marginalised groups. Despite the privilege enjoyed by many Jews in Western societies by virtue of their class, gender or skin colour, Jews as a group suffer from oppression in three forms: first, antisemitic discrimination, violence and marginalisation; second, internalised oppression (including conscious or unconscious negative valuations of Jewish identity and culture, psychological effects such as low self-esteem and, in extreme cases, self-hatred); third, alienation from and illiteracy within their own heritage and culture, stemming from the cultural currency enjoyed by pejorative notions of Judaism (among other religious and minority cultures) and also from concrete phenomena such as failings in the Jewish education system. This oppression also tends to isolate Jews psychologically – creating a siege mentality, for example – and discourages them from correctly analysing their predicament as one instance of broader oppressive dynamics, rather understanding it as sui generis. Consequently, they are deterred from forming alliances with other oppressed groups on the basis of shared self-interest. At the same time, it also prevents them from drawing on their own tradition as a cultural resource for combatting oppression.

This model envisions a clear alternative: an egalitarian, democratic society where power and resources are shared equitably and all are able to participate in political, economic, cultural life, free from discrimination. In this scenario, all individuals and communities would be literate in their own languages and cultures, able to 'read the word and the world', and have the capacity to communicate across linguistic and cultural differences. This kind of cultural literacy is an antidote to alienation and the marginalisation that underpins oppression. It is an act of resistance to being stripped (however subtly) of one's own culture and identity at the hands of a dominant majority. It also represents the expression of a non-utilitarian internal good and, as such, can be seen as a form of humanising Aristotelian *praxis* or *Torah lishmah*. Literacy also enables humanisation in the Freirean sense of conscientisation: the development of subjectivity, critique, agency and solidarity. As well as being inherently liberating, critical cultural literacy also enables organisation and mobilisation in the pursuit of emancipatory structural change or social reform.

For Jews, cultural literacy means being immersed and literate in Jewish culture and tradition. This requires rigorous knowledge of Jewish history, languages and literature and an ability to interpret contemporary society and Jewish culture hermeneutically in light of each other so as to generate critique and conscientisation. This hermeneutical process combined with the inherently pluralistic nature of rabbinic texts encourages literate Jews to arrive at complex understandings of oppression and liberation, recognising for instance that individuals can simultaneously occupy oppressor and oppressed positions, refusing one-sided narratives that privilege other forms of oppression over antisemitism or vice versa, and finding ways to connect with the experiences of other marginalised groups and develop solidarity with them. For example, this kind of position could involve maintaining a liberal Zionist viewpoint which celebrates and affirms Jewish national self-determination in Israel while acknowledging the oppressive role of the Israeli state in relation to Palestinians and simultaneously building alliances with local Muslim groups to fight antisemitism and Islamophobia.

The two approaches outlined previously see community either as a forum for critique and action (where the result of the action, that is, social change, is less important than the fact of acquiring political agency) or as a manifestation of religious and moral values of relationship and caring. The strategy adopted by 'Jewish critical pedagogy for cultural emancipation', in contrast, is to create an egalitarian, humanised society through *praxis*, a dialectical process of politics and education, where the role of education is conscientisation: the development of critique, agency and solidarity. Community organising is seen as a way of building groups for praxical or dialogical political mobilisation in the pursuit of structural change and as settings for emancipatory learning. In a Jewish context this means mobilising people and doing educational work within faith or communal institutions and then using these organisations as a foundation for coalition building and political campaigning.

The educational pole of this dialectic requires a particular form of dialogue: rational discourse in line with Burbules's model of inclusive-convergent inquiry combined with a form of tactical deliberation, where the goal is to enable learners to reach shared conclusions as a basis for collective, radical action. However, this rational discourse must also have an affective component as it implies a commitment to bell hooks' concept of 'speaking out' (since hearing others' voices is crucial to the inclusive nature of the dialogue) as an ingredient of personal and collective psychological liberation. Similarly, in order to be truly emancipatory, rational discourse must enable people to draw on their experiences as members of marginalised groups as a foundation for developing political critique and agency. Sharing and articulating experiences and feelings is clearly rooted in affect, even as it provides ingredients for the primary process of rational deliberation.

This version of dialogue is reinforced by a particular approach to Jewish education. The aim here is to embed learners in Jewish culture as a path to humanisation and conscientisation by conceptualising Jewish learning as *Torah lishmah* – a practice which has intrinsic value – and by employing hermeneutical pedagogies such as *dvar torah* as a way of creating connections between their worldviews and the contents of Jewish tradition, thereby making Judaism more relevant to students' personal and political concerns. This approach is complemented by a midrashic pedagogical hermeneutical orientation which presents to students interpretations of Judaism which highlight the tradition's radical potential, thereby simultaneously creating relevance for learners who have a pre-existing progressive political agenda, and influencing others in the direction of radical politics.

This differs from the previous two models in several important ways. As in the first approach ('Jewish politics in a renewed public sphere'), Jewish texts function as a source of generative or topical themes which enable social and political critique. However, educators in that mode use these themes as triggers for genuinely open, critical dialogue which assumes a dialogical pedagogic hermeneutic orientation and the deployment of *maḥloket*-based pedagogies. Jewish critical pedagogues, conversely, will tend to present texts midrashically (interpreting them so as to catalyse progressive social and political critique) and aim to engender inclusive-convergent dialogue so as to arrive at shared positions as a basis for collective action.

This is, superficially, more similar to 'Jewish education for relational community building' but also differs from that approach in two important respects. First, that model assumed an incremental model of social change in which just communities are built from the ground up by strengthening relationships and improving the way individuals and communities see and treat each other. Its educational approach was therefore to nurture the virtues of caring and relationship-building within individuals and communities. Jewish critical pedagogy, in contrast, believes in the necessity of structural transformation and seeks to develop people and organisations as radical, political change agents. Second, Jewish critical pedagogy as a model of auto-emancipatory cultural education puts a premium on nurturing textual and cultural literacy as an emancipatory end in itself. This requires an emphasis (which does not exist in the previous models) on rigorous linguistic, historical and literary studies and an aversion to using decontextualised snippets of Jewish sources. This model clearly differs, then, from Jewish education for relational community building in terms of curriculum or subject matter: it will tend to select texts and interpret them in such a way as to induct students more thoroughly into the canon and to direct them towards explicitly structural, political critique and action. However, upon reflection it becomes clear that Jewish critical pedagogy also demands a distinctive methodology, one based on a pedagogic hermeneutic orientation which is somewhat different from the midrashic standpoint. While Jewish critical pedagogy still gives the teacher the broadly midrashic role of selecting and presenting texts on the basis of an explicit, ideologically informed, interpretive perspective, its insistence on rigorous, close reading implies a commitment to understanding the original meaning of any given source (i.e. the meaning as understood by the author or original audience – *peshat* rather than *derash* in rabbinic terminology) and to facilitating critical dialogue between students and teacher in pursuit of this meaning.

Jewish critical pedagogy assumes that humanisation can only be achieved by means of auto-emancipation on the part of the oppressed. This means the priority is to carry out educational and organising work with groups whose identity and social position include elements of marginalisation (including groups such as white, middle-class Jews in the UK who are privileged in relation to some aspects of their identity and simultaneously experience forms of oppression). This work also extends to potential allies, some of whom are likely to be subject to similar forms of oppression. In the case of UK Jews, for example, potential natural allies might include British Muslims or members of other religious and ethnic minorities who experience similar forms of marginalisation. The educational and political leaders suited to carry out this work are people who emerge from the oppressed communities in question, who are embedded in the same cultural milieu, and who have the insight and skills required to nurture cultural learning, critical dialogue and conscientisation.

Normative Theories: Summary

See table below.

		JEWISH POLITICS IN A RENEWED PUBLIC SPHERE	JEWISH EDUCATION FOR RELATIONAL COMMUNITY BUILDING	JEWISH CRITICAL PEDAGOGY FOR CULTURAL EMANCIPATION
Critique	Anthropology	Human beings are individual, rational agents	Human beings are fundamentally embedded in and constituted by their relationships	Human beings are defined by social position – oppressor and oppressed identities
	Form of de-humanisation	The subordination of the 'political' to the 'social' renders people unable to engage in social critique and deprived of political agency	Instrumentalisation and objectification – people are seen as means and not ends	Oppressed people are stripped of their culture and forced to see the world through the ideological lens of the oppressors, denying them agency and critical literacy
	Nature of oppression	The exclusion of marginalised groups from public discourse due to failure to communicate across difference	Breakdown of relationships, not seeing in others the image of God, failure to care for and treat others as human subjects	Political and economic oppression – the denial of power and resources – underpinned by cultural marginalisation
	Social/political critique	Degradation of the democratic public sphere (e.g. 'fake news' and populism) leads to anti-democratic policies that fail to pursue the common good A failure to sustain common values means rational deliberation is replaced by chauvinism and power politics	Modernity is characterised by instrumentalisation, inversion of priorities and the undermining of meaning to the detriment of all Social injustice and the breakdown of relationships: inequality, poverty, discrimination, human rights abuses; domestic abuse, sexual harassment, loneliness, poor mental health	Manipulative populism and the inversion of priorities are in the interest of the oppressor class; they serve to perpetuate privilege and inequality Marginalised groups such as Jews suffer from discrimination and exclusion, internalised oppression, divide-and-rule politics

		JEWISH POLITICS IN A RENEWED PUBLIC SPHERE	JEWISH EDUCATION FOR RELATIONAL COMMUNITY BUILDING	JEWISH CRITICAL PEDAGOGY FOR CULTURAL EMANCIPATION
	Educational critique	Education fails to equip students for critical thinking, dialogue and meaningful public life	Instrumentalised, technical, individualistic pedagogies, neglect of arts, humanities, culture and religion as sources of meaning	Oppressive cultural illiteracy for marginalised groups is fed by pejorative notions of minority cultures and systemic failings in the school system
Vision	Social vision	A healthy, diverse, deliberative public sphere; a vibrant civil society with the power to hold state and market to account	A democratic, egalitarian commonwealth of dialogical communities in which people discern the divine image in each other and engage in ethical, caring relationships	An egalitarian, democratic society where all cultures and identities are respected and power, resources and participation are shared equally
	Form of humanisation and *praxis*	Rootedness in a culture, political literacy and agency, and the ability to communicate across difference	Commitment to '*lishmah*' and internal conceptions of the good, seeing work as a collaborative effort aimed at internal goods, seeing the intrinsic human value of oneself and others	Cultural literacy as an act of resistance and a process of conscientisation – coming to a critical understanding of the forces of oppression
	Vision of Judaism	Judaism, in dialogue with Western/secular culture, provides a social foundation for civil society and a values-based cultural framework of pluralism, dialogue, agency and critique	Judaism provides a theology of dialogue and renewal which underpins spiritual growth and moral action	Jewish literature and history are resources for cultural literacy and complex, nuanced social critique

		JEWISH POLITICS IN A RENEWED PUBLIC SPHERE	JEWISH EDUCATION FOR RELATIONAL COMMUNITY BUILDING	JEWISH CRITICAL PEDAGOGY FOR CULTURAL EMANCIPATION
Strategy	Role of community organising	Building civil society organisations as the basis for a democratic public sphere, critical education and political action	Building up grassroots communities within interlinked neighbourhoods and institutions, direct service provision to the poor and the creation of caring relationships, incrementally building a just society	The creation of a multicultural coalition of groups for conscientisation and dialogical, political mobilisation in pursuit of structural social and economic change
	Role of education	Developing individual agency through shared learning and debate between clashing perspectives, clarifying differences and, where possible, mobilising people around a common agenda	Experiential, relationship-based, phronetic service learning that engenders affect-driven attitudinal and behavioural change	Conscientisation – the development of critique, agency and solidarity through cultural literacy and dialogue
	Form of educational dialogue	Rational discourse – pluralistic, divergent-critical, cognitive learning processes – leading to the intellectual development of agents	Primarily caring and existential encounter; where dialogue has a cognitive component it is divergent-inclusive, aimed at sharing and relationship-building	Rational, convergent-inclusive inquiry leading to shared conclusions as a basis for common action, on a foundation of affective 'speaking out' about personal experiences of oppression

	JEWISH POLITICS IN A RENEWED PUBLIC SPHERE	JEWISH EDUCATION FOR RELATIONAL COMMUNITY BUILDING	JEWISH CRITICAL PEDAGOGY FOR CULTURAL EMANCIPATION
Function of Jewish education	Jewish political education – hermeneutical dialogue between learners, texts and contemporary issues that generates critique and action	*Lishmah* conception of induction into a justice-orientated Judaism; Jewish education's role is to embody a relational, caring, dialogical society and to socialise students into it	*Torah lishmah* – Jewish language, literature and culture studied rigorously as an emancipatory act in itself and in order to engage students in dialogue with radical ideas
Jewish pedagogies	Signature pedagogies – *dvar torah* and *mahloket* – within a dialogical pedagogical hermeneutical orientation	Signature pedagogy – *hevruta* – within a combined midrashic/dialogical PHO in which Torah is a source of texts that inspire reflection about relationships and community	Signature pedagogy – *dvar torah* and a midrashic PHO combined with close reading – presenting a radical Judaism and leveraging students' values to develop mutually reinforcing Jewish commitments and radical political agendas
People Agents and beneficiaries	Liberal, egalitarian approach to society that ignores power differentials; the aim is to develop the agency of individuals regardless of identity Jewish communities are one setting for this process, with the particular advantage of being in dialogue with multiple intellectual and cultural traditions	Assumes social justice to have universal benefits, while emphasising the role of privileged educational leaders developing agents from within their own communities who can extend caring to poor/oppressed groups and individuals; Jews are seen primarily in this light	Commitment to auto-emancipation by the oppressed; the priority is therefore working with groups that suffer from marginalisation. Jewish critical pedagogy means working with Jews and allies, led by organisers and educators who emerge from these communities

***

In the final section of the book, I will tease out how Jewish social justice educators working within each of the theories set out above might approach particular political and educational issues: Israel/Palestine, LGBT+ inclusion and the culture wars.

Application 1: Israel/Palestine

Jewish politics in a renewed public sphere. The Israeli-Palestinian conflict is seen as an instance of people being deprived of political agency and prevented from communicating across difference. The principal victims of these phenomena are Palestinians, but they also affect politically progressive Israelis and Diaspora Jews whose positions and identities have been marginalised. Israeli political culture reflects a degradation of the public sphere in which genuine policy debate has been displaced by power politics, emotion and the cult of personality and in which key questions of democracy, human rights and the Occupation tend to be ignored. Discussion of the conflict within Diaspora Jewish communities is marked by a suppression of voices critical of the status quo, Israeli government policy and, more broadly, Zionism.

The antidote to this malaise involves empowering Palestinian and Israeli civil society activists to communicate, critique current reality, develop and advocate for solutions, which must be based on universal, liberal, democratic principles that advance the rights and freedoms of all parties to the conflict. In addition, Diaspora Jews' participation in this discussion should be facilitated through open, critical dialogue within their communities. This approach sees a more pluralistic, empowered Jewish community not only as a tactic for advancing solutions to the Israeli-Palestinian conflict but as an end in itself, and implies that a wide range of views on the conflict is an acceptable outcome to this process. Within UK Jewry this means enabling groups and individuals within the community to understand, analyse and take positions on Israel/Palestine through hermeneutical educational processes and signature pedagogies of *mahloket* and *dvar torah* that enable them to engage critically with multiple narratives: historical accounts of the conflict from various viewpoints; texts drawn from Jewish tradition dealing with topics such as the significance of the land of Israel, Jewish/non-Jewish relations, the ethics of war and peace; visits to relevant sites in Israel/Palestine and meetings with Israeli and Palestinian participants in the conflict; and personal perspectives of other learners from diverse Jewish, Palestinian and other non-Jewish backgrounds.

Jewish education for relational community building. The Israeli-Palestinian conflict is diagnosed here as a failure on both sides to see the humanity of the other and the divine image they embody. As well as preventing people from extending caring across religious, ethnic and political boundaries, this results in objectification of people who are different from ourselves. Within Israeli and Jewish political discourse, Palestinians become a two-dimensional symbol, used as a means for attaining or preserving power or as a way of strengthening particular forms of ethnic and religious identity. Symptoms of this malaise include political violence, terrorism, racism and a refusal to recognise the plight of the other. While this approach does not ignore the fact that Israelis and Palestinians take on oppressor and oppressed roles, respectively, it insists that objectification and failure to care operate in both directions and also within each population. Dehumanisation affects not only the victims but also the oppressors, whose actions strip away their own humanity. A dynamic of objectification cannot easily be confined to one relationship; it tends to proliferate, threatening to push oppressors in one context into the role of the oppressed in another (this applies, for example, to the relationship working-class *Mizrahi* Israelis have with Palestinians on the one hand and with middle-class *Ashkenazi* Israelis respectively).

The solution is to build caring relationships across communal and national divides so that people begin to recognise each other's humanity and are able to take collective and individual action for peace, justice and the common good. This is to be achieved through changing attitudes incrementally and building relationships by facilitating dialogue among joint groups of Israelis and Palestinians. Within UK Jewish communities, this is to be supported by nurturing a caring orientation towards the various parties in the Israel–Palestine conflict through, for example, experiential, affect-driven service learning programmes in Israel and the Occupied Territories. These programmes would combine meeting and doing volunteer work alongside people on all sides of the conflict with text study employing *hevruta* learning and a midrashic pedagogic hermeneutic orientation to focus on the values of justice, compassion and obligations to the Other that emerge from Jewish texts. Other programmatic responses could include interfaith dialogue between British Muslims and Jews, who often find themselves at odds over Israel/Palestine, enabling them to develop a humanised conception of the other and begin building relationships of empathy, care and concern. The relationships between UK Jews and their Israeli, Palestinian and

Muslim counterparts initiated by this process would in turn begin to engender caring dispositions and behaviours within all the communities involved in this project, thereby rippling out and contributing to a more caring, peaceful and humanised world.

Jewish critical pedagogy for cultural emancipation. Dehumanisation operates within and around Israel–Palestine as the result of oppression on several levels: the Occupation, discrimination against Palestinian citizens of Israel and against other marginalised communities – for example, refugees, *mizrahi* Jews, *haredim* (ultra-Orthodox Jews) and women (it should also be noted that oppression also operates within Palestinian society but this is less of a relevant issue for Jewish educators within this paradigm). In all cases, economic and political inequality is underpinned by cultural marginalisation or exclusion of certain identities from normative 'Israeli' discourse. When Diaspora Jewish communities are analysed in similar terms it becomes clear that they are also sites for the marginalisation and exclusion of various groups on grounds of class/economic status, gender, ethnicity and sexual orientation. At the same time, members of Jewish communities are collectively oppressed by antisemitism and by illiteracy in their own Jewish culture. The various forms of oppression affecting Diaspora Jews often serve to reinforce conservative or ethnocentric notions of Jewish identity, thereby further embedding the oppressive dynamics within the community, militating against progressive or radical approaches to the Israel–Palestinian conflict, and blocking the formation of alliances to fight antisemitism.

The solution is radical political change, economic and cultural transformation, leading to a humanised society free of oppression. In this context, guaranteeing equality for Palestinians and ending antisemitism are seen as subsets of the same universal, emancipatory process. (It should be noted that this vision does not prescribe a particular solution to the Israeli-Palestinian conflict and that various formulations, both Zionist and non-Zionist, could be expected to emerge from a Jewish critical pedagogical process.) However, since humanisation can only be achieved by means of auto-emancipation on the part of the oppressed, UK Jews cannot take direct responsibility for the liberation of Palestinians or marginalised Israelis. Instead their role is to liberate themselves from the forms of oppression they themselves face through a process of *lishmah* critical cultural education focused on acquiring a thoroughgoing literacy in Jewish languages and literature, reclaiming a radical conception of Judaism and Jewish culture, and organising the progressive sections of the community and non-Jewish allies to combat the forms of oppression that collectively affect or involve them. This educational process includes a critical examination of Zionism, Israel–Diaspora relations, Israeli society and the Israeli-Palestinian conflict, and enables student-activists to disrupt the dominant, uncritically pro-Israel positions that characterise much of the established Jewish community. This and other forms of action (e.g. lobbying the UK government to exert pressure on the Israeli authorities, campaigning directly against Israeli policy or organising a boycott of settlement goods) depend upon UK Jews recognising their power and privilege and determining to exploit this by acting alongside Palestinians and other oppressed groups as allies.

Application 2: LGBT+ Inclusion

Jewish politics in a renewed public sphere critiques the marginalisation of LGBT+ people, on the basis that their exclusion from community and public life means their views and experiences are silenced and wider public debate is therefore impoverished. This issue is complicated by the difficulty of finding the right balance between creating safe, inclusive spaces and allowing critical debate on controversial issues. For example, how is it possible to have an analytical discussion of the issues surrounding transgender rights and gender-critical feminism, while preventing accusations of misogyny or transphobia from shutting down debate, and ensuring that real discriminatory behaviour does not itself exclude people because of their gender identity or sexual orientation?

This dilemma represents a tension between two different forms of inclusion: on the one hand a pluralism of ideas, and on the other a safe space for the experiences of marginalised, potentially vulnerable people. It also reflects a failure of nuanced, critical engagement. For example, crude, discriminatory views on the place of LGBT+ people within the Jewish community can only be sustained by ignoring the complex intellectual resources provided by Jewish tradition and by the illiteracy – or manipulativeness – of exclusionary faith leaders. There is a correlation between religious fundamentalism and sexist, homophobic thinking based on the fact that both rely on the same binary categories and dichotomous habits of thought.

Creating a diverse, deliberative public sphere where everyone feels able to participate means people need to understand how to express and debate their views in ways that do not cause others to feel excluded. This involves listening as well as speaking, readiness to deliberate and change your mind, focusing on substance not *ad hominem* attacks, and the development of personal resilience in the face of different, sometimes difficult views. It also demonstrates the overlap between different theories of Jewish social justice education, since developing these habits of public debate requires an underlying ethos of respect and care for the other.

Bringing the cultural resources of Judaism to bear is a way of generating complexity. This includes explorations of sex- and gender identity issues in traditional rabbinic texts, but relates more broadly to the practice of bringing different kinds of discourse – religious, scientific, philosophical, political – into dialogue with each other. This process, to be achieved through divergent-critical dialogue, the signature pedagogy of *mahloket* and a dialogical pedagogical hermeneutical orientation, not only helps develop critical thinking on LGBT+ issues but also serves to break down religious fundamentalism and other forms of dogmatic thinking.

Jewish education for relational community building understands discrimination against LGBT+ people and the conflicts that exist around transgender rights as a failure to see people's humanity and to develop attitudes and relationships of caring. Too often, this manifests itself in bullying, discrimination and violence and negatively impacts the relationships and mental health of those involved. This forms part of a cycle of cruelty in which internalised trauma, caused by abuse and oppression, makes it harder to empathise with others and to be sensitive to their individual, human situations. This encourages people to instrumentalise or objectify each other in the service of ideology, as in the case of religiously motivated homophobia, for example, with 'conversion therapy' being the ultimate instance of forcing human beings to conform to ideological demands. It also relates to situations in which exaggerated hostility can be explained by the failure of people on both sides of a conflict to recognise each other's pain and vulnerability, as in the case of debates between some trans activists and gender-critical feminists.

In a Jewish context, LGBT+ people too often find themselves excluded from communal networks of relationship and care because of practices based on exclusionary readings of Judaism, and by their own assumptions, engendered by internalised cruelty and oppression, that they will not be made welcome.

In contrast, a just society will be founded on ethical, caring relationships, emotional intelligence and sensitivity, people's ability to see the humanity in each individual, and genuine dialogical encounters which have the power to break through the objectifying force of ideology. In such a society, people will accept themselves and each other for who they are. Personal identity and interpersonal interactions will be marked by fluidity and a refusal to classify people on grounds of sexuality or gender identity or to punish them for breaching predetermined categories. The building blocks of this society are communities where everyone feels welcome, included and cared for, and where caring is a foundation for dealing compassionately with ideological disagreements.

Jewish education for relational community building therefore seeks to create environments and facilitate experiences in which people of different gender identities, sexual orientations, political and religious views can learn together, in dialogue with Jewish texts. This theory emphasises the signature pedagogy of *hevruta* as a way of helping learners connect with others, overcome prejudice and build trusting relationships across difference. This process works primarily by developing an affective dialogue of care. However, there is also room for cognitive learning. This takes the form of inclusive-divergent dialogue and a midrashic pedagogic hermeneutic orientation in which Torah becomes a source of reflection about gender, sexuality, relationships and community. In particular, Jewish experiences of exclusion and liminality as reflected in the textual tradition and in Jewish history are important analogies or educational resources for creating compassion and flexibility in how we encounter others.

Jewish critical pedagogy for cultural emancipation. The oppression of LGBT+ people is a mechanism for perpetuating social hierarchies on several levels, most obviously between hetero/cis-gender and LGBT+ people. Homophobia and transphobia are also mechanisms for policing the boundaries around stereotypical gender roles, thereby reinforcing patriarchal social relations. Under capitalism, discrimination on the basis of gender and sexual orientation is used to buttress economic and political inequality; labels, stereotypes and stigma are deployed in the service of inequality to deny people opportunity, money and power. More broadly, heteronormativity is associated with a worldview that distinguishes sharply between the 'normal' and the 'abnormal'. The resulting alienation and dehumanisation affect not only the LGBT+ community but other minorities and people with liminal identities of any kind.

Internal divisions and hostility among some feminists and LGBT+ activists is interpreted in this context as a sign of insufficient conscientisation, continued adherence to the kinds of dichotomous, hierarchical thinking that serve social elites, and a failure to analyse the power dynamics of society. This leads to the oppressed turning on each other rather than uniting to fight the oppressor. Within the Jewish community, anti-LGBT+ discourse similarly reinforces anti-pluralist, non-egalitarian norms and practices. It is led by, and strengthens, a certain kind of rabbinic authority, especially within right-wing Orthodox circles; attacking LGBT+ people is a form of manipulative, populist leadership. It tends to alienate and disempower young people and makes the community a more exclusionary place.

The alternative, the world as it should be, is an egalitarian, democratic society, where gender and sexual orientation do not impact on the way power, resources, participation and respect are distributed. The collapse of social hierarchies also means identity markers will lose much of their significance and will be negotiated on their own terms rather than as proxies for privilege and social dominance. A pluralism of gender and sexual identities will therefore emerge. In this setting, cultural literacy will continue to be an ongoing act of resistance and conscientisation: learning to 'read the word and the world' by recovering countercultural, subversive ideas and stories about gender and sexuality in literature, history and art. For Jewish LGBT+ people, reading Jewish culture in this way is a triply emancipatory act. First, applying these lenses is a way of drawing out the emancipatory potential of Judaism. Second, read in this way, Judaism has the power to legitimise LGBT+ identities. Finally, this kind of hermeneutical practice tends to remove the contradictions between LGBT+ and Jewish identities and the associated alienation between a person, her culture and the world.

Achieving these forms of conscientisation and humanisation means engaging in rational, convergent-inclusive dialogue, among the whole range of people who are oppressed or marginalised in different ways in respect of their gender identity or sexual orientation. This cognitive dialogue needs to build on an affective foundation created by people speaking out about their personal experiences of oppression. The aim is to reach shared conclusions and positions as a basis for collective political action.

Jewish LGBT+ people need to do this in their own way and in their own spaces as a prelude to re-engaging with a broader, solidary movement (this applies to all oppressed groups, who are only able to enlist in the wider struggle for social justice once they have initiated *praxis* and dialogue among themselves). This means a pedagogy of Torah *lishmah*, acquiring Jewish literacy and performing close readings of texts that deal with issues of sex and gender as an intrinsically emancipatory act. This process of education, conscientisation and *praxis* involves midrashically teasing out Judaism's radical potential on these issues, and a signature pedagogy of *dvar torah* which enables these ideas to be applied, in a critical, empowering way, to the world.

Application 3: Populism and the Culture Wars

Jewish politics in renewed public sphere. The cultural critic and educationalist Neil Postman distinguishes between 'digital' and 'analogue' societies but uses these terms in an unconventional way, arguing that in recent times the analogue has displaced the digital.[1] Postman's digital society is based on symbols and texts which indirectly signify objects in the real world, and is reflected in verbal, literary forms of discourse – books, newspapers, political pamphlets and speeches – which were culturally dominant until the 1960s. Since then, the analogue has been in the ascendant. Rather than representing the world using symbols, this cultural form works through analogy – images which directly reflect reality, embodied in the dominance of television. Postman argues that this kind of image-based, non-linear, personality-obsessed culture is deeply damaging for analytical, deliberative educational and political practices. His critique can be extended to the world of smartphones and social media which are implicated in processes of social atomisation, the development of 'echo chambers' and anonymisation, a further decline of meaningful verbal interaction and dialogue, and the consequent impossibility of action and *praxis*.

These developments lie behind two interrelated phenomena. First, the hyper-partisanship and tribalism which have increasingly characterised Western politics in the twenty-first century. This is evident in public discourse, in the media and among elected representatives. It expresses itself in the intentional exclusion of people – primarily people of colour, religious and ethnic minorities, and poor people – from the democratic process by means of gerrymandering, the perpetuation of faulty electoral systems and political violence.

The second phenomenon is the failure of rational deliberative politics. Policy debates take up ever-decreasing space within political discourse, which focuses instead on personalities, process and palace intrigue. Politics has come to be dominated by populist messaging in which the connection between problems (some real, some concocted or exaggerated) and proposed solutions is insubstantial at best, as in the case of disingenuous debates over migration as the cause of economic problems. This is fed by fake news, conspiracy theories, the decline of critical journalism and the failure of the education system to equip students for critical thinking, dialogue and meaningful public life.

The solution to this malaise is a renewal of deliberative, participative democracy, embodied in institutions and processes like people's assemblies, sortition and community organising, which involve face-to-face participation in respectful, critical, evidence-based public debate. This also requires democratic electoral reform and devolution; the re-adoption of a deliberative, issue-based and less partisan culture by elected representatives; curbing the power of social media; and resuscitating a critical journalism which would have the capacity to de-emphasise personality and refocus on policy.

The foundation for a renewed political culture is a re-energised civil society populated by reinvigorated community institutions, where people are able to learn how to deliberate, debate public issues and take collective action. These might include faith institutions, youth movements, student unions, neighbourhood groups, parents' organisations, union branches and charities. While digital communication should not be ruled out as a component of this activity, it is vital to reduce dependence on social media and get people back into face-to-face dialogue. Schools are a valuable part of this mosaic, since they have access to thousands of young people and parents in every neighbourhood. Finding ways for schools to become relational, *praxis*-orientated community hubs is therefore vital.

Similarly, Jewish communities are an important instance of this approach. Synagogues are – or should become – places where people can come together, build relationships, learn and debate against the background of a values-driven tradition which prioritises critical thinking, pluralism and hearing minority voices. These educational processes will enable people to come together to take action, but only if politics and social activism come to be seen within the Jewish community as a legitimate part of religious life. This requires a hermeneutical, divergent-critical dialogue grounded in the signature pedagogies of *dvar torah* and *mahloket*. This model uses the dissonance between learners' values, ideas derived from the tradition and contemporary problems to generate complexity of debate. It helps students see through fake news and conspiracy theories, supports them in generating well-grounded policy positions and motivates them to act. While faith communities and certain other cultural, ethnic and political groups are embedded in the kinds of tradition that enable this process, other secular civil society institutions, including schools, will need to create or renew a values-driven culture or tradition within which to engage in *praxis*.

Jewish education for relational community building adds to the previous model in that the breakdown of *praxis* and deliberative politics it identifies are understood to be underpinned by dehumanisation. People fail to realise the humanity in themselves and to see it in others and therefore find it difficult to engage in dialogue with people from different social tribes or who hold unfamiliar views. Rational dialogue in this view depends on an underpinning dialogue of care, which in our society has been undermined by social atomisation, the breakdown of face-to-face relationships, and the anonymising effects of social media in which the affective, caring and human element of interactions are stripped away. When only the semantic content is left, discourse quickly becomes violent and abusive.

Dehumanisation, the failure to see the humanity of the other and to act like human beings ourselves, is the basis of populism: seeing people as a mass or as homogeneous groups, blaming the moral failings of individuals rather than economic and political systems for social injustice, seeking division rather than unity, scapegoating, racism and antisemitism. These phenomena apply to the populist Left as well as to the Right. The decline of humanised, interpersonal relationships also leads to the weakening of moral obligations and is related, via moral carelessness and shamelessness on the part of political leaders, to the phenomena of 'post-truth' and fake news.

The alternative to this is a society where more people are involved in face-to-face community life, engage in relationships, care and feel cared for, and perceive others as being of infinite value. For people of religious faith this might mean seeing them as created in the image of God, while secularists will prefer the Kantian injunction to see people always as ends and never as means. This requires not only a strengthening of existing community and civil society groups, enabling them to reach out and welcome even more people, but also finding ways to make other places where people gather – schools, gyms, healthcare centres, pubs – more relational. These relationships are to be developed both within and between community groups, straddling differences of race, religion and social class. Jewish communities are an important instance of this. Synagogues need to become intentional, relationship-building hubs, both internally and in partnership with other neighbourhood institutions, focused on mobilising their members to care for each other and for other local people.

It is envisaged that involving people in caring relationships will generate a compassionate politics of the common good where policy is debated with an eye to the impact on human well-being. Once people have got to know, and helped refugees, for example, they are unlikely to continue tolerating manipulative, anti-immigrant political discourse. The habits of empathy and compassion will undermine the populism and the politics of hate and will stifle people's appetite for conspiracy theories and fake news.

In strategic terms, this theory relies on community organising in parallel with Ignatian or 'street Torah' service learning, wrapping up volunteering, study and relationship-building into one integrated process. The signature pedagogies here are *dvar torah* and *ḥevruta*, with a focus on developing learners' affective, empathetic responses to each other and more broadly to the human beings affected by social injustice. A concrete example of this might involve a soup kitchen at which members of local Jewish and Muslim communities prepare and serve food to homeless people, where community members build relationships with each other and with the people they serve, through collective action, dialogical study of relevant Jewish and Muslim texts, and joint reflection on issues of homelessness and poverty.

Jewish critical pedagogy for cultural emancipation. Culture wars are a mechanism by which social elites obscure their political agenda of preserving privilege and inequality, manipulate people into misunderstanding their own self-interest thereby generating support for oppressive political projects, and develop false consciousness among oppressed groups, creating enmity between them and eroding the possibility of solidarity and resistance. Understood in intersectional terms, culture wars encourage people to focus on oppressor/oppressed tensions between marginalised groups (e.g. white working class vs people of colour, Muslims vs Jews, disadvantaged locals vs immigrants, women vs transgender people), rather than on the power dynamics of society as a whole. This involves a form of ideological colonialism in which marginalised people are trained to see the world – and other oppressed groups – from the dominant group's perspective and using its language. They are thereby prevented from using their own cultures and unmediated experiences as resources for developing critique, self-confidence, agency and radical political agendas.

An egalitarian, democratic, multicultural society can only be realised if oppressed people join together, with allies from the oppressor class, to build the power needed to fight privilege and enact structural change. This requires relationship-building and the identification of common self-interest among oppressed groups and the articulation of radical social and economic policies that address the genuine interests of the majority. Since the ideal society is marked by ongoing *praxis* – critique and action – which prevent the crystallisation of power and the emergence of new dominant groups and forms of oppression, this is a never-ending process. In such a society, conspiracy theories, fake news and manipulative populism would wither away since the elites who propagate and benefit from them would lose their power to do so and a humanised, conscientised population would have no need or appetite for them.

Pedagogically, this theory is somewhat similar to 'Jewish politics in renewed public sphere' in that it emphasises critical dialogue as a means of engendering social critique and political agency. However, since this model is focused on collective action not individual agency, it employs convergent rather than divergent dialogue and de-emphasises the signature pedagogy of *maḥloket*. Moreover, the way in which Jewish critical pedagogy seeks to combat populism is different. Here, resistance comes not only from critical thinking but from the conscientisation of oppressed people. This involves cultural emancipation, which is achieved through *lishmah*-driven literacy education carried out among groups with shared cultures and who experience similar forms of oppression. As part of this process, Jews (in common with other groups) are able to analyse and come to a nuanced understanding of their own relationship with privilege and disadvantage. Learning to 'read the word and the world' in this kind of homogeneous socio-cultural context provides a foundation for dialogue and *praxis* among a broad alliance of groups fighting for social justice.

Conclusion

Throughout this book I have asked what the phrase 'Jewish social justice education' might mean and have sought to articulate a range of theoretical foundations for this field of practice. My method has been to develop a hermeneutical dialogue between a number of texts and contexts: the tradition of Freirean critical pedagogy, models of social justice education inspired by Catholic social teaching and liberation theology, contemporary theological and political writing on the relationship between Judaism and social justice, and interviews with thinkers and practitioners who consider themselves to be part of the Jewish social justice education enterprise. Analysing these sources has enabled me to draw out and explore a secondary layer of philosophical, political and educational themes and, ultimately, to propose three possible normative theories of Jewish social justice education.

The important components of these theories – both descriptive and normative – have been set out in the body of the book and there is no need to recapitulate them here. However, I do want to highlight several particularly important insights unearthed by the discussion, which advance this area of research in significant ways. As a preliminary comment, it is important to note that in contrast to other well-developed academic fields such as those I have drawn on – Catholic approaches and Freirean critical pedagogy – Jewish social justice education is a new area of research. This book is a first attempt to create an overarching theoretical and disciplinary framework for this political–religious–educational phenomenon.

The first striking finding has been the centrality of *praxis*. The concept of *praxis* in either its Freirean/Marxist version or in more Aristotelian manifestations is vital to understanding the meanings attributed to the constitutive elements that make up this semantic field: Judaism, social justice and education, as well as the various intersections of these terms: radical or progressive education, Jewish pedagogy and specifically Jewish conceptions of social justice. An important insight has been my analysis of the connection between the Greek concept of *praxis* and the rabbinic notion of *lishmah*, in particular the value of *Torah lishmah* (the study of Torah for its own sake) and the implications of this relationship for developing a meaningfully Jewish social justice pedagogy.

Another key area of insight emerges from my analysis of the nature of dialogue, relationships and community, and the intersection of various interpretations of these concepts with ideas of religious faith, social justice and education. The polarity of models associated with the work of Arendt and Buber has been particularly important in articulating and developing a range of distinctively Jewish approaches to social justice and social justice pedagogy.

A further set of findings relates to my discussion of the connection between pluralism and social justice, in particular the importance of epistemological pluralism as a foundation for progressive politics and social justice education. Given the dialectical, pluralistic nature of rabbinic texts and signature Jewish pedagogies and the consequent potential of Jewish education to influence students' ability and desire to accommodate difference and diversity, hear the voice of the other and engage in nuanced social and cultural critique, this highlights the potential power of Jewish education as a social justice strategy.

This study has, I hope, made a significant contribution to the field of Jewish education in its discussion of what makes a pedagogy distinctively Jewish. With this as a foundation, I have raised and explored a hitherto entirely neglected issue: what are the markers of a pedagogy in which both progressive politics and Jewishness are deeply embedded?

Inevitably, there are many important topics which I have not managed to address. I hope that this book has laid the groundwork for further research in some of the following areas.

I have scarcely addressed the biographies and personal identities of my interviewees. An interesting topic for further research would be the relationship between practitioners' personal narratives and the ideological positions they articulate. Empirical research projects could be designed to examine approaches to Jewish social justice education as reflected in observed practice or in curricular materials, or to assess the impact of these approaches on students and the contexts (institutions, communities, society) within which they operate. Expanded studies on specific areas of Jewish social justice practice such as LGBT+ issues, Israel/Palestine, racism, gender, poverty and environmental justice would be valuable. Finally, the methods employed here could fruitfully be extended and adapted to study practitioners working in other locations, primarily the Jewish communities of the United States and Israel, and could also be adopted for the study of social justice education in other faith, cultural and political traditions.

In addition to my theoretical findings, this study provides several important resources for educators. First, it offers the basic insight that a clear theoretical foundation is a vital precondition for any practical educational work, and provides a conceptual framework, a menu of options and a range of stimulating ideas from other thinkers and practitioners as scaffolding for the development of normative theories. Next, it lays out four basic strategic approaches that are available to social justice activists – teaching and learning, activism and campaigning, community organising, and speaking out or personal transformation. These strategies emphasise the importance of adopting a coherent theory of change and of shaping and locating any educational initiative within it. Finally, often drawing on the work of other scholars, it provides a set of concepts which can help shape Jewish and other educators' thinking on practical pedagogical questions: open, directive, cognitive and affective teaching methods, signature pedagogies and pedagogical hermeneutical orientations. I hope these resources will support and influence educators and activists and, perhaps, have a galvanising effect on the practice of Jewish, faith-based and other forms of social justice education.

Notes

Introduction

1 Terry Eagleton, *Ideology: An Introduction* (Verso, 1991).

1 Paulo Freire's Critical Pedagogy – a Theory of Social Justice Education

1 Paulo Freire, *Education for Critical Consciousness* (Continuum International Publishing Group, 1974).
2 Paulo Freire, *Pedagogy of Hope: Reliving Pedagogy of the Oppressed* (Continuum International Publishing Group, 2004), 14.
3 Paulo Freire, *Pedagogy of Freedom: Ethics, Democracy, and Civic Courage* (Rowman & Littlefield, 1998).
4 Freire, *Education for Critical Consciousness*, 3–16; Paulo Freire, *Pedagogy of the Oppressed* (Continuum International Publishing Group, 2000), 27–56.
5 Paulo Freire, *Cultural Action for Freedom* (Harvard Educational Review, 2000); Paulo Freire and Donaldo Macedo, *Literacy: Reading the Word & the World* (Routledge, 1987), 51–3.
6 Donaldo Pereira Macedo, *Literacies of Power: What Americans Are Not Allowed to Know* (Westview Press, 2006), 37–90.
7 Freire and Macedo, *Literacy*; Freire, *Education for Critical Consciousness*.
8 Henry A. Giroux, *Theory and Resistance in Education: Towards a Pedagogy for the Opposition*, 2nd revised edn (Greenwood Press, 2001), 7–41.
9 Ira Shor, *Empowering Education: Critical Teaching for Social Change* (University of Chicago Press, 1992), 112–34.
10 Paulo Freire, *Pedagogy of the Heart* (Continuum International Publishing Group, 1998), 104–5.
11 Miguel Escobar, *Paulo Freire on Higher Education: A Dialogue at the National University of Mexico* (SUNY Press, 1994), 149–51.
12 Freire, *Pedagogy of the Heart*, 46.
13 Paulo Freire, *Teachers as Cultural Workers: Letters to Those Who Dare Teach* (Westview Press, 2005), 1–15.

14 Freire, 87–9; Freire, *Pedagogy of Freedom*, 87.
15 Freire, *Pedagogy of the Oppressed*, 124–5.
16 Freire, 124–7, 184–5.
17 Freire, *Pedagogy of Hope*, 29.
18 Paulo Freire, *The Politics of Education: Culture, Power, and Liberation* (Greenwood Publishing Group, 1985), 186; Escobar, *Paulo Freire on Higher Education*, 38–40.
19 Macedo, *Literacies of Power*, 91–124.
20 Henry A. Giroux, *Border Crossings: Cultural Workers and the Politics of Education*, 2nd edn (Routledge, 2005).
21 Freire, *Pedagogy of the Oppressed*, 57–64; Ira Shor and Paulo Freire, *A Pedagogy for Liberation: Dialogues on Transforming Education* (Greenwood Publishing Group, 1987), 97–103.
22 Escobar, *Paulo Freire on Higher Education*, 77–9; Peter McLaren, *Capitalists and Conquerors: A Critical Pedagogy against Empire* (Rowman & Littlefield, 2005), 75–112.
23 Macedo, *Literacies of Power*, 9–36.
24 Giroux, *Theory and Resistance in Education*.
25 Drew W. Chambers, 'Is Freire Incoherent? Reconciling Directiveness and Dialogue in Freirean Pedagogy', *Journal of Philosophy of Education* 53, no. 1 (2019): 21–47.
26 Freire, *Pedagogy of the Oppressed*, 76–7.
27 Freire, *Cultural Action for Freedom*, 3–4.
28 Paulo Freire, *Pedagogy of the City* (Continuum, 1993), 44–5; Freire, *Pedagogy of Freedom*, 115.
29 Paulo Freire, *Pedagogy in Process: The Letters to Guinea-Bissau* (Continuum, 1983), 25.
30 Giroux, *Theory and Resistance in Education*.
31 Giroux, *Border Crossings*, 157–84.
32 Henry A. Giroux, *On Critical Pedagogy* (Bloomsbury Academic, 2011), 108–29.
33 Freire, *Cultural Action for Freedom*, 2–3; Freire, *Pedagogy of the Oppressed*, 35–7.
34 Freire and Macedo, *Literacy*, 47–9; Freire, *Cultural Action for Freedom*, 92–3.
35 Freire, 2–3.
36 Freire, *Pedagogy of the Oppressed*, 52–6; Escobar, *Paulo Freire on Higher Education*, 29–36.
37 Freire, *The Politics of Education*, 31–2.
38 Freire, 40–1.
39 Freire, *Education for Critical Consciousness*, 14–16.
40 Escobar, *Paulo Freire on Higher Education*, 40; Freire, *Pedagogy of the Oppressed*, 40.
41 Giroux, *Theory and Resistance in Education*, 234–42.
42 McLaren, *Capitalists and Conquerors*.

2 Catholic Social Teaching and Liberation Theology – Theories of Religious Social Justice Education

1 While scholarship on religious social justice education relates almost exclusively to Catholicism, the literature also includes some research on the relationship between religious education and citizenship education and a small number of articles dealing with human rights and peace education from Muslim, Jewish and Protestant perspectives. See Hanan A. Alexander and Ayman K. Agbaria, *Commitment, Character, and Citizenship: Religious Education in Liberal Democracy* (Routledge, 2012); Linda L. Baratte, 'Religious Education and Peace Education: A Partnership Imperative for Our Day', in *International Handbook of the Religious, Moral and Spiritual Dimensions in Education*, ed. Marian de Souza, Gloria Durka, Kathleen Engebretson, Robert Jackson and Andrew McGrady, vol. 1 (Springer Netherlands, 2013), 243–57; Kalwant Bhopal, 'Islam, Education and Inclusion: Towards a Social Justice Agenda?', *British Journal of Sociology of Education* 33, no. 5 (2012): 783–90; Liam Gearon, 'Human Rights and Religious Education: Some Postcolonial Perspectives', in *International Handbook of the Religious, Moral and Spiritual Dimensions in Education*, ed. Marian de Souza, Gloria Durka, Kathleen Engebretson, Robert Jackson and Andrew McGrady, International Handbooks of Religion and Education 1 (Springer Netherlands, 2006), 375–85; Frederick W. Guyette, 'Human Rights Education and Religious Education: From Mutual Suspicion to Elective Affinity', *British Journal of Religious Education* 31, no. 2 (2009): 129–39; Mustafa Köylü, 'Peace Education: An Islamic Approach', *Journal of Peace Education* 1, no. 1 (2004): 59–76; Kenneth Strike and Jeffrey Pegram, 'Religion and Citizenship: The Prophetic Tradition and Public Reason', in *Commitment, Character, and Citizenship: Religious Education in Liberal Democracy*, ed. Hanan A. Alexander and Ayman K. Agbaria (Routledge, 2012), 63–83; Deborah Weissman, 'Jewish Religious Education as Peace Education: From Crisis to Opportunity', *British Journal of Religious Education* 29, no. 1 (2007): 63–76.
2 The primary sources of CST have been collected in David J. O'Brien and Thomas A. Shannon, eds, *Catholic Social Thought: The Documentary Heritage* (Orbis Books, 1992).
3 For a brief historical and theological introduction, see Leonardo Boff and Clodovis Boff, *Introducing Liberation Theology* (Orbis Books, 1987).
4 Fred Kammer, *Doing Faithjustice: An Introduction to Catholic Social Thought* (Paulist Press, 1991).
5 Christopher Rowland, *The Cambridge Companion to Liberation Theology* (Cambridge University Press, 2007), 26.

6 Karen Eifler, Jeff Kerssen-Griep and Peter Thacker, 'Enacting Social Justice to Teach Social Justice: The Pedagogy of Bridge Builders', *Catholic Education: A Journal of Inquiry and Practice* 12, no. 1 (1 September 2008): 55–70.
7 Roger Bergman, *Catholic Social Learning: Educating the Faith That Does Justice* (Fordham University Press, 2011).
8 Fitzgerald in Rowland, *The Cambridge Companion to Liberation Theology*, 248–64.
9 Rowland, 19–38; Rowland, 278–303.
10 Kammer, *Doing Faithjustice*.
11 O'Brien and Shannon, *Catholic Social Thought*.
12 Michael Kirwan, 'Liberation Theology and Catholic Social Teaching', *New Blackfriars* 93, no. 1044 (2012): 246–58.
13 Rowland, *The Cambridge Companion to Liberation Theology*, 19–38.
14 Roger Bergman, 'Teaching Justice after MacIntyre: Toward a Catholic Philosophy of Moral Education', *Catholic Education: A Journal of Inquiry and Practice* 12, no. 1 (2008): 7–24.
15 O'Brien and Shannon, *Catholic Social Thought*.
16 Fitzgerald in Rowland, *The Cambridge Companion to Liberation Theology*, 248–64.
17 Joseph Ratzinger, 'Instruction on Certain Aspects of the "Theology of Liberation"' (1984), www.vatican.va; O'Brien and Shannon, *Catholic Social Thought*.
18 Bergman, *Catholic Social Learning: Educating the Faith That Does Justice*.
19 Bergman, 62.
20 The kind of character education advocated by Bergman finds expression in much of the research on Catholic approaches to social justice education. For approaches that prioritise intellectual or classroom-based aspects of the students' moral development, see James B. Ball, Zaida Martinez and Brian Toyne, 'Catholic Social Teaching: Addressing Globalization in Catholic Business Education', *Journal of Catholic Higher Education* 28, no. 1 (2009): 63–82; Gerald Grace, 'Catholic Social Teaching Should Permeate the Catholic Secondary School Curriculum: An Agenda for Reform', *International Studies in Catholic Education* 5, no. 1 (2013): 99–109; Nancy G. Calley, Sheri Pickover, Jocelyn M. Bennett-Garraway, Simon J. Hendry and Garbette M. Garraway, 'Integrating Social Justice across the Curriculum: The Catholic Mission and Counselor Education', *Journal of Catholic Higher Education* 30, no. 2 (2011): 289–308. Scholars who have emphasised the experiential and affective aspects of Catholic social justice education include Susan Crawford Sullivan and Margaret A. Post, 'Combining Community-Based Learning and Catholic Social Teaching in Educating for Democratic Citizenship', *Journal of Catholic Higher Education* 30, no. 1 (2011): 113–31; Rachel Collopy, Connie Bowman and David A. Taylor, 'The Educational Achievement Gap as a Social Justice Issue for Teacher Educators', *Catholic Education: A Journal of Inquiry and Practice* 16, no. 1 (2012): 4–25; Mary Lynne Gasaway Hill and Andrew J. Hill, 'Catholic Social

Teaching and Civic Engagement: Grounding Civic Praxis in Catholic Theory', *Journal of Catholic Higher Education* 27, no. 1 (2008): 97–115.
21 Daniel S. Schipani, *Religious Education Encounters Liberation Theology* (Religious Education Press, 1988).
22 For further discussion of the respective roles of, and interaction between, experiential/praxical and scriptural knowledge, see Antonio on James Cone's Black Theology and Hebblethwaite on more conservative, text-based epistemological approaches – in Rowland, *The Cambridge Companion to Liberation Theology*, 79–104, 209–28.
23 Rowland, 139–58.
24 Ann Curry-Stevens, 'New Forms of Transformative Education Pedagogy for the Privileged', *Journal of Transformative Education* 5, no. 1 (1 January 2007): 33–58.
25 Diane J. Goodman, *Promoting Diversity and Social Justice: Educating People from Privileged Groups*, 2nd edn (Routledge, 2011).
26 Ricky Lee Allen, 'Pedagogy of the Oppressor: What Was Freire's Theory for Transforming the Privileged and Powerful?' (Annual Meeting of the American Educational Research Association, New Orleans, LA, 2002).
27 Alice F. Evans, Robert A. Evans and William B. Kennedy, *Pedagogies for the Non-Poor* (Wipf and Stock, 2000).
28 Thomas H. Groome, *Educating for Life: A Spiritual Vision for Every Teacher and Parent* (T. More, 1998).

3 Judaism and Social Justice – Religion, Culture and Progressive Politics

1 Howard M. Sachar, *Course of Modern Jewish History*, 2nd edn (Random House, 1990), 102–13.
2 Jonathan Frankel, 'The Roots of "Jewish Socialism" (1881–1892)', in *Essential Papers on Jews and the Left (Essential Papers on Jewish Studies): 10*, ed. Ezra Mendelsohn (New York University Press, 1997); Sachar, *Course of Modern Jewish History*, 332–43.
3 Paul R. Mendes-Flohr and Jehuda Reinharz, *The Jew in the Modern World: A Documentary History* (Oxford University Press, 1995), 419–22.
4 Arthur Hertzberg, *The Zionist Idea: A Historical Analysis and Reader* (Atheneum, 1972), 388–96; Gideon Shimoni, *The Zionist Ideology* (Brandeis University Press, 1997), 309–12.
5 Hertzberg, *The Zionist Idea*, 395.
6 Hertzberg, 372–83; Shimoni, *The Zionist Ideology*, 208–16.

7 Marc Silverman, *Ha-Hinukh Ba-Kibbutz Ha-Dati: Historiyah ve-Ideologiyah* (Jerusalem, Hebrew University, 1982).
8 The impact of multiculturalism on Jewish identity and politics is discussed from various perspectives in David Biale, Michael Galchinsky and Susannah Heschel, eds, *Insider/Outsider: American Jews and Multiculturalism* (University of California Press, 1998).
9 Abraham Sagi, *Jewish Religion After Theology* (Academic Studies Press, 2009), 205–34.
10 Michael Walzer, *Exodus and Revolution* (Basic Books, 1986).
11 www.tikkun.org (retrieved 25 November 2021).
12 Michael Lerner, *Jewish Renewal: A Path to Healing and Transformation* (G.P. Putnam's Sons, 1994).
13 Eugene B. Borowitz, *Exploring Jewish Ethics: Papers on Covenant Responsibility* (Wayne State University Press, 1990), 320–31.
14 Abraham Joshua Heschel, *The Insecurity of Freedom: Essays on Human Existence* (Jewish Publication Society of America, 1966), 101–11; Abraham Joshua Heschel and Susannah Heschel, *Moral Grandeur and Spiritual Audacity: Essays* (Farrar, Straus and Giroux, 1997), 216–18.
15 Levine in Nathan J. Diament, *Tikkun Olam: Social Responsibility in Jewish Thought and Law (Orthodox Forum Series)* (Jason Aronson, 1997), 265–308.
16 Arthur Waskow, *Down-To-Earth Judaism: Food, Money, Sex, and the Rest of Life* (William Morrow, 1995).
17 Benstein in Or Rose, Margie Klein, Jo Ellen Green Kaiser and David Ellenson, *Righteous Indignation: A Jewish Call for Justice* (Jewish Lights, 2009), 76–8.
18 Shmuly Yanklowitz, *Jewish Ethics and Social Justice: A Guide for the 21st Century* (Derusha, 2012).
19 Judith Plaskow, *Standing Again at Sinai: Judaism from a Feminist Perspective*, repr. edn (Bravo, 1991); Judith Plaskow, *The Coming of Lilith: Essays on Feminism, Judaism, and Sexual Ethics, 1972–2003* (Beacon Press, 2005).
20 Tamar Ross, *Expanding the Palace of Torah – Orthodoxy and Feminism*, 2nd edn (Brandeis University Press, 2021).
21 Laurie Zoloth, *Health Care and the Ethics of Encounter: A Jewish Discussion of Social Justice*, 1st edn (University of North Carolina Press, 1999).
22 Marla Brettschneider, *Jewish Feminism and Intersectionality* (SUNY Press, 2016).
23 Jill Jacobs, *There Shall Be No Needy: Pursuing Social Justice Through Jewish Law & Tradition* (Jewish Lights, 2010).
24 Tamari in Diament, *Tikkun Olam: Social Responsibility in Jewish Thought and Law (Orthodox Forum Series)*, 239–63.
25 Yanklowitz, *Jewish Ethics and Social Justice*.
26 Elliot N. Dorff, *The Way Into Tikkun Olam: Repairing the World* (Jewish Lights, 2007).

27 Jonathan Sacks, *The Politics of Hope* (Vintage, 2000), 243.
28 Aryeh Cohen, *Justice in the City: An Argument from the Sources of Rabbinic Judaism* (Academic Studies Press, 2013).
29 Babylonian Talmud, Bava Batra 7a-b.
30 Waskow, *Down-To-Earth Judaism*.
31 David Birnbaum and Martin S. Cohen, eds, *Tikkun Olam* (New Paradigm Matrix, 2015).
32 David Jaffe, *Changing the World from the Inside Out: A Jewish Approach to Personal and Social Change* (Trumpeter, 2016).
33 Lerner, *Jewish Renewal*.
34 Dorff, *The Way Into Tikkun Olam*, 21–44.
35 Heschel, *The Insecurity of Freedom*, 85–100.
36 Heschel, 97.
37 Lerner, *Jewish Renewal*.
38 Walzer, *Exodus and Revolution*.
39 Borowitz, *Exploring Jewish Ethics*, 295–307.
40 Sidney Schwarz, *Judaism and Justice: The Jewish Passion to Repair the World*, repr. edn (Jewish Lights, 2008), 259.
41 Schwarz, 41.
42 Schwarz, *Judaism and Justice*.
43 Jacobs, *There Shall Be No Needy*.
44 Yanklowitz, *Jewish Ethics and Social Justice*.
45 Yehudah Mirsky, 'Tikkun Olam: Basic Questions and Policy Directions', January 2008, www.bjpa.org.
46 Waskow, *Down-To-Earth Judaism*.
47 Rose et al., *Righteous Indignation*, 185–94.
48 Tamar Ross, 'The Feminist Contribution to Halakhic Discourse Kol Beisha Erva as a Test Case', *Emor*, no. 1 (2010): 37–69.
49 Hermann Cohen, *Religion of Reason Out of the Sources of Judaism* (Scholars Press, 1972).
50 Erich Fromm, *You Shall Be as Gods: A Radical Interpretation of the Old Testament and Its Tradition* (Open Road Media, 2013).
51 Joseph Dov Soloveitchik, *Fate and Destiny: From Holocaust to the State of Israel* (KTAV Publishing House, 2000).
52 Sidney Schwarz, 'Welcome to the Tribe' (www.rabbisid.org/hello-world, 2012); Sidney Schwarz, *Jewish Megatrends: Charting the Course of the American Jewish Future* (Jewish Lights, 2013).
53 Borowitz, *Exploring Jewish Ethics*.
54 Mirsky, 'Tikkun Olam'; Lerner in Rose et al., *Righteous Indignation*, 38–44; Sherwin, 'Tikkun Olam'; Wolf, 'Repairing Tikkun Olam'.

55 Yeshayahu Leibowitz, 'The Social Order as a Religious Problem', in *Judaism, Human Values, and the Jewish State*, trans. Eliezer Goldman (Harvard University Press, 1992), 145–57.
56 Ross, 'The Feminist Contribution to Halakhic Discourse Kol Beisha Erva as a Test Case'.
57 Diament, *Tikkun Olam*.
58 Blidstein in Diament, 17–59.
59 Jacobs, *There Shall Be No Needy*.
60 For similar approaches see Cohen, *Justice in the City*; Dorff, *The Way Into Tikkun Olam*; Walzer, *Exodus and Revolution*; Waskow, *Down-To-Earth Judaism*; Yanklowitz, *Jewish Ethics and Social Justice*.

Part 2 Jewish Social Justice Education – Interviews with Practitioners

1 For a few isolated examples, see Martin Buber, 'Education', in *Between Man and Man*, trans. Ronald Gregor-Smith (Routledge, 2002), 98–122; Zvi Lamm, *The Educational Method of Hashomer Hatzair Youth Movement* (Hebrew University Magnes Press, 1998); Lerner, *Jewish Renewal*; Michael Lerner, *Spirit Matters*, vol. 2002 (Hampton Roads, 2002); Matt Plen, 'Pedagogiyah bikortit ve-ideologiyot shel tzedek ḥevrati: Paulo Freire ve-ha-ideologiyot shel Hashomer Hatzair ve-Hakibbutz Hadati' (Hebrew University, 2008); Schwarz, *Judaism and Justice*; Silverman, 'Ha-Ḥinukh Ba-Kibbutz Ha-Dati: Historiyah ve-Ideologiyah'; Weissman, 'Jewish Religious Education as Peace Education'.
2 Lamm, 'Ideologiyah ve-maḥshevet ha-ḥinukh'.
3 William K. Frankena, 'A Model for Analyzing a Philosophy of Education'. *High School Journal* 50, no. 1 (1966): 8–13.

4 Critique – the World as It Is

1 Peggy McIntosh, 'White Privilege', in *Independent School* (1 January 1990): 31–6.
2 Amartya Sen, *Identity and Violence: The Illusion of Destiny* (Penguin, 2007).
3 Zygmunt Bauman, 'From Pilgrim to Tourist – or a Short History of Identity', in *Questions of Cultural Identity* (SAGE, 2011), 18–36.
4 See Chapter 8 for further discussion of Buber's and Levinas's positions.
5 An elected umbrella body representing most UK synagogues and Jewish organisations.
6 Mishnah Gittin, Chapter 4.

7 Berkovitz in Birnbaum and Cohen, *Tikkun Olam*; Borowitz, *Exploring Jewish Ethics*, 95–105; Diament, *Tikkun Olam*, 17–59; Jonathan Sacks, *To Heal a Fractured World: The Ethics of Responsibility* (Continuum, 2005); Schwarz, *Judaism and Justice*.
8 Peter Beinart, *Crisis of Zionism* (Picador Paper, 2013).
9 Schwarz, *Judaism and Justice*.
10 A bill designed to anchor the Jewish character of the State of Israel in law. See www.timesofisrael.com/final-text-of-jewish-nation-state-bill-set-to-become-law/ (retrieved 20 July 2018).
11 Ali Dawabshe was killed in an arson attack by Israel settlers on his family's home in the West Bank village of Duma. See www.guardian.com/world/2015/jul/31/death-18-month-old-in-arson-attack-heightens-tensions-west-bank-israel (retrieved 16 March 2017).
12 Maggid in Rose et al., *Righteous Indignation*, 260–9.
13 The Bund and the Autonomist movement both advocated forms of non-territorial cultural autonomy for Jewish communities within the multinational empires of late-nineteenth- and early-twentieth-century Eastern and Central Europe. The Workmen's Circle developed similar ideas in the Jewish community of the United States in the early twentieth century. Mordecai Kaplan was the founder of Reconstructionist Judaism, an American Jewish movement which sought to redefine Judaism the all-encompassing civilisation of the Jewish people rather than merely a religion. For primary sources and background information see Mendes-Flohr and Reinharz, *The Jew in the Modern World*, 419–22.
14 A north London theatre which cancelled screenings of the UK Jewish Film Festival while it was sponsored by the Israeli embassy. See www.theguardian.com/stage/2014/aug/15/tricycle-theatre-u-turn-jewish-film-festival-ban (retrieved 16 March 17).
15 David Biale, *Power and Powerlessness in Jewish History*, new edn (Random House, 1988).

5 Vision – the World as It Should Be

1 On the polarity of Jewish and Greek thinking, see Victor Seidler, *Jewish Philosophy and Western Culture: A Modern Introduction* (I.B. Tauris, 2007).
2 Jonathan Sacks, 'The Spirit of Community (Vayakhel 5775)' (2015), www.rabbisacks.org/the-spirit-of-community-vayakhel-5775 (accessed 21 June 2016).
3 Saul David Alinsky, *Reveille For Radicals*, 2nd edn (Vintage Books, 1989); Saul David Alinsky, *Rules For Radicals*, 2nd edn (Vintage Books, 1989).
4 Babylonian Talmud, Eruvin 13b.

6 Strategy – Education, Activism and Community Organising

1. Schwarz, *Judaism and Justice*.
2. This idea is inspired by the following insight by Fischer and Ravizza, cited in Judith Suissa, 'Tiger Mothers and Praise Junkies: Children, Praise and the Reactive Attitudes', *Journal of Philosophy of Education* 47, no. 1 (1 February 2013): 1–19:

    > Even before children are fully responsible for their actions, we often find ourselves taking certain attitudes to them that are in many respects similar to the full-blown attitudes of indignation and resentment (which are of course only appropriately applicable to morally responsible agents). … By adopting certain attitudes towards a child (and expressing them suitably) – by acting as if the child were a fully developed moral person – we begin to teach the child what it means to be such a person. Of course, this sort of training, with its characteristic set of parental attitudes and responses, is a central feature of the moral education of children.

3. Cohen, *Justice in the City*.
4. Chabad is a Hasidic outreach group which aims to involve secular Jews in Orthodox religious life. See Philip Wexler, 'Chabad: Social Movement and Educational Practice', in *Educational Deliberations; Studies in Education Dedicated to Shlomo (Seymour) Fox*, by Mordecai Nisan and Oded Schremer (Keter, 2005), 196–206; Sue Fishkoff, *The Rebbe's Army: Inside the World of Chabad-Lubavitch*, repr. edn (Schocken Books, 2005).
5. See www.ijv.org.uk (retrieved 31 March 2017).
6. On this debate see Dov Waxman, *Trouble in the Tribe: The American Jewish Conflict over Israel* (Princeton University Press, 2016); Keith Kahn-Harris, *Uncivil War: The Israel Conflict in the Jewish Community* (David Paul, 2014).
7. However, the nature of this relationship and the rationale for involvement in Israeli politics requires further clarification. The majority of activists interviewed here fit into what might be described as a liberal-Zionist paradigm in which involvement in Israeli justice issues emerges from a sense of responsibility to the people of Israel and from a commitment to shaping Israel as a Jewish and democratic state. An alternative conception is articulated by Joe who displays concern for the Palestinians as part of a broader, universalist conception of justice which also leads him to reject the very idea of Jewish statehood. These positions map neatly onto Leonie Fleischmann's typology of Israeli peace activists, which distinguishes between 'moderates' and 'radicals' – see Leonie Fleischmann, 'Beyond Paralysis: The Reframing of Israeli Peace Activism Since the Second Intifada', *Peace & Change* 41 (July 2016): 354–85.

8 Hélder Câmara was a Brazilian archbishop, liberation theologian and outspoken opponent of Brazil's military dictatorship from 1964 to 1985; see Alex Bellos, 'Hélder Câmara', *The Guardian*, 31 August 1999.
9 Dorff, *The Way Into Tikkun Olam*.
10 bell hooks, *Talking Back: Thinking Feminist, Thinking Black* (South End Press, 1989), 9.
11 Cohen, *Justice in the City*, 41–62.
12 Menachem Mendel of Kotzk, better known as the Kotzker Rebbe (1787–1859), was a Hasidic rabbi and leader in eastern Poland.
13 Rebecca Tarlau, 'From a Language to a Theory of Resistance: Critical Pedagogy, the Limits of "Framing," and Social Change', *Educational Theory* 64, no. 4 (1 August 2014): 369–92.
14 Tarlau, 386.
15 Tarlau, 380.
16 Myles Horton and Paulo Freire, *We Make the Road by Walking: Conversations on Education and Social Change* (Temple University Press, 1990), 115.

7 People – Agents and Beneficiaries of Social Change

1 For example, various interviewees name Arik Ascherman, Shoshana Boyd-Gelfand, Dyonna Ginsburg, Herschel Gluck, Ari Hart, Abraham Joshua Heschel, Jill Jacobs, Laura Janner-Klausner, Levi Lauer, Aharon Ariel Lavi, Natan Levy, Jay Michaelson, Shaiya Rothberg, Sheila Shulman, Ari Weiss, Jonathan Wittenberg and organisations in the United States and Israel including Be-ma'agalei Tzedek, Olam, the Shuva community, Siach and Uri Letzedek.
2 Mishnah Avot 4:17.
3 Pope Francis, *Encyclical on Climate Change and Inequality: On Care for Our Common Home* (Melville House, 2015).

8 Philosophical, Theological and Political Themes

1 Freire, *Pedagogy of the Oppressed*, 119.
2 Hannah Arendt, *The Human Condition*, 2nd edn (University of Chicago Press, 2013); Joseph Dunne, *Back to the Rough Ground: Phronesis and Techne in Modern Philosophy and in Aristotle* (University of Notre Dame Press, 1993).
3 Yeshayahu Leibowitz, 'The Reading of Shema', in *Judaism, Human Values, and the Jewish State*, trans. Eliezer Goldman (Harvard University Press, 1992), 37–47.
4 Dunne, *Back to the Rough Ground*.

5 Dunne.
6 Martin Buber, *Paths in Utopia* (Syracuse University Press, 1950), 129–38.
7 Martin Buber, *I and Thou* (Touchstone, 1996).
8 Hannah Arendt, 'Labor, Work, Action', in *The Portable Hannah Arendt* (Penguin, 2003), 167–81.
9 Arendt, *The Human Condition*, 22–7.
10 Arendt, 28–49.
11 Hannah Arendt, *On Revolution* (Penguin Classics, 2006), 49–105.
12 See, for example, Arendt's discussion of desegregation in the southern United States in the 1950s. Hannah Arendt, 'Reflections on Little Rock', in *The Portable Hannah Arendt* (Penguin, 2003), 231–46.
13 Arendt, *The Human Condition*, 50.
14 Birnbaum and Cohen, *Tikkun Olam*.
15 Lerner, *Jewish Renewal*.
16 Michael Lerner, 'Heschel's Legacy for the Politics of the Twenty-First Century', *Modern Judaism* 29, no. 1 (13 May 2009): 34–43; Waskow, *Down-To-Earth Judaism*; Yanklowitz, *Jewish Ethics and Social Justice*.
17 Rose, Klein, Kaiser and Ellenson, *Righteous Indignation*, 23–30; Rabbi Avraham Weiss, *Spiritual Activism: A Jewish Guide to Leadership and Repairing the World*, 1st edn (Jewish Lights, 2008).
18 Ryan Urbano, 'Approaching the Divine: Levinas on God, Religion, Idolatry, and Atheism', *Logos: A Journal of Catholic Thought and Culture* 15, no. 1 (1 January 2012): 50–81.
19 Freire, *Pedagogy in Process*, 103–4; Freire, *The Politics of Education*, 105.
20 Bauman, 'From Pilgrim to Tourist – or a Short History of Identity'.
21 Alasdair MacIntyre, *After Virtue: A Study in Moral Theory* (Gerald Duckworth, 2007).
22 Fraser, 'Social Justice In the Age of Identity Politics'; for a similar discussion in an explicitly Jewish context see Michael Walzer, 'Multiculturalism and the Politics of Interest', in Biale, Galchinsky and Heschel, *Insider/Outsider*, 88–100.
23 For nuanced discussions of pluralism, multiculturalism and Jewish identity, see Mitchell Cohen, 'In Defense of Shaatnez: A Politics for Jews in a Multicultural America', in Biale, Galchinsky and Heschel, *Insider/Outsider*, 34–54; Cheryl Greenberg, 'Pluralism and Its Discontents: The Case of Blacks and Jews', Biale, Galchinsky and Heschel, *Insider/Outsider*, 55–87.
24 Freire, *Cultural Action for Freedom*, 51–3.
25 Macedo, *Literacies of Power*, 37–90; Giroux, *Border Crossings*, 83–119; Giroux, 123–36; Giroux, *On Critical Pedagogy*, 48–68.
26 Freire, *Pedagogy of Hope*, 29, 133–4; Freire, *The Politics of Education*, 186; Escobar, *Paulo Freire on Higher Education*, 38–40; Freire, *Pedagogy of the Heart*, 86; Macedo, *Literacies of Power*, 91–124.
27 Giroux, *Border Crossings*, 11–30; Giroux, 137–53.
28 McLaren, *Capitalists and Conquerors*, 75–112.

29 Bergman, *Catholic Social Learning*.
30 Charles Taylor, 'The Politics of Recognition', in *Multiculturalism: Examining the Politics of Recognition*, ed. Amy Gutmann, expanded paperback edn (Princeton University Press, 1994), 25–73.
31 Tony Beavers, 'Introducing Levinas to Undergraduate Philosophers' (1995), faculty.evansville.edu/tb2/PDFs/UndergradPhil.pdf; Simon Critchley and Robert Bernasconi, *The Cambridge Companion to Levinas* (Cambridge University Press, 2002), 1–32, 63–81.
32 Nicholas C. Burbules, *Dialogue in Teaching: Theory and Practice* (Teachers College Press, 1993).
33 Buber, 'Education'.
34 Nel Noddings, *Caring: A Feminine Approach to Ethics and Moral Education* (University of California Press, 2003).
35 Noddings, 75.
36 Nel Noddings, *Starting at Home: Caring and Social Policy* (University of California Press, 2002), 230–47.
37 Noddings, *Caring*, 171–202; Noddings, *Starting at Home*, 283–300.
38 Buber, *I and Thou*, 156–7.
39 Luke Bretherton, *Resurrecting Democracy: Faith, Citizenship, and the Politics of a Common Life* (Cambridge University Press, 2015).
40 Franz Rosenzweig, *The Star of Redemption* (University of Wisconsin Press, 2004), 169–220.
41 Jenni Frazer, 'Rabbi, You May Bore Us but Stay out of Politics', *The Jewish Chronicle*, 13 August 2009; Marc Saperstein, ' "Rabbis, Stay out of Politics": Social Justice Preaching and Its Opponents, 1848–2014', *Jewish Culture and History* 16, no. 2 (4 May 2015): 127–41.
42 Leibowitz, 'The Social Order as a Religious Problem'.
43 Sacks, 'The Spirit of Community (Vayakhel 5775)'.
44 MacIntyre, *After Virtue*; Alasdair MacIntyre, 'Alasdair MacIntyre on Education: In Dialogue with Joseph Dunne', *Journal of Philosophy of Education* 36, no. 1 (February 2002): 1–19.

9 The Jewishness of Social Justice Pedagogies

1 Groome, *Educating for Life*.
2 Seymour Fox, Israel Scheffler and Daniel Marom, *Visions of Jewish Education* (Cambridge University Press, 2003).
3 Jonathan Cohen, 'Jewish Thought for Jewish Education: Source and Resources', in *International Handbook of Jewish Education* (Springer Science & Business Media, 2011), 219–36.

4 For a fascinating discussion of a similar question – what makes a philosophy Jewish? – see Seeskin 1990, 1–7.
5 Lee S. Shulman, 'Pedagogies of Interpretation, Argumentation, and Formation: From Understanding to Identity in Jewish Education', *Journal of Jewish Education* 74, no. suppl (5 December 2008): 5–15.
6 Elie Holzer, 'What Connects "Good" Teaching, Text Study and Hevruta Learning? A Conceptual Argument', *Journal of Jewish Education* 72, no. 3 (1 December 2006): 183–204.
7 Marjorie Lehman and Jane Kanarek, 'Talmud: Making a Case for Talmud Pedagogy – The Talmud as an Educational Model', in *International Handbook of Jewish Education* (Springer Science & Business Media, 2011), 581–96.
8 Inbar Galili-Schachter, 'Pedagogic Hermeneutic Orientations in the Teaching of Jewish Texts', *Journal of Jewish Education* 77, no. 3 (1 July 2011): 216–38.
9 MacIntyre, *After Virtue: A Study in Moral Theory*, 187.
10 MacIntyre himself denies that teaching is a practice and insists it is merely a method for inducting people into practices. Dunne, however, argues convincingly that teaching clearly fits MacIntyre's own definition of a practice. See Alasdair MacIntyre, 'Alasdair MacIntyre on Education: In Dialogue with Joseph Dunne', *Journal of Philosophy of Education* 36, no. 1 (February 2002): 1–19; Joseph Dunne, 'Arguing for Teaching as a Practice: A Reply to Alasdair MacIntyre', *Journal of Philosophy of Education* 37, no. 2 (May 2003): 353–69.
11 For a detailed discussion of the relationship between particular schools of educational and political thought, namely Freirean critical pedagogy and two varieties of socialist Zionist ideology (the secular Marxist Zionism of Hashomer Hatzair and the Orthodox socialism of the Religious Kibbutz movement) see Plen, '*Pedagogiyah bikortit ve-ideologiyot shel tzedek ḥevrati: Paulo Freire ve-ha-ideologiyot shel Hashomer Hatzair ve-Hakibbutz Hadati*'.
12 Norman Lamm, *Torah Lishmah: Torah for Torah's Sake in the Works of Rabbi Hayyim of Volozhin and His Contemporaries* (KTAV Publishing House, 1989).
13 Luis Lugo et al., 'A Portrait of Jewish Americans' (Pew Research Center), 1 October 2013.
14 Hertzberg, *The Zionist Idea*, 262–9.
15 Lehman and Kanarek, 'Talmud: Making a Case for Talmud Pedagogy – The Talmud as an Educational Model'; Cohen, *Justice in the City*.

10 Normative Theories of Jewish Social Justice Education

1 Neil Postman, *Teaching as a Conserving Activity* (Delta, 1980).

Bibliography

Alexander, Hanan A., and Ayman K. Agbaria. *Commitment, Character, and Citizenship: Religious Education in Liberal Democracy*. Routledge, 2012.

Alinsky, Saul David. *Reveille for Radicals*, 2nd edn. Vintage Books, 1989.

Alinsky, Saul David. *Rules for Radicals*, 2nd edn. Vintage Books, 1989.

Allen, Ricky Lee. 'Pedagogy of the Oppressor: What Was Freire's Theory for Transforming the Privileged and Powerful?' Paper presented at the Annual Meeting of the American Educational Research Association, New Orleans, LA, 2002. https://files.eric.ed.gov/fulltext/ED467424.pdf.

Arendt, Hannah. 'Labor, Work, Action'. In *The Portable Hannah Arendt*, edited by Peter Baehr, reissue edn, 167–81. Penguin, 2003.

Arendt, Hannah. *On Revolution*. Penguin Classics, 2006.

Arendt, Hannah. 'Reflections on Little Rock'. In *The Portable Hannah Arendt*, edited by Peter Baehr, reissue edn, 231–46. Penguin, 2003.

Arendt, Hannah. *The Human Condition*, 2nd edn. University of Chicago Press, 2013.

Ball, James B., Zaida Martinez and Brian Toyne. 'Catholic Social Teaching: Addressing Globalization in Catholic Business Education'. *Journal of Catholic Higher Education* 28, no. 1 (2009): 63–82.

Baratte, Linda L. 'Religious Education and Peace Education: A Partnership Imperative for Our Day'. In *International Handbook of the Religious, Moral and Spiritual Dimensions in Education*, edited by Marian de Souza, Gloria Durka, Kathleen Engebretson, Robert Jackson and Andrew McGrady, 1:243–57. Springer Netherlands.

Bauman, Zygmunt. 'From Pilgrim to Tourist – or a Short History of Identity'. In *Questions of Cultural Identity*, edited by Stuart Hall and Paul du Gay, 18–36. SAGE, 2011.

Beavers, Tony. 'Introducing Levinas to Undergraduate Philosophers', 1995. https://www.academia.edu/281338/Introducing_Levinas_to_Undergraduate_Philosophers (accessed 24 April 2022).

Beinart, Peter. *Crisis of Zionism*. Picador Paper, 2013.

Bergman, Roger. *Catholic Social Learning: Educating the Faith That Does Justice*. Fordham University Press, 2011.

Bergman, Roger. 'Teaching Justice after MacIntyre: Toward a Catholic Philosophy of Moral Education'. *Catholic Education: A Journal of Inquiry and Practice* 12, no. 1 (2008): 7–24.

Bhopal, Kalwant. 'Islam, Education and Inclusion: Towards a Social Justice Agenda?' *British Journal of Sociology of Education* 33, no. 5 (2012): 783–90.

Biale, David. *Power and Powerlessness in Jewish History*. Random House, 1988.

Biale, David, Michael Galchinsky and Susannah Heschel, eds. *Insider/Outsider: American Jews and Multiculturalism*. University of California Press, 1998.

Birnbaum, David, and Martin S. Cohen, eds. *Tikkun Olam*. New Paradigm Matrix, 2015.

Borowitz, Eugene B. *Exploring Jewish Ethics: Papers on Covenant Responsibility*. Wayne State University Press, 1990.

Bretherton, Luke. *Resurrecting Democracy: Faith, Citizenship, and the Politics of a Common Life*. Cambridge University Press, 2015.

Brettschneider, Marla. *Jewish Feminism and Intersectionality*. SUNY Press, 2016.

Buber, Martin. 'Education'. In *Between Man and Man*, translated by Ronald Gregor-Smith, 98–122. Routledge, 2002.

Buber, Martin. *I and Thou*. Touchstone, 1996.

Buber, Martin. *Paths in Utopia*. Syracuse University Press, 1950.

Burbules, Nicholas C. *Dialogue in Teaching: Theory and Practice*. Teachers College Press, 1993.

Calley, Nancy G., Sheri Pickover, Jocelyn M. Bennett-Garraway, Simon J. Hendry and Garbette M. Garraway. 'Integrating Social Justice across the Curriculum: The Catholic Mission and Counselor Education'. *Journal of Catholic Higher Education* 30, no. 2 (2011): 289–308.

Chambers, Drew W. 'Is Freire Incoherent? Reconciling Directiveness and Dialogue in Freirean Pedagogy'. *Journal of Philosophy of Education* 53, no. 1 (2019): 21–47.

Cohen, Aryeh. *Justice in the City: An Argument from the Sources of Rabbinic Judaism*. Academic Studies Press, 2013.

Cohen, Hermann. *Religion of Reason Out of the Sources of Judaism*. Scholars Press, 1972.

Cohen, Jonathan. 'Jewish Thought for Jewish Education: Source and Resources'. In *International Handbook of Jewish Education*, 219–36. Springer Science & Business Media, 2011.

Collopy, Rachel, Connie Bowman and David A. Taylor. 'The Educational Achievement Gap as a Social Justice Issue for Teacher Educators'. *Catholic Education: A Journal of Inquiry and Practice* 16, no. 1 (2012): 4–25.

Critchley, Simon, and Robert Bernasconi. *The Cambridge Companion to Levinas*. Cambridge University Press, 2002.

Curry-Stevens, Ann. 'New Forms of Transformative Education Pedagogy for the Privileged'. *Journal of Transformative Education* 5, no. 1 (1 January 2007): 33–58.

Diament, Nathan J. *Tikkun Olam: Social Responsibility in Jewish Thought and Law (Orthodox Forum Series)*. Jason Aronson, 1997.

Dorff, Elliot N. *The Way Into Tikkun Olam: Repairing the World*. Jewish Lights, 2007.

Dunne, Joseph. 'Arguing for Teaching as a Practice: A Reply to Alasdair MacIntyre'. *Journal of Philosophy of Education* 37, no. 2 (May 2003): 353–69.

Dunne, Joseph. *Back to the Rough Ground: Phronesis and Techne in Modern Philosophy and in Aristotle*. University of Notre Dame Press, 1993.

Eagleton, Terry. *Ideology: An Introduction*. Verso, 1991.

Eifler, Karen, Jeff Kerssen-Griep and Peter Thacker. 'Enacting Social Justice to Teach Social Justice: The Pedagogy of Bridge Builders'. *Catholic Education: A Journal of Inquiry and Practice* 12, no. 1 (1 September 2008): 55–7.

Escobar, Miguel. *Paulo Freire on Higher Education: A Dialogue at the National University of Mexico*. SUNY Press, 1994.

Evans, Alice F., Robert A. Evans and William B. Kennedy. *Pedagogies for the Non-Poor*. Wipf and Stock, 2000.

Fishkoff, Sue. *The Rebbe's Army: Inside the World of Chabad-Lubavitch*, repr edn. Schocken Books, 2005.

Fleischmann, L. 'Beyond Paralysis: The Reframing of Israeli Peace Activism Since the Second Intifada'. *Peace & Change* 41 (July 2016): 354–85.

Fox, Seymour, Israel Scheffler and Daniel Marom. *Visions of Jewish Education*. Cambridge University Press, 2003.

Francis, Pope. *Encyclical on Climate Change and Inequality: On Care for Our Common Home*. Melville House, 2015.

Frankel, Jonathan. 'The Roots of "Jewish Socialism" (1881–1892)'. In *Essential Papers on Jews and the Left (Essential Papers on Jewish Studies): 10*, edited by Ezra Mendelsohn. New York University Press, 1997.

Frankena, William K. 'A Model for Analyzing a Philosophy of Education'. *The High School Journal* 50, no. 1 (1966): 8–13.

Fraser, Nancy. 'Social Justice in the Age of Identity Politics: Redistribution, Recognition and Participation'. In *The Tanner Lectures on Human Values*. Stanford University, 1996.

Frazer, Jenni. 'Rabbi, You May Bore Us but Stay out of Politics'. *Jewish Chronicle*, 13 August 2009. https://www.thejc.com/news/world/rabbi-you-may-bore-us-but-stay-out-of-politics-1.10840 (accessed 24 April 2022).

Freire, Paulo. *Cultural Action for Freedom*. Harvard Educational Review, 2000.

Freire, Paulo. *Education for Critical Consciousness*. Continuum International Publishing Group, 1974.

Freire, Paulo. *Pedagogy in Process: The Letters to Guinea-Bissau*. Continuum, 1983.

Freire, Paulo. *Pedagogy of Freedom: Ethics, Democracy, and Civic Courage*. Rowman & Littlefield, 1998.

Freire, Paulo. *Pedagogy of Hope: Reliving Pedagogy of the Oppressed*. Continuum International Publishing Group, 2004.

Freire, Paulo. *Pedagogy of the City*. Continuum, 1993.

Freire, Paulo. *Pedagogy of the Heart*. Continuum International Publishing Group, 1998.

Freire, Paulo. *Pedagogy of the Oppressed*. Continuum International Publishing Group, 2000.

Freire, Paulo. *Teachers as Cultural Workers: Letters to Those Who Dare Teach*. Westview Press, 2005.

Freire, Paulo. *The Politics of Education: Culture, Power, and Liberation*. Greenwood Publishing Group, 1985.
Freire, Paulo, and Donaldo Macedo. *Literacy: Reading the Word & the World*. Routledge, 1987.
Fromm, Erich. *You Shall Be As Gods: A Radical Interpretation of the Old Testament and Its Tradition*. Open Road Media, 2013.
Galili-Schachter, Inbar. 'Pedagogic Hermeneutic Orientations in the Teaching of Jewish Texts'. *Journal of Jewish Education* 77, no. 3 (1 July 2011): 216–38.
Gearon, Liam. 'Human Rights and Religious Education: Some Postcolonial Perspectives'. In *International Handbook of the Religious, Moral and Spiritual Dimensions in Education*, edited by Marian de Souza, Gloria Durka, Kathleen Engebretson, Robert Jackson and Andrew McGrady, 375–85. International Handbooks of Religion and Education 1. Springer Netherlands, 2006.
Giroux, Henry A. *Border Crossings: Cultural Workers and the Politics of Education*, 2nd edn. Routledge, 2005.
Giroux, Henry A. *On Critical Pedagogy*. Bloomsbury Academic, 2011.
Giroux, Henry A. *Theory and Resistance in Education: Towards a Pedagogy for the Opposition*, 2nd revised edn. Greenwood Press, 2001.
Goodman, Diane J. *Promoting Diversity and Social Justice: Educating People from Privileged Groups*, 2nd edn. Routledge, 2011.
Grace, Gerald. 'Catholic Social Teaching Should Permeate the Catholic Secondary School Curriculum: An Agenda for Reform'. *International Studies in Catholic Education* 5, no. 1 (2013): 99–109.
Groome, Thomas H. *Educating for Life: A Spiritual Vision for Every Teacher and Parent*. T. More, 1998.
Guyette, Frederick W. 'Human Rights Education and Religious Education: From Mutual Suspicion to Elective Affinity'. *British Journal of Religious Education* 31, no. 2 (2009): 129–39.
Hertzberg, Arthur. *The Zionist Idea: A Historical Analysis and Reader*. Atheneum, 1972.
Heschel, Abraham Joshua. *The Insecurity of Freedom: Essays on Human Existence / by Abraham Joshua Heschel*. Essays on Human Existence. Jewish Publication Society of America, 1966.
Heschel, Abraham Joshua, and Susannah Heschel. *Moral Grandeur and Spiritual Audacity: Essays*. Farrar, Straus and Giroux, 1997.
Hill, Mary Lynne Gasaway, and Andrew J. Hill. 'Catholic Social Teaching and Civic Engagement: Grounding Civic Praxis in Catholic Theory'. *Journal of Catholic Higher Education* 27, no. 1 (2008): 97–115.
Holzer, Elie. 'What Connects "Good" Teaching, Text Study and Hevruta Learning? A Conceptual Argument'. *Journal of Jewish Education* 72, no. 3 (1 December 2006): 183–204.
hooks, bell. *Talking Back: Thinking Feminist, Thinking Black*. South End Press, 1989.

Horton, Myles, and Paulo Freire. *We Make the Road by Walking: Conversations on Education and Social Change*. Temple University Press, 1990.

Jacobs, Jill. *There Shall Be No Needy: Pursuing Social Justice through Jewish Law & Tradition*. Jewish Lights, 2010.

Kahn-Harris, Keith. *Uncivil War: The Israel Conflict in the Jewish Community*. David Paul, 2014.

Kammer, Fred. *Doing Faithjustice: An Introduction to Catholic Social Thought*. Paulist Press, 1991.

Kirwan, Michael. 'Liberation Theology and Catholic Social Teaching'. *New Blackfriars* 93, no. 1044 (2012): 246–58.

Köylü, Mustafa. 'Peace Education: An Islamic Approach'. *Journal of Peace Education* 1, no. 1 (2004): 59–76.

Lamm, Norman. *Torah Lishmah: Torah for Torah's Sake in the Works of Rabbi Hayyim of Volozhin and His Contemporaries*. KTAV Publishing House, 1989.

Lamm, Zvi. *The Educational Method of Hashomer-Hatzair Youth Movement: The Story of Its Formation*. Hebrew University Magnes Press, 1998.

Lamm, Zvi. '*Ideologiyah ve-mahshevet ha-hinukh*'. In *Lahatz ve-hitnagdut ba-hinukh*, edited bt Yoram Harpaz, 217–54 Sifriat Poalim, 2000.

Lehman, Marjorie, and Jane Kanarek. 'Talmud: Making a Case for Talmud Pedagogy – The Talmud as an Educational Model'. In *International Handbook of Jewish Education*, 581–96. Springer Science & Business Media, 2011.

Leibowitz, Yeshayahu. 'The Reading of Shema'. In *Judaism, Human Values, and the Jewish State*, translated by Eliezer Goldman, 37–47. Harvard University Press, 1992.

Leibowitz, Yeshayahu. 'The Social Order as a Religious Problem'. In *Judaism, Human Values, and the Jewish State*, translated by Eliezer Goldman, 145–57. Harvard University Press, 1992.

Lerner, Michael. 'Heschel's Legacy for the Politics of the Twenty-First Century'. *Modern Judaism* 29, no. 1 (13 May 2009): 34–43.

Lerner, Michael. *Jewish Renewal: A Path to Healing and Transformation*. G.P. Putnam's Sons, 1994.

Lerner, Michael. *Spirit Matters*. Vol. 2002. Hampton Roads, 2002.

Lugo, Luis, Alan Cooperman, Erin O'Connell, Gregory A. Smith and Sandra Stencel. 'A Portrait of Jewish Americans'. Pew Research Center, 1 October 2013.

Macedo, Donaldo Pereira. *Literacies of Power: What Americans Are Not Allowed to Know*. Westview Press, 2006.

MacIntyre, Alasdair. *After Virtue: A Study in Moral Theory*. Gerald Duckworth, 2007.

MacIntyre, Alasdair. 'Alasdair MacIntyre on Education: In Dialogue with Joseph Dunne'. *Journal of Philosophy of Education* 36, no. 1 (February 2002): 1–19.

McIntosh, Peggy. 'White Privilege: Unpacking the Invisible Knapsack'. *Independent School* (1 January 1990): 31–6.

McLaren, Peter. *Capitalists and Conquerors: A Critical Pedagogy against Empire*. Rowman & Littlefield, 2005.

Mendes-Flohr, Paul R., and Jehuda Reinharz. *The Jew in the Modern World: A Documentary History*. Oxford University Press, 1995.

Mirsky, Yehudah. 'Tikkun Olam: Basic Questions and Policy Directions', January 2008. www.bjpa.org.

Noddings, Nel. *Caring: A Feminine Approach to Ethics and Moral Education*. University of California Press, 2003.

Noddings, Nel. *Starting at Home: Caring and Social Policy*. University of California Press, 2002.

O'Brien, David J., and Thomas A. Shannon, eds. *Catholic Social Thought: The Documentary Heritage*. Orbis Books, 1992.

Plaskow, Judith. *Standing Again at Sinai: Judaism from a Feminist Perspective*, repr. edn. Bravo, 1991.

Plaskow, Judith. *The Coming of Lilith: Essays on Feminism, Judaism, and Sexual Ethics, 1972–2003*. Beacon Press, 2005.

Plen, Matt. '*Pedagogiyah bikortit ve-ideologiyot shel tzedek ḥevrati: Paulo Freire ve-ha-ideologiyot shel Hashomer Hatzair ve-Hakibbutz Hadati*'. Hebrew University, 2008.

Postman, Neil. *Teaching as a Conserving Activity*. Delta, 1980.

Rose, Or, Margie Klein, Jo Ellen Green Kaiser and David Ellenson. *Righteous Indignation: A Jewish Call for Justice*. Jewish Lights, 2009.

Rosenzweig, Franz. *The Star of Redemption*. University of Wisconsin Press, 2004.

Ross, Tamar. *Expanding the Palace of Torah – Orthodoxy and Feminism*, 2nd edn. Brandeis University Press, 2021.

Ross, Tamar. 'The Feminist Contribution to Halakhic Discourse Kol Beisha Erva as a Test Case'. *Emor*, no. 1 (2010): 37–69.

Rowland, Christopher. *The Cambridge Companion to Liberation Theology*. Cambridge University Press, 2007.

Sachar, Howard M. *Course of Modern Jewish History*, 2nd edn. Random House, 1990.

Sacks, Jonathan. *The Politics of Hope*. Vintage, 2000.

Sacks, Jonathan. 'The Spirit of Community (Vayakhel 5775)'. Rabbi Sacks, 8 March 2015. www.rabbisacks.org/the-spirit-of-community-vayakhel-5775.

Sacks, Jonathan. *To Heal a Fractured World: The Ethics of Responsibility*. Continuum, 2005.

Sagi, Abraham. *Jewish Religion after Theology*. Academic Studies Press, 2009.

Saperstein, Marc. '"Rabbis, Stay out of Politics": Social Justice Preaching and Its Opponents, 1848–2014'. *Jewish Culture and History* 16, no. 2 (4 May 2015): 127–41.

Schipani, Daniel S. *Religious Education Encounters Liberation Theology*. Religious Education Press, 1988.

Schwarz, Sidney. *Jewish Megatrends: Charting the Course of the American Jewish Future*. Jewish Lights, 2013.

Schwarz, Sidney. *Judaism and Justice: The Jewish Passion to Repair the World*, repr edn. Jewish Lights, 2008.

Schwarz, Sidney. 'Welcome to the Tribe'. Rabbi Sid Schwarz, 2012. http://www.rabbisid.org/hello-world/ (accessed 27 July 2018).

Seeskin, Kenneth. *Jewish Philosophy in a Secular Age*. State University of New York Press, 1990.

Seidler, Victor. *Jewish Philosophy and Western Culture: A Modern Introduction*. I.B.Tauris, 2007.

Sen, Amartya. *Identity and Violence: The Illusion of Destiny*. Penguin, 2007.

Sherwin, Byron L. 'Tikkun Olam: A Case of Semantic Displacement'. *Jewish Political Studies Review* 25, nos. 3/4 (2013): 43–58.

Shimoni, Gideon. *The Zionist Ideology*. Brandeis University Press, 1997.

Shor, Ira. *Empowering Education: Critical Teaching for Social Change*. University of Chicago Press, 1992.

Shor, Ira, and Paulo Freire. *A Pedagogy for Liberation: Dialogues on Transforming Education*. Greenwood Publishing Group, 1987.

Shulman, Lee S. 'Pedagogies of Interpretation, Argumentation, and Formation: From Understanding to Identity in Jewish Education'. *Journal of Jewish Education* 74, no. suppl (5 December 2008): 5–15.

Silverman, Marc. 'Ha-Hinukh Ba-Kibbutz Ha-Dati: Historiyah ve-Ideologiyah'. Hebrew University, 1982.

Soloveitchik, Joseph. *Fate and Destiny: From Holocaust to the State of Israel*. KTAV Publishing House, 2000.

Strike, Kenneth, and Jeffrey Pegram. 'Religion and Citizenship: The Prophetic Tradition and Public Reason'. In *Commitment, Character, and Citizenship: Religious Education in Liberal Democracy*, edited by Hanan A. Alexander and Ayman K. Agbaria, 63–83. Routledge, 2012.

Suissa, Judith. 'Tiger Mothers and Praise Junkies: Children, Praise and the Reactive Attitudes'. *Journal of Philosophy of Education* 47, no. 1 (1 February 2013): 1–19.

Sullivan, Susan Crawford, and Margaret A. Post. 'Combining Community-Based Learning and Catholic Social Teaching in Educating for Democratic Citizenship'. *Journal of Catholic Higher Education* 30, no. 1 (2011): 113–31.

Tarlau, Rebecca. 'From a Language to a Theory of Resistance: Critical Pedagogy, the Limits of "Framing," and Social Change'. *Educational Theory* 64, no. 4 (1 August 2014): 369–92.

Taylor, Charles. 'The Politics of Recognition'. In *Multiculturalism: Examining the Politics of Recognition*, edited by Amy Gutmann, 25–73. Princeton University Press, 1994.

Urbano, Ryan. 'Approaching the Divine: Levinas on God, Religion, Idolatry, and Atheism'. *Logos: A Journal of Catholic Thought and Culture* 15, no. 1 (1 January 2012): 50–81.

Walzer, Michael. *Exodus and Revolution*. Basic Books, 1986.

Waskow, Arthur. *Down-To-Earth Judaism: Food, Money, Sex, and the Rest of Life*. William Morrow 1995.

Waxman, Dov. *Trouble in the Tribe: The American Jewish Conflict over Israel*. Princeton University Press, 2016.

Weiss, Avraham. *Spiritual Activism: A Jewish Guide to Leadership and Repairing the World*, 1st edn. Jewish Lights, 2008.

Weissman, Deborah. 'Jewish Religious Education as Peace Education: From Crisis to Opportunity'. *British Journal of Religious Education* 29, no. 1 (2007): 63–76.

Wexler, Philip. 'Chabad: Social Movement and Educational Practice.' In *Educational Deliberations; Studies in Education Dedicated to Shlomo (Seymour) Fox*, by Mordecai Nisan and Oded Schremer, 196–206. Keter, 2005.

Wolf, Arnold Jacob. 'Repairing Tikkun Olam.' *Judaism* 50, no. 4 (2001): 479.

Yanklowitz, Shmuly. *Jewish Ethics and Social Justice: A Guide for the 21st Century*. Derusha, 2012.

Zoloth, Laurie. *Health Care and the Ethics of Encounter: A Jewish Discussion of Social Justice*, 1st edn. University of North Carolina Press, 1999.

Index

Abraham (biblical character) 44, 130
action 10, 18, 26, 38, 119, 121–5, 147–51, 152–5, 170, 212
    Political 13, 31, 42, 103, 131, 150–1, 155, 164, 173, 191, 211
activism 111–17
Adorno, Theodor 12
affect 16, 27–8, 104–8, 170–1, 192, 195, 210, 213–14
agency 40, 190, 203, 205
    of students 16
Ahad Ha'am (Ginsberg, Asher) 188
Alinsky, Saul 86, 131, 137, 184
Allen, Ricky Lee 30
altruism 121, 176
America *see* United States, Latin America
American Jews *see under* United States
analogue society 211–12
anthropology 193–4, 201
antisemitism 1, 37, 64–5, 143, 162–3, 188, 197, 214
anti-Zionism 34, 93, 106
apartheid 69, 121
Aquinas, Thomas 27
Arendt, Hannah 148, 151–6, 169, 175, 190, 218
Aristotelian 27, 41, 100, 148–51, 194, 197, 217
Arrupe, Pedro, 22, 26
authority 13, 40, 152, 159, 181, 182, 184, 210
    teacher's 15–16
autonomy, communal or cultural 34, 96–7, 141, 189

Bakhtin, Mikhail 14
Bal tashhit 102
banking pedagogy 14–15, 29, 100, 108, 150, 175, 186
Baumann, Zygmunt 59, 159
Beinart, Peter 70
Benjamin, Walter 15, 183

Bergman, Roger 22, 25–8, 164
Bet Midrash 48, 181
Bible 24, 28–9, 38, 46, 175–6
Binding of Isaac 44
Black Lives Matter 37
Bloom, Allan 11, 162
Blue Labour 83, 184
Board of Deputies of British Jews 65, 71
border pedagogy 14
Borochov, Ber 35
Borowitz, Eugene 39, 45, 48
Buber, Martin 61–2, 151–5, 157, 165–6, 170, 172–6, 218
Bund 34, 74, 83, 96, 183–4
Burbules, Nicholas 169–70
bureaucratisation 63, 153, 190

Câmara, Hélder 118
capitalism 15, 18, 23, 36, 45, 39–40, 59–62
caring 170–3, 203, 206, 214
Catholic social teaching (CST) 5, 21–32, 133, 163, 217
Catholicism 21–32, 175
character education 21, 166–8, 195
charity 99–101, 163
Christianity 23, 25, 28, 31, 42, 158, 179
Christians 97, 142–3, 164, 177
churches 63–4, 121
civil rights 37, 45
civil society 13, 41–2, 85–7, 176–7, 191, 202–3, 205, 213–14
class, socio-economic 60, 196
cognitive learning 32, 169, 192, 210
cognitive liberation 131
Cohen, Aryeh 41, 110, 188
Cohen, Hermann 47
Cohen, Jonathan 179
colonialism 10–11
    ideological 215
coming to voice 125
common good 24, 25, 41, 62, 163–6, 176, 206

244   *Index*

communism 34, 37
communitarianism 21, 25, 41–2
community 41, 62–4, 151–6, 193–6,
    201–4, 206–7, 209–10, 213–15, 218
community organising 85, 118–25, 137,
    164, 173, 195, 203, 212
complexity 38, 47, 79, 103, 167–8,
    190, 209
conscientisation 17–18, 28, 197–8, 200,
    202–3, 210–11, 215
consciousness
    critical 17–18, 30
    naïve 17
conspiracy theories 212–15
covenant 24, 41, 71, 164
    brit goral, brit ye'ud 47
critical pedagogy 9–19, 131, 133, 217
    Jewish 196–200, 201–4, 207–8,
        210–11, 215–16
cultural emancipation 187–8, 196–200
culture 10–12, 17–18, 159, 160–2, 190–1,
    196–7, 201–4
    Jewish 34, 43, 73–4, 97, 183–4, 188,
        191, 197–8, 207
    of silence 11, 161
    students' 16
culture wars 211–16

Darwin, Charles 176
De Tocqueville, Alexis 85–6, 176
Declaration of Independence, Israeli 72–3
dehumanisation 9–10, 19, 30, 190, 193–4,
    201, 206, 214
deliberation 109–11, 190, 198, 212
democracy 12–13, 19, 97, 169, 183–4
    in Israel 70–1, 205
    participative 212
democratic public sphere 190–3, 189–93,
    201–6, 208–9, 211–13
depth structures 31, 179
dialectics 19, 10, 49
dialogue 18, 127, 154–5, 168–73, 182,
    206, 213, 218
    of care 170–3, 195, 203, 213
    educational 15, 203
    as existential encounter 173–4,
        195, 203
    as rational discourse 168–70, 192, 198,
        203, 210–11, 213

Diaspora 34, 36–7, 74–5, 97, 116–17
    Jews 187, 205
    nationalism 183
difference 10, 14, 92, 160, 164–5, 184,
    195–6, 205, 210, 218
digital society 211–12
divine image 19, 22, 43, 58, 129, 156,
    161, 194, 201, 206, 214 (*see also
    under* God)
Dorff, Elliot 40, 43, 125
Dunne, Joseph 149, 187
dvar torah 19, 180, 183, 184, 192, 199,
    205, 211, 213, 214

Eagleton, Terry 4
Ecclesial Base Communities (EBCs) 29
economic justice 23–4, 39, 80–2
Economic Justice for All 25
environment 40, 67, 102
epistemological privilege (of the
    oppressed) 29
epistemology 166–70
exclusion 55, 190, 194, 201, 209, 212
Exodus 28, 38, 44, 47
experience 100–3, 198

fake news 190, 212–15
feminism 14, 37
    gender-critical 208–9
    and Judaism 40, 47, 56–8, 68, 139
Fraser, Nancy 159
Freire, Paulo 3, 9–19, 28, 38, 131, 133,
    147–51, 158, 161–2, 170, 184,
    192, 217
Fromm, Erich 47
fundamentalism 166, 208–9

Galili-Schachter, Inbar 182, 184
gender identity 58, 209, 58, 139,
    142, 210
Giroux, Henry 12–18, 161–2
God 22, 24, 43, 90–1, 152, 156–8, 173
    image of 19, 22, 43, 58, 129, 156,
        161, 194, 201, 206, 214 (*see also
        divine image*)
Gordon, A. D. 35–6
Groome, Thomas 31, 179
Gutierrez, Gustavo 22–5

Habermas, Jurgen 150
halakhah 40, 48, 102
Hasidism 42, 157
Hebrew 187–8
hermeneutics 5, 33, 43, 47, 183, 192, 197, 217
Heschel, Abraham Joshua 39, 44, 90, 119, 157
Hess, Moses 34
ḥevruta 19, 181, 184, 195, 206, 210, 214
hidden curriculum 184
Hirsch, E. D. 11, 162
Hirsch, Samson Raphael 83
Holocaust 45, 66, 94, 165
Holzer, Elie 181
homelessness 101–2, 214–15
homophobia 208, 210
hooks, bell 125, 198
Horton, Myles 131
human rights 25, 60, 138, 194, 205
    and Torah 95
humanisation 9–10, 13, 17, 19, 191, 202

I and Thou 152, 165, 172
identity politics 13–14, 58, 160–2
ideology 4, 11, 18, 17, 52–3, 209
idolatry 23
Ignatian pedagogy 26, 103, 148, 214 (*see also* pastoral cycle)
Imitatio Dei 24, 29, 43, 156
inclusion 55–8
inequality 59–62, 194
instrumentalisation 193–4, 201, 209
interfaith 86–7, 142–3
internal goods 185–7, 194–5, 197
international development 24, 59, 94, 115
intersectionality 13–14, 30, 142–3, 196, 215
Isaiah (biblical prophet) 94, 80–1, 101
Israel 2, 37, 60, 70–5, 138
    Diaspora relations 74–5, 116–17
    and Palestine 71, 103–6, 205–8 (*see also* Occupation, Palestinians)

Jacobs, Jill 45, 48
Jaffe, David 42
Jewish education 1–2, 52, 67, 83, 101, 175, 179, 183–8, 192, 196, 198, 218

Jewish law *see halakhah*
Jubilee year 24

Kammer, Fred 24
Kanarek, Jane 181, 188
Kaplan, Mordecai 74
Katznelson, Berl 35
Kibbutz, religious 36
King, Martin Luther 90
Kingdom of God 23, 25

Latin America 12, 17, 21, 24, 29, 31, 161, 164
Lamm, Norman 186–7
Lamm, Zvi 52
leadership 13, 18, 57, 63, 142, 177
Lehman, Marjorie 181, 188
Leibowitz, Yeshayahu 48, 174
Lerner, Michael 39, 42, 44, 46, 157
Levinas, Emmanuel 61–2, 110, 158, 165–6, 173, 176
LGBT+ 1, 46, 55–6, 79, 89, 107–11, 126–7, 141, 208–11
liberalism 33, 48–9, 73, 160–1, 189, 192–3
liberation theology 5, 21–32, 118, 133, 217
Libertatis Nuntius 25
lishmah 149, 194–5, 202, 216, 218 (*see also under Torah*)
literacy 17, 187, 197, 199, 202, 211, 216
Living Wage 60
lobbying 115–17

Macedo, Donald 11, 161
MacIntyre, Alasdair 25, 27, 159, 177, 186, 193
Maḥloket 19, 181, 184, 192, 205, 213
Maimonides, Moses 40, 41, 179
Mao Zedong 16
Marxism 3, 23, 34, 121, 150, 161–3
Masorti Judaism 2, 92, 95
mass society 152
McIntosh, Peggy 55
McLaren, Peter 162
Mensch 83, 140, 166
mental landscape 119, 176
Michaelson, Jay 46
Midrash 97, 182, 184–5, 196, 199, 200, 206, 210–11

Miliband, David 116
mipnei darkei shalom 66
mitzvot 119
modernity 32–4, 59, 151–3, 159, 201
Moses (biblical character) 38
multiculturalism 13–14, 30, 66, 96, 184, 215
Muslims 88, 103, 124–5, 137, 142–3, 164, 198, 200, 206, 214–15
Mussar movement 42

narratives 104, 119–20, 129–30, 205
nationalism 59, 73, 188
neo-colonialism 11
neoliberalism 16
Neo-Orthodoxy 83, 184
Noahide laws 48
Noddings, Nel 170–3
non-poor 21, 29–32

Occupation (of Palestinian territories) 70, 72–3, 116, 138, 205–6 (*see also under* Israel)
oppression 29–32, 125, 133–4, 141–3, 193, 196, 201, 206, 215–16
of Jews 196–7 (*see also* antisemitism)
Orthodox Judaism 36, 46, 48, 57, 67–9, 91, 102, 139, 210
Other, the 78, 90–1, 152, 156–7, 164–7, 206

Pacem in Terris 24
Palestinians 1, 103–6, 116, 138, 206, 208 (*see also under* Israel)
pastoral cycle 26, 103, 148 (*see also* Ignatian pedagogy)
pedagogic hermeneutic orientation (PHO) 182–4, 196, 219
dialogical 192, 196, 199, 204
midrashic 199, 206, 210
Pedagogies for the Non-Poor 31
pedagogy
Jewish 19, 179–83, 218
social justice 26–9, 144, 183–8, 218
talmudic 188
Pedagogy of the Oppressed 30
personal development 82–5, 125–30, 140, 158, 169, 195
peshat 192, 200

Petrella, Ivan 23
philanthropy 81, 135
phronesis 27, 172, 195–6
Plaskow, Judith 40
pluralism 38–9, 66, 77–80, 102, 159–68, 184, 197–8, 205
epistemological 218
of gender and sexual identities 211
Jewish 91–3
poiesis 148, 152–3, 186
political education 28–9, 106, 183–5
politics 18, 56, 153, 212
faith/religion and 69, 174–7, 213
left wing 111–13, 111
progressive 35, 37, 44, 48, 64, 69, 72, 112, 159, 161, 167, 183, 218
radical 140–1
of redistribution and recognition 159–60
poor, the 21–2, 61–2, 138, 177
Pope Francis 134
populism 11–13, 18, 190, 201, 214, 211–16
Populorum Progressio 24
post-truth 214
postcolonialism 161–3
Postman, Neil 211–12
postmodern 14, 30, 59, 162
poverty 81, 156, 161, 194, 215
as a religious category 22
practice, education as a 186
praxis 4, 10, 13, 17, 21, 29, 38, 147–53, 159, 170, 186, 191, 202, 212–16
Aristotelian 27, 148–51, 194, 197, 217
Freirean/Marxist 147–8, 149–51, 217
prayer 69, 92, 97
privilege 26, 46, 60, 122, 196, 211, 215
problem-posing education 9
Progressive Judaism 91, 68–9 (*see also* Reform Judaism)
Prophetic Judaism 82, 196
psychotherapy 63, 158
public sphere *see* democratic public sphere

Quadragesimo Anno 24

Rabbinic Judaism 149, 166
rabbis 82, 126–7, 134–5
racism 1, 44, 72, 214

Ratzinger, Joseph 26
recognition, politics of 159–60, 164
redistribution, politics of 159–60, 164
Reform Judaism 92 (*see also* Progressive Judaism)
refugees 60, 65, 138, 214
relationships 112–13, 118–25, 151–6, 193–6, 169, 201, 214, 218
  between rich and poor 61–2, 81–2, 88–9, 123, 142, 159, 163–6, 172
  Covenantal 87–91
  with God 90–1
religious education 21
revelation 45, 173
role models 102, 126
Rosenzweig, Franz 173
Ross, Tamar 40, 47–8

Sacks, Jonathan 41, 85–6, 176
Sagi, Avi 38
Schipani, Daniel 28–9
schools 18–19, 99
  Jewish 63, 79, 97
Schwarz, Sid 45, 70, 101–2
scripture 29, 175–6
self-interest 60, 165
sermons 126
service learning 26–8, 163–6, 172, 195, 203, 206, 214
Shabbat 56–7, 69, 88, 92, 128
Shor, Ira 12, 192
Shulman, Lee 180
signature pedagogies 180–1, 183, 192, 204, 205, 209–15, 218–19
Simon, Roger 16
sin 22
  structural 25, 155
social action 32, 63, 67, 78, 87–8, 95, 98, 102, 121, 129, 148–9, 151, 157–8, 168, 173, 185, 195
  and Jewish identity 139, 175–6 (*see also under* social justice)
social atomisation 214
social democracy 38
social harmony 163–6, 163
social justice
  disconnect from Judaism 65–70
  and Jewish continuity 66–7 (*see also under* social action)
  personal and structural conceptions 18, 21, 25–8, 32, 39–43, 59–60, 78, 128, 197–9, 203
social justice pedagogy 25–9, 144, 183–8, 218
social media 190, 212–14
social sphere (in Buber and Arendt) 152–3, 155, 175
socialism 3, 12, 33–6
  Jewish 34–6, 69–70
Soloveitchik, J. B. 47
South Africa 63, 119–21, 142
speaking out 198, 203
speech 125–30
spirituality 156–9, 195
state authority 40, 135–6
street Torah 102, 214
survivalist Judaism 70
synagogue 93, 97, 118, 213–14
Syrkin, Nahman 34

Talmud 42, 45, 78, 102, 110, 181
Tarlau, Rebecca 130
teachers 1, 4, 15–16, 102, 109, 113, 136–7, 142, 170, 182, 192, 196
texts
  Jewish 179–80, 181, 187–8, 211
  rabbinic 185, 197, 209, 218
  religious 166–7, 175–6
textual study 175–6
themes, generative or topical 192, 199
theology 129
  apophatic 157, 176
  dialogical 176, 194
  negative 176
theory 1–2, 150–1, 219
  normative 189–204, 189, 217
tikkun 139, 158
  ha-nefesh 42, 129
  olam/ha-olam 38, 41, 44, 48, 68, 129
Tikkun magazine 39
Torah 36, 101, 210
  im derekh eretz 83
  lishmah 32, 185–7, 197–8, 211, 218 (*see also lishmah*)
tradition 25, 33, 127, 159, 177, 187, 197
  Greek 41
  Jewish 43
  rabbinic 45

training 107–11
transgender 208–10
trauma 72, 209
Tutu, Desmond 121
Twersky, Isadore 179, 181
tzedakah 36–7, 40
tzimtzum 39

United States 11, 31, 37, 46, 153, 162, 176
   Jews and Judaism in 44–6, 48, 70, 116
universal basic income 82
universalism 3, 33–4, 36, 45–6, 49, 66, 95, 160–1, 195–6, 205, 207
Utopia 4, 37–9

volunteering 83–5, 99–101, 99, 214

Walzer, Michael 38, 44
Waskow, Arthur 42
Wittenberg, Jonathan 42, 157
women 115, 139
workers' rights 24, 41, 60, 81, 88

Yanklowitz, Shmuly 45–6
Yiddish 34, 37, 97, 183

Zionism 2, 70–5, 205, 207–8
   liberal 70, 73
   socialist 34–6

www.ingramcontent.com/pod-product-compliance
Lightning Source LLC
Chambersburg PA
CBHW062134300426
44115CB00012BA/1922